D1040235

PRAYERS
FOR A
PLANETARY
PILGRIM

DEDICATED

with deepest affection
in this the year of his 70th birthday
to

WILLEM BERGER

priest, psychologist and professor,
who has been my mentor, spiritual director
and friend for 25 years

PRAYERS
FOR A
PLANETARY
PILGRIM

A Personal
Manual for
Prayer and
Ritual

EDWARD HAYS

Forest of Peace Publishing, Inc.

Other Books by the Author:
(available through the publisher or your favorite bookstore)

Prayers and Rituals
Prayers for the Domestic Church
Prayers for the Servants of God

Contemporary Spirituality
The Old Hermit's Almanac
Feathers on the Wind
Holy Fools & Mad Hatters
A Pilgrim's Almanac
Pray All Ways
In Pursuit of the Great White Rabbit
The Lenten Labyrinth
Secular Sanctity
The Ascent of the Mountain of God

Parables and Stories
The Gospel of Gabriel
St. George and the Dragon
The Quest for the Flaming Pearl
The Magic Lantern
The Ethiopian Tattoo Shop
Twelve and One-Half Keys
Sundancer
The Christmas Eve Storyteller

PRAYERS FOR A PLANETARY PILGRIM

Library of Congress Catalog Card Number: 88-83763
ISBN: 0-939516-10-1

published by
Forest of Peace Publishing, Inc.
PO Box 269
Leavenworth, KS 66048-0269 USA
1-800-659-3227

printed by
Hall Directory, Inc.
Topeka, KS 66608-0007

1st printing: February 1989
2nd printing: August 1989
3rd printing: February 1990
4th printing: December 1990
5th printing: February 1992

6th printing: September 1993
7th printing: October 1994
8th printing: September 1995
9th printing: September 1996
10th printing: April 1998

The photograph that appears on the front cover of the dust jacket of this book is the spiral galaxy Messier 81 (NGC 3031), and the Pleiades cluster is on the back cover. The photograph on the front fly page is the Andromeda galaxy Messier 31 (NGC 224). The shadow page has the Earth's moon, and the dedication page Halley's Comet. The title page is a photograph of the moon. The photograph on the back fly page is the spiral galaxy Messier 81 (NGC 3031).

All the photographs that appear in this book, other than that of the planet Earth, are reproduced with permission from the Lick Observatory, University of California at Santa Cruz 95064. The photograph of Earth from space is reproduced with permission from NASA. We gratefully thank both NASA and the Lick Observatory for their permission to use these photographs.

GRATEFUL ACKNOWLEDGEMENT

There's an old expression that no feast comes to the table on its own feet. And it can equally be said that no book comes to you, the reader, on its own wings. As a good meal requires the loving attention of caring hands, the work of many hours and often the effort of many hands, so it is with this book.

I wish first of all to express my gratitude to my friend and fellow community member, THOMAS SKORUPA, who labored long hours in editing this text. His creative and poetic touch is upon each page of this book.

Another member of the community to which I am privileged to belong deserves my heartfelt thanks, the final editor and publisher of this book, my longtime friend, THOMAS TURKLE. I am grateful to him for the long hours of keen and careful attention to the technical and professional aspects required in order that this book might become a reality.

And I am grateful to those who shared in the work of editing, to RUTH SLICKMAN who was involved in the early stages and PAULA DUKE who continued in the task of editing and proofreading.

I am indebted as well to my friends and community members, JENNIFER SULLIVAN and PAULA DUKE, who wrote the beautiful prayers for the women's Seasons of Change.

And to the other members of the community of Shantivanam belongs my gratitude for their input, support and assistance in the various stages of this book.

And finally, I wish to express my thanks to STEVE HALL in his capacity of advisor and printer of this book, along with the able staff at Hall Directory, Inc. and to DAVID DE ROUSSEAU for his assistance as an art advisor.

The love, work and effort of these many hands and hearts have made possible the book that is in your hands. It is my prayer that the labor of making this book a reality bears fruit in your personal prayer pilgrimage home.

Edward Hays
January 6, 1989
Epiphany, Feast of the Stars

TABLE OF CONTENTS

THE SEASON OF AUTUMN

THE SEASON OF WINTER

PRAYERS BEFORE AND AFTER PRAYING

PSALMS FOR THE 21ST CENTURY

SEASONAL PSALMS

PSALMS FOR SACRED SEASONS

DAILY PRAYERS FOR THE 21st CENTURY

Regardless of the calendar date, we have already entered into the 21st century, into another age. In this new era our attention is turned from this small planet outward to the boundless space that surrounds us. Our prayer needs a new vocabulary that reflects such new vistas, that helps us understand more correctly who we truly are.

Words like sunset and sunrise which still remain in our daily vocabulary are in reality pre-Galilean terms. They were logical for flat-earth people who saw themselves as the center of the universe. Earth was perceived as stationary and the sun, moon and stars as the objects that moved around our planet. Such an attitude is much like that of children who perceive themselves as the center of all life.

Today we realize that Earth and the sun in company with the other planets of our solar system are a cosmic colony moving outward into infinite space. Our earth is a living spaceship, a conscious interlocking organism on a voyage. From such a realization comes a flood of new prayers with new terms that fit our daily experience.

Instead of sunset, we might speak of an evening "turn-around," as our small planet slowly turns around to face the horizonless space into which we are moving. And night could be called "look-out," as we see before us the billions of stars and those limitless vistas of the universe.

Look-out is a sacred time, filled with mystery and also with fear. The hours of look-out, when the darkness of space engulfs our earth, is a time filled with crime and deeds of darkness, but it is also the time for love, prayer, relaxation and reflection. And we are among the living creatures who choose to use look-out as a time for sleep. The hours of look-out also give us an opportunity to see ahead to where we as a cosmic colony are traveling. But while we enjoy gazing outward at the stars, we can easily grow tired of looking through the windshield of look-out. At such times we wish to turn our attention back to the often trivial but necessary matters of our life aboard the space vessel. We then await the coming of the first signs of morning turn-around, or as it was called in olden days, sunrise.

A great relief for the sick person who has endured the restless hours of darkness, morning turn-around is a welcome happening for all of us. As the planet earth slowly turns around from its vision of the billions of stars in unlimited space, it is filled with the light of one single star, the brilliant and beautiful daystar that we call the sun. We are no longer exposed to that awesome vision which is beyond our comprehension. The light of day enables us to view our lives and the tiny ship upon which we are traveling with more definition. We rise from sleep and begin to go about our daily duties as crew members. The frontiers of the universe shrink to the manageable dimensions of that which touches only our personal lives. While this morning turn-around focusing-of-vision helps us to get on with our lives, it can also contribute to the narrow vision of envy, bickering, greed and the fighting that breaks out among the crew members of our tiny space vessel.

Look-back, as day might be called, turns our attention away from our larger destination and gives us an opportunity to look at that massive nuclear-powered star we call the sun. It is the engine that propels our cosmic colony of planets, the solar system, out into the darkness of space. We rely so fully on its majestic power and seemingly endless endurance that we have made this daystar divine, or at least a symbol of that mystery we call by countless names.

Countless ancient ones and many of our planet's present crew members have realized that they and the earth are somehow part of that mystery of God. Sacred—at one with the Divine Mystery—is the tiny earthen vessel and we the crew. So too are the billions of stars, planets, comets and other creations that travel together with our solar space colony. It seems that the Sacred Essence is at the heart of the interstellar interconnection of all space travelers. We can wonder, then, if the Divine Mystery is also our ultimate destination. We wonder at the God-seed buried deeply within each member of the crew, a compass and map of our final destination. Or perhaps the real mystery is that it is God who is on a journey into space, forever pushing outward the cellophaned confines of the cosmos, the transparent tissue of nothingness, ever expanding the edges of the universe by constantly casting outward newly created, wondrously beautiful galaxies and undiscovered worlds.

The prayers that follow could be a beginning toward the creation of a breviary, or prayer book, for those who see themselves as members of the space vessel Earth, part of a cosmic traveling colony. Such psalms and prayers serve as an inner compass for those who see themselves as co-explorers and co-creators with the Divine Mystery, which at this very moment is playing at the ever-expanding edges of the universe.

A PLANETARY PILGRIM

Our senses tell us that the earth stands still and that the sun, moon and stars move around it. But while we know this is not true, our daily speech reveals that ancient belief. This is a handbook for a traveler on a sacred journey, a pilgrim who lives on a planet traveling in three different ways at the same time.

The earth spins around her axis at the speed of 1,000 miles an hour at the equator. To spin around once takes 23 hours, 56 minutes and 4.1 seconds. The spinning of the earth makes our days and nights. But as we spin we are also on another circle journey as we orbit around our daystar, the sun. Traveling at the speed of 66,600 miles an hour, this second journey takes 365 days, 6 hours, 9 minutes and 9.54 seconds to complete. In the annual pilgrimage around our great star we travel 595,000,000 miles. Finally, Earth, as a member of a solar family composed of the sun and nine planets and their moons, is also racing outward into space at 43,000 miles an hour.

In the space of one turnaround we travel a million miles outward into space in a gigantic helic path which spirals like a winding staircase. Yet our usual language of prayer is pre-Copernican, as if the great discoveries of Copernicus and Galileo had never taken place. This manual for a planetary pilgrim is an attempt to awaken us to the reality of our earth's threefold movements at this very moment. Such an awareness of distance, speed and order creates a sense of awe and wonder. To what sacred destination is our planet traveling, together with the rest of our cosmic colony and the other colonies of stars and planets of this great universe?

THE SACRED JOURNEY

Three great questions present themselves to those who travel and live upon this planet: "Where did I come from?" "Where am I going?" and "Why am I here?" To seek a sacred answer to these questions is to be a planetary pilgrim. Such a person believes that all life came from the Divine Mystery and is forever on a spiraling journey back to that Sacred Source of creation. The earth, with her three movements of spinning on her axis at the same time as she circles the sun and also travels outward into space with the rest of the solar family, becomes a sacred sign of the threefold aspect of our personal pilgrimages.

The planet's 24-hour circular journey, while one continuous movement, is divided into day and night. And each of us, though one reality, is a twofold mystery of body and spirit. These are not separate realities but a blended mystery which makes each pilgrim a cosmic amphibian. As such we experience both an interior and exterior life. To know only one aspect of existence makes the space traveler incomplete. This manual seeks to balance these twin natures of our humanity and to provide a means to experience the unity of body and soul as we have been designed to do.

The earth is a bearer of life only because of her unique and creative relationship with the sun. Without our daystar life would be impossible. So the yearly pilgrimage of the earth around this source of life becomes a sacrament celebrating our intimate relationship with the Divine Mystery. The prayers in this manual are addressed to God, the Eternal Source from which we have come and the destination toward which we are moving.

Finally, the earth and her companion planets that circle the sun as a family are also moving a million miles a day outward into space. None of us travels home alone. Together with our companion pilgrims, the entire solar family and the other sun colonies of the universe, we are involved in a cosmic dance which is a corporate mystical quest. While this is a personal manual of prayer, it is not one of private prayer! We may pray apart from others but we never pray alone. May the words written in this book awaken the pilgrim who uses it to the sacred mystery of the interconnectedness of all creation.

THE SOLAR JOURNEY
THROUGH THE SEASONS

This Planetary Pilgrim's manual has four sections of prayers for our daily circle journey as our planet rotates on her axis. Since our planet tilts 23½ degrees with respect to the sun in her annual pilgrimage around it, we experience the influence of the sun in different ways at different times in various parts of the world. The number of daylight hours and changes in temperature divide our year into four periods we call seasons: spring, summer, autumn and winter.

If you are using this handbook as a pilgrim in space in the northern hemisphere of our planet, spring begins about March 21 and ends around June 21. In a leap year it is slightly earlier than in the other three years. Summer begins June 21, 22 or 23 and ends on September 22, 23 or 24. The autumn season officially begins then and ends around December 21 when winter begins.

As we circle the sun, the 23½ degree tilt of our planet causes the light of the sun to strike the northern half at a more direct angle in the season of summer, bringing warmer temperatures. In winter the light and heat of our daystar strikes that part of the earth at a less intense angle.

In the southern hemisphere the seasons are reversed. Spring begins in September, summer in December, autumn in March and winter in June. For prayer pilgrims near the middle of the planet, there are only two seasons, dry and wet. And those at the polar regions have only light and dark seasons. In using this manual near the equator or at either of the polar regions, adaptations will be necessary.

An awareness of the different seasons that our companions experience in other regions of our planet can be a ritual of realizing communion with our brothers and sisters who are co-pilgrims, sharing this eternal journey in space.

Since the most ancient times the pilgrims of this planet have welcomed the changing of the seasons with rituals of celebration. This guidebook for space travel will provide an opportunity for you to step into that river of tradition and allow you to be enriched by an awareness of the changes that come about through the movements of the earth on her sacred journey around the sun.

IMPORTANT NOTES ON THE USE OF THIS BOOK

This book is divided into two parts. The first is composed of daily prayers for each of the four seasons of the year. These prayers provide a pattern or framework for a regular personal prayer of meditation and devotion to God. (Each daily prayer begins and ends with the instruction "sacred gesture." This can be a profound bow of the head or body or perhaps the sign of the cross. Whatever form it takes, it should be done slowly and with devotion.) The daily prayers are followed by a collection of contemporary psalms, prayers and rituals that can be used at special occasions or seasons of your life, or they can serve to give body to the daily prayer times. They appear in a wide variety of themes that give expression to a full spectrum of human feelings and longings in our relationship with God. (There is an index of these themes at the back of the book to assist you in finding a psalm that expresses what is in your heart and mind at a given moment.)

The second part of this book is a manual of instruction on the art of prayer and meditation and other aspects of the sacred journey. It includes suggestions about creating a prayerful environment, both inner and outer, and other aids for making your daily prayer and your pilgrim journey home to God both a source of joy and a way of responding to our deepest calling.

REFERENCES AND NAMES FOR THE DIVINE MYSTERY

For Jesus Christ, the awareness of God as a Divine Parent, his Father, made a deep impression on his spirituality and theology. If God is the single parent from whom all life has come, then it follows that we are a single family. All beings are our brothers and sisters. This awareness makes Jesus' disciples political mystics. Their pilgrimage back to their Divine Parent cannot be indifferent to the social and political conditions of their brothers and sisters or to the ecological concerns of our planet and all the creatures that live upon it. Once we understand this underlying connection, then prayers for justice and peace for all who dwell on this planet must be an essential element of our practice.

The use of such names for the Divine Mystery as "Beloved" or "Sacred Energy" allow the pilgrim who uses this book to explore other aspects of her or his personal relationship with God. But the pilgrim who uses this manual should be cautious not to abandon a parental title "Father" or "Mother" in praying to God, lest the corporate, family consciousness of all life be lost.

The Moon

THE SEASON
OF SPRING

A SPRING EQUINOX RITUAL

As the sun's rays strike our planet more directly, the earth responds with newness and freshness. Prehistoric priesthoods set this day apart as sacred, as a feast to celebrate the resurrection of the earth. The sun, radiant and healing, revitalizes the dark and dormant, as days and nights are again of equal length on the day of equinox. May the eternal experience of spring prepare each of us for a personal rebirth and resurrection. May it be a pledge-sign that life rises out of death.

A true planetary pilgrim experiences this feast not as a spectator but as a concelebrant with the earth and all creation. This day is both holy and magical, filled with hidden spirits and sounds. May your ears, eyes and nose be attentive to the rebirth of green life pushing up through the earth, even if it is still hidden from view. May you feel in your body the energy of the sun calling for newness and life.

The Ancient Ones danced like children to the mystery of new life and sprouting vegetation. They lit great fires to banish the tired, aged spirits of winter and darkness. They built their bonfires to ward off the half-hidden fears that perhaps this time, this year, winter would not leave and they would die in the barren, icy darkness.

With reverence, let yourself be touched by this hidden memory as you respond to the tidal-gravitational tug of the planet Earth on this feast. Rejoice with all the Web of Life, woven so tightly, as the season of spring begins.

SONG OF WELCOMING
MARCH 21

Sacred Parent, creator of the sun which makes the seasons,
    I rejoice in the gift of ever-growing light
    as the earth daily leans closer to our daystar.
With joyfulness I greet this new season of spring
    that rises from the gray death chamber of winter.

As my ancestors of old
    lit feasting fires to banish the darkness
    and to call forth the fire of the sun,
    may I enkindle in my heart
    the flames of hope in new life.

Hope rides on the springtime air,
    carried aloft upon the wind,
    filling field and forest, city and town,
    with the incense of excitement.

With awe-filled joy
    I sing of the sun, mysterious daystar
    that warms and feeds our planet
    with energy and light.
I sing with joy that your son, the sun,
    has signaled once again
    the beginning of a new season of life.

Great and generous are you, my God,
    who has given us the rich variety
    of ever-changing seasons.

Amen+

SONG OF AWAKENING

as one lights a candle

Listen, all you seeds in the earth,
    buried in your dark earthen tombs.
As this flame of my spring candle
    penetrates the darkness,
    may your young tender stems pierce the earth
    to dance in wind and rain
    just as this flame, like a tiny sun,
    now dances before me.

Father of fire, Mother of mystery,
    teach me the lesson of spring
    as all creation comes alive—
    tree and bush, flower and plant—
    in the alleluia richness
    of the resurrection of creation.
Grant me the gift, O God,
    to do the same.

Teach me, O glorious Spring,
    the lesson that nothing dies completely.
At the death of my body help me to know
    that I have not entered an endless winter,
    but simply a stage in the unfolding mystery
    whose name is Life.

On this feast of the spring equinox
    may I taste with delight
    the freshness and vitality of new birth
    and come forth from the womb of winter
    youthful with hope
    and fully alive
    in the presence of my God.

Amen+

SUNDAY MORNING PRAYER

sacred gesture

As the earth once again turns to face the sun on this first day of the week, I rejoice in this season of spring. I give thanks, O God, that each day grows longer in light and that the earth has been liberated from the grip of winter.

On this day that remembers the resurrection of your son Jesus from the depths of death's decay in the tomb, I lift my heart to you in gratitude. I thank you for the gift of a day of worship and all the graces it holds. I thank you for the healing touch of sleep as I begin this day refreshed and renewed. With a full heart, I enter now into the prayer of silence.

period of silent prayer or meditation

I now unite myself with all the peoples of this earth, my companion pilgrims, as I pray.

a psalm, spiritual reading or personal prayer

As I begin this first day of a new week, I ask for the grace, my God, to live in a new way. Grant me fresh dreams and new visions. May this day come upon me like Spring herself, so that my heart may be filled with hope.

Remind me, as I begin this day, to discipline myself so that it may be a day of rest from my usual labors. May I thus taste more deeply the joys of simply being alive. May I find the countless hidden treasures that you have scattered throughout this day.

On this day of worship and prayer, I pause to pray especially for the intentions of: _____, as well as all those whom I love. May your peace rest upon all the members of the earthen family with whom you have made me one.

I begin this day
    in your Holy Name
    and in the name of your son Jesus
    and in the name of the Holy Spirit,
    as I bow before you. Amen.

sacred gesture

SUNDAY EVENING PRAYER

sacred gesture

O Divine Parent, in harmony with all the earth, with sun and moon, stars and comets, I thank you for this day that is now ending. As the earth turns away from the sun, and night comes to visit me, I bow down before you in adoration and gratitude.

I pause to recall how I have responded to your gifts of persons and events this Sunday.

pause for silent examination of conscience

I ask pardon from you, O God, for any haste or lack of kindness on my part that may have been a cause of pain or separation. I bow in wonder before your love that forgives me instantly and unconditionally. In a like way, may I now pardon all who may have caused me pain this day. . . .

At peace with you and with all, I enter now into a time of silent affection and union with you.

period of silent prayer or meditation

With love I join myself with all those on this planet Earth who at the beginning of night praise you, as I now pray.

a psalm, spiritual reading or personal prayer

Once again, Beloved God, this planet has turned outward in its unknown destination into space. I look with wonder upon the vastness of the universe as the family of our sun's planets travels onward in its galactic pilgrimage.

Come and be with me in a sleep that will refresh me for a new day and for the work that it holds for me. Grant comfort to all who face the darkness of this night with fear. Give shelter to those without a home and peace to all.

With gratitude and faith, I conclude this day
in your Holy Name
and in the name of your Son
and in the presence of your Spirit. Amen.

sacred gesture

MONDAY MORNING PRAYER

sacred gesture

My Beloved Divine Parent, the earth is turning from its vision of countless star-suns to look once again with great joy upon one star, our sun. A new day has dawned, and with it come fresh challenges to grow more mindful of you and of the web that unites me with all life.

I pause now in the midst of this springtime morning to be in a conscious communion with you, my God, so that I will use wisely this gift of a day of life. Wrap me in your Spirit as I now enter into silent prayer.

period of silent prayer or meditation

You who alone know the secrets of hearts, look with love upon my feeble attempts at silent prayer. I am grateful that you do not measure my effort but look only upon my love for you. As springtime life quickens upon this planet, may this morning prayer express my devotion.

a psalm, spiritual reading or personal prayer

I know that your love for me, O God, is ever-constant and that you know all my needs, but as I begin this new spring day, I awaken my reliance on you as I pray for the following personal intentions: _____.

My happiness is not divorced from the well-being of others, and so I pray now for these persons: _____.

Grant me the grace to look with respect upon all I will meet this day and upon every event I encounter. Mindful that I am a pilgrim, may I treat each and every one with reverence and love, as a manifestation of you to whom I journey. May the work of my hands be part of the redemption of the world and its eternal springtime liberation.

As your priestly pilgrim, I dedicate this day and all that I shall do as an act of sacrifice to you, my God. I begin this day in a holy way
in your Holy Name
and in the name of your son Jesus
and in the name of the Spirit. Amen.

sacred gesture

MONDAY EVENING PRAYER

sacred gesture

O Beloved One, Divine Parent of each of us, so quickly has this spring day come to an end. I rejoice in the signs of new life that are appearing and only regret that your spring comes so slowly in me. I lift my heart to you in gratitude for all the numerous blessings and gifts of this day that is now ending.

As this part of our planet turns away from the sun, and the darkness grows, I ask forgiveness for any lack of the Light in myself this day. I am sorry if my patterns of behavior have prevented me from loving uncondi-tionally or have caused me to judge others. I pause now to take inventory of my day. . . .

Wrap me, O Holy One, in your absolution as I readily give full pardon to all who may have caused me pain this day. In peace now, I enter into silent prayer.

period of silent prayer or meditation

O Blessed Silence, Divine Presence, after the toil of this day I am refreshed by your touch. With a grateful heart I now pray.

a psalm, spiritual reading or personal prayer

From every corner of this green planet, from every place of worship and from every heart wrapped in prayer comes a single chorus of praise to you, O God. Oceans, mountains, prairies and valleys add their praise to my prayer of adoration and love.

I surrender myself to your safekeeping as night draws close to me. Bless with your presence those I love and especially this night: _____. Bless as well those who have no bed in which to sleep or who fear the coming of tomorrow. With your grace, I pledge to strive with more love to make my tomorrow better than this day.

I seal myself now in your presence
in your Holy Name
and in the name of your Son
and the Holy Spirit,
One God, forever and ever. Amen.

sacred gesture

TUESDAY MORNING PRAYER

sacred gesture

O Divine Parent, vest me in prayerfulness as I join with all
the earth on this springtime morning to lift up my
heart to you. With splendor, our daystar, the sun, now
floods this planet with light and energy. May your
presence flood my heart with light eternal as I rejoice
in this dawn.

As a planetary pilgrim, I marvel that I have traveled over a
million miles in space since yesterday morning. My
personal journey this day will be small in distance, but
I pray that it will be significant and sacred in my drawing closer to you. As the earth turns toward the sun, I
turn my whole self toward you, my God, as I now enter
into silent prayer.

period of silent prayer or meditation

Your Word is written large across all the universe, in the
wonders of creation and in the holy books, written by
the pen of your Spirit. Open my heart to your Word as
I now pray.

a psalm, spiritual reading or personal prayer

May this morning prayer and all my prayers this day be one
with all this earth which you have ordained to prayer.
May my day be prayerfully one with jungle rivers, hills
and valleys and crowded cities as they all raise their
prayerful praise to you, Most Holy.

I dedicate this new day to you and ask that as spring
unfolds before me, I may unfold according to your
ancient dream. As I reflect upon my personal needs
this day, I ask the following blessing: _____. I ask
that you would look upon my work this day as a
sacrifice performed in solidarity with: _____, who is
(are) in need of your grace and assistance.

Imprint upon my body, and upon all that I shall touch, your
sacred signature as I conclude this prayer
in your Holy Name
and in the name of your Son
and of the Holy Spirit,
One God, forever and ever, ages without end. Amen.

sacred gesture

TUESDAY EVENING PRAYER

sacred gesture

Beloved God, Eternal Womb from which all life has come, I
greet the arrival of night with gratitude and faith in
you. As this part of the earth turns away from the sun
and darkness shadows us, dawn is breaking aglow in
golden light on the other side of this small planet.
One with those who are now awakening, united with
those of us who are preparing to enter into sleep, I
pause to reflect on how I have used the hours of
daylight that have been given to me. . . .

I am filled with gratitude that your love is unconditional
and that you have forgiven me the moment that I
stumbled in my journey to be your living presence in
my world. Grant me the grace to forgive others as you
have forgiven me. One with your Spirit who prays continuously in my heart, I now enter into the prayer of
silence.

period of silent prayer or meditation

This night is filled with the sounds of life. To all those
sounds I now join my voice in a prayer of devotion.

a psalm, spiritual reading or personal prayer

With faithfulness, this planet earth has traveled over a
million miles in its orbit around the sun since I last
slept. Because of its life-path, this planet flourishes
with living beings, plants and animals. I pray that my
life path this day has also enriched and given life to
all with whom I have come in contact.

As I prepare to enter into the sacrament of sleep, I lift up
into your divine heart the following intentions: _____.
I pray as well for my brothers and sisters who have no
roof over them this night and for those who are imprisoned by the chains of fear, doubt or addiction.

Grant me a restful sleep, and if it be your will, may I rise
tomorrow to the gift of a new day of life. With trust I
place myself in confidence
in your Holy Name
and in the name of your Son
and of the Holy Spirit. Amen.

sacred gesture

WEDNESDAY MORNING PRAYER

sacred gesture

O Beloved Sacred Parent, I rise from sleep to join the great dance of life. One with stars and planets no longer visible because of the dawning light of our one star, the sun, yet which are still blazing in beauty all about me, I enter into prayer. One with this whole planet, whose northern hemisphere is awakening to the season of spring, I now awake to your hidden presence in my life as I descend into my heart to be one with you.

period of silent prayer or meditation

As darkness slides around this planet to the other side and the light of our daystar reveals a springtime world, I put flesh upon my silent song of love as I pray.

a psalm, spiritual reading or personal prayer

I rejoice that this simple expression of my affection for you, Beloved One, rises in harmony with temple chants, with the prayers of hermits as well as the life-prayer of those preparing to begin a new workday. While silent to my ears, I acknowledge the cosmic chorus of adoration of which my prayer has been a part.

Open as well my third eye that I may see you hidden in countless forms in the springtime beauty of creation and in my brothers and sisters, each made in your image. Remember my needs this day, especially the need to grow in patience. Enlarge my heart that I may love more and with greater zeal. I place before you at the beginning of this new day the following intentions: _____. I pray on this springtime Wednesday morning especially for the conversion of my society. May I, by simple deed and word, be part of the redemptive work begun by your son Jesus and so bring about justice and peace on this small planet.

May I live in the spirit of hope, so alive in this season of rebirth, as I begin my day
in your Holy Name
and in the name of your Son
and in the Spirit of the Holy. Amen.

sacred gesture

WEDNESDAY EVENING PRAYER

sacred gesture

O Beloved One who never sleeps, I prepare to conclude this day in a oneness with you. This side of our planet has turned away from the sun, but the evenings grow warm as the earth tilts toward our daystar. May this springtime evening, so fertile with life, enrich my prayer as I now recall the gifts of this day. . . .

Grant me as well the light of your Spirit that I may now search this day that is concluding for any words, thoughts or deeds that were devoid of love. . . .

May others forgive me for any way I may have caused them pain. Let this day not end without me forgiving those who have injured me. Graced with your never-ending forgiveness and at peace with all, I enter now into the prayer of silence.

period of silent prayer or meditation

As I come forth from the cave of my heart, I thank you, Beloved One, for your patience as I struggle to sit in silence, with its emptiness of sound but fullness of you. I thank you for all the expressions of yourself that I tasted this day in my work, my struggles and my loves. Like a fish in the ocean, I have been immersed in your presence this day. I proclaim that communion as I pray.

a psalm, spiritual reading or personal prayer

As death's shadow, sleep, approaches, may I embrace it with faith and peace. I pray that these twin gifts be also given to all who are in need of your touch in their lives, especially:_____. Into your hands I place all those this night who are in need in body or spirit.

As this planet and all the solar family travel endlessly outward into space as I sleep, may I, day and night, asleep and awake, journey without ceasing toward you, the source of life. I place myself and all those I love under your blessing,
in your Holy Name
and in the name of your Son
and in the name of the Holy Spirit,
One God forever and ever. Amen.

sacred gesture

THURSDAY MORNING PRAYER

sacred gesture

Once again, as it has done for endless ages, the earth is slowly turning around toward the sun. Dawn comes with the freshness of that first day of creation. May my worship at the beginning of this day be united with that of birds and wild animals, with clouds and sky. May my rising be a rehearsal for my resurrection from the dead. With gratitude for the wonder of this day, for the rich gift of life itself, I enter into silent prayer.

period of silent prayer or meditation

In harmony with all the earth as it soaks up the fire of the sun, I express the gratitude and devotion of my heart as I now pray.

a psalm, spiritual reading or personal prayer

In the quiet of this spring-touched morning, I absorb the light of this new day and soak up the love that ceaselessly flows out of your divine heart. As a cosmic pilgrim traveling with the earth and her sister planets outward into space, I ask you to accept my sacrifice of this day in solidarity with the special needs today of: _____.

May I embrace with joy my pilgrim work of unity. May I, with your grace, be an instrument of your peace to all I will meet and in every situation of this day. May our tiny planet, divided in a multitude of nations, races and religions, be united in its love of you. May my prayer and all the prayers, sacrifices and deeds of compassion performed on this planet today be blend-ed together as one and reach you through the mystery of your son Jesus, the cosmic Christ.

O Divine Giver of Life, you in whom we breathe and live, show yourself to me this day in countless ways. And grant me the grace to bow in wonder and in joy wherever and whenever I discover you. Boldly trace your sacred sign upon me in love as I begin this day
in your Holy Name
and in the name of your Son
and in the abiding presence of your Spirit,
One God forever and ever. Amen.

sacred gesture

THURSDAY EVENING PRAYER

sacred gesture

O Beloved Sacred Parent, this spring evening is green-edged with hope and filled with promise. With each passing day, the light of the sun lingers longer upon this planet. Even in the darkness of this night, one can feel the earth stirring with life. The night wind is full of promise as I reflect upon my actions this Thursday. I ponder if they, like this season of spring, have been full of hope and rich in life.

Open my heart and pour in all that is lacking. Saturate my words with love and encouragement, so that I may be truly an expression of your presence in this world. I thank you for the countless blessings of this day: gifts of sight, sound, hearing and smell, for wonders without end. I thank you as well for your endless patience with me and your pardon of my failings. Robed in your peace, my heart ripe with gratitude, I now enter into the prayer of silence to be one with you.

period of silent prayer or meditation

O Gracious Creator of the moon and stars, of galaxies spreading outward beyond the vision of our tiny telescopes, I marvel that you have chosen to dwell within the temple of my heart. I ask your understanding, for that temple is a crowded place where I have stored concerns and conflicts, work and worries as well as all the content of this day. I take springtime hope that all those things that clutter my heart, while they seem so distant from you, in reality hold your presence, my God. In that confidence, I now express my gratitude as I pray.

a psalm, spiritual reading or personal prayer

Mindful of the needs of others, before I retire I lift up into your divine heart the needs of all who are in need of your protection, healing and care this night, especially: _____. Encircle my bed, my home and all those I love with your divine love. I ask this
> in your Holy Name
> and in the name of your Son
> and the Holy Spirit. Amen.

sacred gesture

FRIDAY MORNING PRAYER

sacred gesture

O Beloved Parent, be near as I begin this new day of life. The work of this spring day knocks at my door, anxious for me to begin. But let this present moment be as still as a stone as I rest my heart in you. May past and future meet in the peace of this springtime morning prayer. Quiet my restless heart as I now enter into silence.

period of silent prayer or meditation

May this spirit of silence be like a golden thread woven into every work of this new day that is dawning. May I feel the touch of that thread in everything and so recall the fullness of this moment. May my love for you now find expression as I pray.

a psalm, spiritual reading or personal prayer

This planet, O Gracious Creator, has made one complete turn since yesterday morning and continues its sacred spin as I pray. Together with this movement, it circles the sun and with her sister planets continues outward in a cosmic pilgrimage into space. Grant that in my personal journey and the complex turnings of this day I may remain balanced in you, my God. May I, with your assistance, use every opportunity this day to grow in love and service. I pray this morning for these personal needs: _____, as well as the special needs of: _____.

May this prayer and all my labors this day be united with the prayers of all my Moslem brothers and sisters on this their weekly day of prayer and worship at the mosque. May my sacrifice and worship today be in communion with that of all peoples of this planet.

More precious than gold or silver are the prayers of your children, my companion pilgrims on this planet earth. May we all be one in you as I begin this day
    in your Holy Name
    and in the name of your son Jesus
    and in the Holy Spirit,
    One God forever and ever. Amen.

sacred gesture

FRIDAY EVENING PRAYER

sacred gesture

O Gracious God, Divine Beloved, as this part of the earth turns away from the sun, I turn toward you. I lift up to you my song of thanksgiving for all the gifts and blessings of this day. Among those gifts are the trials and tribulations that serve as opportunities to strengthen my love for you. As the earth comes alive in this season of spring, I remind myself that there is no true growth without struggle, effort and even pain. May my pain this day reflect the labor of springtime that gives birth to new life. Before I conclude this day, I desire that all things be at peace with me. I reflect on my relationships with the earth, with others and with you, my God. . . .

As the darkness of outer space surrounds me, heal me and all the earth of our failings this day. Absolve us of our sluggish delays in bringing about an age of peace and justice, of our blindness to the sufferings and plight of our brothers and sisters. May your pardon be the tent of peace I enter as now I descend into silent prayer.

period of silent prayer or meditation

Love sings many songs; may this prayer be the song of my heart.

a psalm, spiritual reading or personal prayer

How wondrous, O God, is the universe that you have made. To reach the nearest star would take several lifetimes, so vast is the distance that separates us. As I prepare to sleep, your act of creation continues as new stars are born amidst a swirl of dust and gases, exploding in an ecstasy of light. May the work of my re-creation continue as you rest my mind and body in sleep. With trust, I turn over my world and all I love to you. I place before you the concerns of all those who are alone and abandoned this night, especially the needs of:_____.

Encompass me in your presence as I pray
in your Holy Name
and in the name of your Son
and of the Holy Spirit. Amen.

sacred gesture

SATURDAY MORNING PRAYER

sacred gesture

O Divine One who never slumbers, smile on me as I awake
to greet this seventh day of the week. I arise from
sleep united with all of the House of Israel who greet
this dawn as a sacred day. Holy is this Saturday, holy
have been each of the days of this week that concludes today. That I may live in that sense of holiness
and fullness, I now enter into silent prayer. Wrap me
in your Spirit as I enter the cave of my heart.

period of silent prayer or meditation

Splendorous is the song of silence, for how can words
speak of you who are beyond all names, beyond the
concepts of my mind yet nearer to me than I am to
myself. I celebrate the wonder of your being as I pray.

a psalm, spiritual reading or personal prayer

As this earth spins around at thousands of miles an hour,
my mind spins with plans for this day. At the same
time as I use your gift of organizing, grant me also the
gift of openness to what you, my God, may have in
store for me on this new spring day. May I be open to
sacred surprises. Grant me the readiness to set aside
my plans when life proposes another agenda or the
needs of others invite me to unexpected service. I present to you these my personal needs this day: _____,
as well as the special needs of: _____.

Mindful this day of the great commandment that you gave
to Moses, that we are to love you with all our heart,
mind, soul and body, help me this Saturday to love in
such a way. How easily do I live but half a life and
love with but half a heart, but with your grace, this
day will be different. May a zeal for life and for you
consume me as it did your son Jesus and all the great
saints of this earth.

May the new life of spring that fertilizes the earth be but a
mirror of your ever-new life within my heart. I begin
this day with joy and gratitude
in your Holy Name
and in the name of your Son
and of the Holy Spirit. Amen.

sacred gesture

SATURDAY EVENING PRAYER

sacred gesture

O Holy Father and Divine Mother, from whom all life and
creation has come, I bow before you in wonder and
adoration. As this seventh day of the week concludes,
I marvel that within this week I have traveled seven
million miles outward into the mystery of the night of
space. Where is this cosmos, which you have shaped,
traveling? Why have you placed me here at this place
on this planet, at this precise moment in history? The
only answer I hear is silence—and so only silence can
be my response. With all my heart, I now enter into
the prayer of stillness, one with you and all the earth.

period of silent prayer or meditation

How patient are you, my God, with my infant efforts to sit
in silence before you. Pardon my restless mind and
receive the gift of my desire to sit still. As this week
concludes, while this planet once again looks outward
at the great sea of stars and the beauty of the moon, I
pray the following prayer.

a psalm, spiritual reading or personal prayer

May my ears and eyes be open to the marvel of green life
pushing up through the skin of the earth and struggling free in buds on branches. This is the season of
lovers, so let my heart freshly fall in love with you, my
God. May the growing presence of ever-virgin Spring
speak of the perennial possibilities for new beginnings
in my life. And so I prepare to conclude a week now
grown old. May this night be alive with springtime
hope for the new week that will begin tomorrow.

I reach out to the web of life that binds all that you, my
God, have created in a sacred unity. May I be united
with all living beings on this planet, with the sun,
planets and moons of our solar family and all the glit-
tering colonies of night stars. May I sleep this night,
and at the hour of my death, in that sacred oneness.

Seal me this Saturday night with yourself, as I pray
in your Holy Name
and in the name of your son Jesus Christ
and in the Spirit of the Holy. Amen.

sacred gesture

The Moon

THE SEASON
OF SUMMER

SUMMER SOLSTICE CELEBRATION

In the northern hemisphere the season of summer begins on about June 21 and extends to about September 23. The intense rays of the sun reach the northernmost tip of our planet on the June summer solstice. And because the northern half of our planet tilts fully toward the sun, the hours of sunlight are the longest on this day and the hours of darkness the shortest. From our vantage point, it appears that the sun stops at the peak of its northward journey. For several days it lingers at this point and then slowly appears to move southward.

Our ancient ancestors, who lived in harmony with the sun and the moon, knew within their bones the sacredness of such times. The eve of June 21 or midsummer's eve was a night of magic and feasting. Deep within our bodies the memories of those sun feasts are still alive. We are children of the sun, the daystar that makes all life possible as we travel in the icy darkness of frozen space. It is only fitting that we celebrate this turning point of our planet, even if we have a more sophisticated knowledge of the earth, sun, moon and planets than our ancestors.

It was believed that on midsummer's eve, the walls separating the worlds of the spirits and humans became as thin as tissue paper. The spirits of field and forest, of river and stream—all the inhabitants of that inner world—were free to pass back and forth between those walls and play among humans. It was a festival of fire, celebrating the full force of the sun-star. It was a time for feasting, a summer Christmas for play and pretending.

Summertime allows us opportunities for celebrations outside—ideal for a fire feast. Whether you celebrate the solstice alone or with family or friends, you are in communion with all peoples, ancient and modern, who are touched by the magic of the feast and who gratefully honor the blazing gift of the sun.

THE RITUAL
OF THE SUMMER SOLSTICE FIRE

a fire or a simple candle flame may be used

Holy is this fire of midsummer's eve,
    and holy are you, O God,
    who from your burning heart
    drew forth a fiery ball
    and flung it into space.

Your laughter shook the empty cosmos
    and echoed again and again
    until the darkness of space resounded
    with your love and with fire.

You reached in again and drew forth fire
    and seeded it like yeast
    in each atom, plant and animal,
    each bird, fish, man and woman.

And you gave us a special star, our sun,
    aflame with a life-evoking energy
    to make our planet green and fertile,
    sun-soaked in your love.

As we celebrate this magic feast,
    open our eyes to the countless wonders
    and to the sparks of fire-life
    that you have planted in each of us.

May this holy and magical night
    be aglow with star-fire and God-light
    as we once again begin
    the sacred season of summer.

Amen+

NOTE: To dance about or to jump over the solstice fire was said in ancient times to be a cure for disease, a prevention against snake bites and a blessing.

A RITUAL BLESSING OF THE SUN-FEAST

Sun-drenched food and drink,
>saturated with solar energy and sparks of life,
>we are grateful that you share
>your radiant life-force with us.

Your rays have traveled 93 million miles
>to sun-bathe this food and drink.
We are thankful for this long journey
>that makes us more alive with fire.

May you set our hearts aflame
>and our feet playfully a-dancing
>as in fun we circle-dance like the sun
>and delight in this festival of our star.

Hidden light, invisible power of our sun,
>we acknowledge with great gratitude
>your gift to us of all the planets
>who journey with us in the solar family.

Let the feast begin.

Amen+

A BLESSING OF THE SUN-FEAST FOOD

a circle is slowly traced over the food and drink of the feast as the blessing is pronounced

O Sacred Source of all the stars,
>we thank you for placing our small planet
>in such a course about our daystar, the sun,
>that we are neither fried nor frozen.

This food we are about to share
>is sun-kissed, drunk with starlight,
>and so full of life.

May we eat and drink of these gifts
>in your company and in great gratitude.

May this food and drink be blessed
>in the circle-sign of the sun,
>in the sign of our orbit around it,
>and in the holy sign of your unbroken unity.

Amen+

SUNDAY MORNING PRAYER

sacred gesture

I bow before you in adoration, O my God, on this first day
of the week, the day of your son Jesus' resurrection
from the dead. The earth also rises to new life this
morning and has turned round once again to face the
sun. Yet I hear not a sound; silent to my ears is the
revitalizing energy of the roaring nuclear furnace of
our daystar, the sun. You too, my God, are silent, yet
the sole source of my life. I seek your quiet presence
in my life as I now descend into the cave of my heart
to be one with you.

period of silent prayer or meditation

On this Sunday may I be aflame with love for you, my Beloved, like the sun which praises you with fire and
light. I unite myself with all those who have set aside
this day as holy, as I now lift up my heart to you in
prayer.

a psalm, spiritual reading or personal prayer

I rejoice in this season of warmth and growth, so full of
life. As plants and animals soak up the sun's life-
energy, may I absorb your Life this day in countless
ways. On this day of rest from work, may I find healing in the absence of my usual duties. By the touch of
leisure, may I be restored in creativity and new vision.
As I worship you on this summer day, may my heart
dance in wonder at all that you have ever made and
all you are bringing forth in this moment.

Present in my heart this morning are my concerns for the
needs of: _____, as well as my own needs
for:_____. May I be one this day with all believers
and with all unbelievers, with peoples of all religions
and races. Grant me a holy unity with all living beings, with life in every shape and form.

I bow before you, Divine Father, Holy Mother,
Eternal Source of my existence.
Your heart is my home,
from you I have come
and to you I journey this day.

sacred gesture

SUNDAY EVENING PRAYER

sacred gesture

As the darkness of space slowly enfolds the earth and the
light of the sun disappears, I come before you, O God,
to conclude this day of pilgrimage. I marvel that since
this time last summer, the earth, in company with her
sun and the other planets, has traveled outward over
300 million miles into the uncharted darkness of
space. As your pilgrim, I also have traveled closer this
day to my destination in you, my hidden God. I pause
now to be consciously one with you as I enter into
silent prayer.

period of silent prayer or meditation

The summer night is filled with sounds of life. I add my
voice to them with a song of devotion and love.

a psalm, spiritual reading or personal prayer

The earth is traveling on a threefold mystical journey, as it
whirls in the dance of day and night, makes its annual
pilgrimage around the source of its life, the sun, and
moves outward into boundless space. I too have traveled this day on my pilgrim's path. I pause to examine
whether on my way I have failed to remember who I
am and how I am to respond if I would be faithful to
you, my God. . . .

In your pattern of absolution which is unconditional and
without end, I grant pardon to all who have caused me
pain or injury. May tomorrow find me more awake to
the Way and to your presence in all of life.

Grant me a sleep of refreshment, a rest that heals and
restores the body and freshens my soul. I entrust into
your holy hands and heart the following intentions: _____. And when the earth has completed its
circle-journey and again faces the sun, I look forward
to once again sitting in your silence, one with you in
the prayer of love.

I bow before you, Divine Father, Holy Mother,
Eternal Source of my existence.
Your heart is my home,
from you I have come
and to you I journey this night.

sacred gesture

MONDAY MORNING PRAYER

sacred gesture

Our great daystar floods the earth with fire in this season of summer. The heart of the sun prays at 40 million degrees; grant me a heart of such fierce fire as I now begin this new day in an act of devotion and adoration. Wrap me in the silence of your Spirit and lead me into quiet prayer.

period of silent prayer or meditation

Like comets, various thoughts and concerns of my life have circled in my silent prayer. I consecrate these concerns which have been present without my permission in this time. By your presence, O God, you have touched them and made them the timeless fuel of my journey to you. Great is your love for me; may this prayer echo my deep affection for you, my Beloved.

a psalm, spiritual reading or personal prayer

This summer day is heated by the intense nuclear fires of the sun. May my day be alive with love and compassion for all, as it is fueled by this prayer and my communion with you, O God. Remind me frequently that I am a pilgrim. May I see all the events of this day as hidden lessons, directions for the unfolding map of my sacred journey. Grant me these graces this day: _____. And grant me assistance in these practical matters which are part of my task for this Monday: _____. I pray as well for the needs of: _____.

By thought, speech and deed, may I be concerned for the needs of the helpless. May justice for all be my will so that I may truly do your divine will on earth this day. As I prepare to begin the tasks of this summer day, let me never forget your presence within me. May all I do delight your heart.

I bow before you, Divine Father, Holy Mother,
    Eternal Source of my existence.
    Your heart is my home,
    from you I have come
    and to you I journey this day.

sacred gesture

MONDAY EVENING PRAYER

sacred gesture

We have named the darkness of our planet's turning outward, "night." I enter into the mystery of this summer
night, which is alive with the sound of my brothers
and sisters, the insects. How short is their life. But let
me not screen out the reality that my life is also brief.
May I now be busy with the real business of my short
life, as I enter into silent communion with you, O God.

period of silent prayer or meditation

In this prayer of mine now concluded, I have let go of
words and ideas about you who are beyond all words
and names. In my attempt to be still I have been naked before you, aware of my creaturehood. But my
heart dances in the knowledge that you delight in my
simplest attempts to be one with you. I now join my
voice to the many sounds of praise this night as I
pray.

a psalm, spiritual reading or personal prayer

Unlike the earth, which is traveling at over 66,000 miles an
hour in its pilgrimage around the sun, I feel that I
have covered little ground in my pilgrimage to you. I
pause to reflect on how I may have been detoured this
day because I forgot that I was a pilgrim, homeward
bound to you. . . . I lift up my heart in a song of
gratitude that you forgive me even as I ask. May I now
do the same for all who have presented difficulties to
me this day.

The chorus of insects, this summer night's concert, is
nature's night prayer of praise. Brief is their song, but
so is mine compared to the age of mountains. Grant
me the gift, O God, to not take my life for granted, to
live ready to depart this planet, homeward bound for
you. I surrender to death's sister, sleep, at peace with
others and one with you.

I bow before you, Divine Father, Holy Mother,
Eternal Source of my existence.
Your heart is my home,
from you I have come
and to you I journey this night.

sacred gesture

TUESDAY MORNING PRAYER

sacred gesture

I bow before you, my hidden but beloved God, as I begin
this day. An alarm rings in my heart to awaken me to
the fact that I am a pilgrim who travels a sacred path.
I now answer that call to mindfulness, as I prepare to
enter into silent prayer. I join myself with all who are
in prayer at this sacred hour when the earth once
again faces its source of life, the sun. I now turn fully
to face you, O God, the source of the universe and of
my life, as I enter into silence.

period of silent prayer or meditation

With fidelity I have tried to still my restless heart in you,
the divine source of all I am. May this effort bear fruit
by my living more fully in the present moment this
day. I join my voice to all the awakening sounds of
the earth at this hour, as I pray.

a psalm, spiritual reading or personal prayer

This summer day is growing warmer as we turn to face the
fullness of our daystar, the sun. Plants, animals and
we humanfolk are all solar-powered in the marvel of
your clever creation. May this morning prayer give me
the energy to act at all times this day with love and
kindness. May I treat each person and each living being as a brother or sister, as a member of your sacred
family. I pray now for these personal needs: _____,
and for the special needs this day of: _____.

May the business of this Tuesday never eclipse my real
work as a pilgrim on the sacred path. Open my eyes
and ears to the miracles you have hidden along my
path this day. Let my mind find its joy in the present
moment, the only place where you dwell.

I bow before you, Divine Father, Holy Mother,
    Eternal Source of my existence.
    Your heart is my home,
    from you I have come
    and to you I journey this day.

sacred gesture

TUESDAY EVENING PRAYER

sacred gesture

O Holy Parent, in the magnificent splendor of its setting the sun has slipped from my view, as the earth turns outward on its ageless journey among the stars. As we drink in the coolness of the eternal night of space, those in another part of this earth are rejoicing in the warmth of the sun on a new winter day. One with those who are awakening as well as those who prepare for sleep, I enter now into silent prayer.

period of silent prayer or meditation

My heart was full of the cares of this day as I returned again and again to the stillness of your presence within me. Cleanse my heart of any thoughts that might separate me from others so that I may be one in you. I pause to take inventory of the gift of this day of life. . . .

May the coolness of your touch heal all that is broken and mend all that is divided, as I express my praise in this prayer.

a psalm, spiritual reading or personal prayer

While darkness hides the light of the sun, the earth retains the warmth of its solar fires. May my heart likewise retain the fire of your love as I prepare to close my eyes in sleep. As this summer day ends, I place before you these needs: _____. I pray as well for those who face this night with fear and dread and for all who end this day hungry, alone or prisoners of pain. May the sun of your justice rise on all who suffer from oppression, slavery or the hatred of their brothers and sisters.

Come, Beloved of my heart. Be with me in sleep, that I may rise in glory. As I prepare to end this day, I look forward to the restoring prayer of tomorrow, when I shall greet a new day one with you.

I bow before you, Divine Father, Holy Mother,
    Eternal Source of my existence.
    Your heart is my home,
    from you I have come
    and to you I journey this night.

sacred gesture

WEDNESDAY MORNING PRAYER

sacred gesture

O Blessed One, as it has done each day for millions of years, the earth once again has circled around to face the sun. Yet the appearance of that great daystar is like the first time: forever new, forever fresh. May the freshness and the coolness of this summer morning inspire me as I enter into silent prayer.

period of silent prayer or meditation

As I come forth from the refreshment of my solitude in you, all the earth arises, revived by the night, to the work of this day. Plants and trees, fields and forests are busy with the work of this summer day, the work of Life. To their songs of love, I join this prayer.

a psalm, spiritual reading or personal prayer

Enriched by your touch, O loving God, I now prepare to join my tasks on this Wednesday to the work of birds, flowers and plants, to the labors of all the human family. I am aware of how easily I forget to live in communion with all your creation, so I now pray for these personal needs: _____. May my work this day be done as a prayerful sacrifice in solidarity with those who also are in need of your constant presence, especially: _____.

As the sun pours forth its life that we on this earth may live, may I pour forth my life this day in service to others and in love of you, my beloved God. Remind me in countless ways as I walk the sunlit hours of this day that I am on a sacred journey; along with the stars traveling through space, I am on a pilgrim path.

I bow before you, Divine Father, Holy Mother,
    Eternal Source of my existence.
    Your heart is my home,
    from you I have come
    and to you I journey this day.

sacred gesture

WEDNESDAY EVENING PRAYER

sacred gesture

Beloved Father, the light of this day has lingered long as our earth drinks in the great heat of the sun. I rejoice in these long hours of sunlight and hope that I have used them well. Holy Mother, with great care you have helped me in my feeble attempts this day to walk as your child, a pilgrim on a sacred path. One with you and with all your children, I enter now into silent prayer.

period of silent prayer or meditation

Rich is your silence, full of peace, even if mixed with the thoughts that zig-zag through my silent prayer. The sounds of this summer night rise up in a canticle to you. I ask that my voice harmonize with them, as I now pray.

a psalm, spiritual reading or personal prayer

As you plunge your thermometer deep into my heart, may you find there the same intense heat which burns in the nuclear blast furnaces of the stars that illuminate the night of outer space. May the presence of your fiery Spirit, who prays continuously within my heart, make up for all the zeal my heart may lack. I conclude this day mindful of my poverty before you, as I lift up the special needs of: _____.

All of creation in this part of the earth has been busy this day growing to maturity. Have I been in concert with them in my efforts to grow in patience, hope and faith? I pause in this prayer to reflect upon my activities this day. . . . I thank you, O God, for the opportunities that you have placed on my sacred path this day to grow in maturity of heart and spirit. I thank you for the times that took me to the limit in my efforts to love and to serve. Wrapped in gratitude as clothing for my sleep, I rest in you.

I bow before you, Divine Father, Holy Mother,
Eternal Source of my existence.
Your heart is my home,
from you I have come
and to you I journey this night.

sacred gesture

THURSDAY MORNING PRAYER

sacred gesture

O Sacred Source of sleep, Creator of night stars and
oceans deep, I arise to this new day to sing of my love
for you. Glorious is the light of our daystar, the sun,
full of life and heat. As this summer day is sun-kissed
into awakening, I seek to live it fully awake. I enter
now into sacred silence, one with all who live in your
light.

period of silent prayer or meditation

My ears ring with the songs of silence, as the melodies of
this summer day counterpoint that ancient silent song
of the universe. To all the sounds of this new day, I
add my voice as I pray.

a psalm, spiritual reading or personal prayer

How easily, my God, come the words of my prayer. Pour
forth your Spirit, the fire of your heart, into each of
them so that they may express your Word, as I strive
this day to put flesh upon the prayer I sing to you.

I know you will give me all I need for the success of the
labors of this day and for the work of my sacred
journey to you. But your son Jesus told us to pray for
our daily needs, so I place before you these Thursday
intentions: _____.

Whatever this summer day holds for me, may I find,
among its many events, signs to confirm and direct
me in my primary vocation of pilgrimhood. May I be
eager to assist my sister and brother pilgrims in their
journeys. May I do nothing by word or deed that will
detour them on their homeward path to you. May I
burn with the fire of the sun in loving all the earth and
all the members of your sacred family.

I bow before you, Divine Father, Holy Mother,
Eternal Source of my existence.
Your heart is my home,
from you I have come
and to you I journey this day.

sacred gesture

THURSDAY EVENING PRAYER

sacred gesture

> O Divine Parent, how wondrous is my view of the universe
> as our planet earth turns outward into space once
> again. Beyond counting are the stars that congregate
> in colonies of distant galaxies. May my heart blaze
> with their brilliance as I enter now into sacred silence.

period of silent prayer or meditation

> Oh that my prayer may be as silent as the stars spread
> across this summer night sky. Grant me patience as I
> strive to sit in stillness, listening to your song of
> silence. I join my small voice to the symphony of the
> stars as I now pray.

a psalm, spiritual reading or personal prayer

> The sun and her planets travel tonight, as they have for
> billions of years, on their eternal night journey in
> space. As I look out toward their unknown destination,
> I reflect on how I have used the gift of this day. . . .

> As marvelous as the universe is your gift of conscience, a
> beacon for my pilgrimage. I thank you for that gift
> which keeps me on course and continually calls me to
> give more and to be more. Tomorrow may I follow it
> with still greater devotion.

> With great beauty you created our sun among a family of
> stars, in a great cloud of interstellar matter, gas and
> fire. Somewhere out in the starscape of this summer
> night, the brothers and sisters of our sun, born five
> billion years ago, are traveling their own mysterious
> paths, known only to you. I easily forget that, like our
> daystar, I too have brothers and sisters who are far
> distant but who share the same sacred Womb. I pray
> for them tonight, especially the lonely and afflicted,
> the dying and the sick. Wrap me in the cloud of your
> compassion and love as I soon will surrender to sleep.

> I bow before you, Divine Father, Holy Mother,
> > Eternal Source of my existence.
> > Your heart is my home,
> > from you I have come
> > and to you I journey this night.

sacred gesture

FRIDAY MORNING PRAYER

sacred gesture

Beloved God, as the call to prayer is heard by your
children of Islam on this their sacred day of the week,
I hear in my heart the call to bow down before you in
adoration and surrender at the beginning of this Friday. One with all, I wrap myself in silent prayer.

period of silent prayer or meditation

Many are the voices that speak their love for you, O
Sacred Parent of all the earthen family. I now join my
prayer to theirs.

a psalm, spiritual reading or personal prayer

With this prayer I dedicate this new day in the season of
summer to you, the creator of day and night, of the
seasons and endless cycles of life. May the work of
this day and all my daily duties be a living sacrifice of
love.

In the midst of the heat of this day, grant me the grace to
be at peace and centered in you. I ask for the grace
to faithfully do your will so that all may enjoy the
fruits of your bounty and justice. I pray now for those
who are in urgent need of your care and love,
especially: _____.

As the cool and quiet of this morning is slowly joined by
the sounds of summer life, I prepare to set forth on
this day's journey. May your Spirit, the Spirit of the
Holy, be with me. So escorted, I shall make holy all
the work of my day. May I strive to do all that is required of me with an awareness that I dwell constantly
within your great cosmic temple. So mindful, each act
will be a sacred ritual, each word a prayer and all my
life worship. Grant that when this day concludes and
the earth turns slowly outward to gaze into the night
of space, I may bring a harvest of light and love as my
gift to you.

I bow before you, Divine Father, Holy Mother,
Eternal Source of my existence.
Your heart is my home,
from you I have come
and to you I journey this day.

sacred gesture

FRIDAY EVENING PRAYER

sacred gesture

Divine Beloved, I ask your seal upon this summer day
before I close my eyes in sleep. I began this day one
with you and have struggled to live it in your harmony. Now I seek to bring it to conclusion in unity
with you. Invest me with a spirit of prayer as I enter
now into silence.

period of silent prayer or meditation

From this shrine of prayer the web of worship extends outward and touches all peoples—black, brown, yellow,
red and white—and all creation on this planet and the
far distant stars of the universe, all your holy family.
May my desire echo the eternal design of unity and
peace as I now pray.

a psalm, spiritual reading or personal prayer

In the heat of this day, in the crowded events of my work, I
may have rushed past you, my Beloved, in blindness.
Quiet of heart, I look back upon this day . . . .

Unite me now in a holy communion with all those I love
and with those I do not know personally but whose
needs I include as my own. I pray now for: _____.
As together we watch the night sky, pondering the
unanswered questions of our lives, calm our fears and
anxieties as you encircle us in your divine compassion
and love. We are all pilgrims on our way to you:
pilgrims with different orbits, different dreams and different burdens to bear, but each homeward bound to
you. Teach us to be like the sun and her planets, that
we might travel together with trust into the darkness
of the future.

May I surrender to sleep, filled with the joyful music of the
universe, with your melody that plays in ten thousand
tongues as if in one and whose sweetest song is silence.

I bow before you, Divine Father, Holy Mother,
Eternal Source of my existence.
Your heart is my home,
from you I have come
and to you I journey this night.

sacred gesture

SATURDAY MORNING PRAYER

sacred gesture

Blessed are you, Creator of the Universe. After a night of viewing the moon and a million stars, our earth turns so that we might look with wonder upon a single star, the sun. Large and orange it appears, as in turquoise twilight the sunrise leaves behind the darkness of space at dawn. Silent and golden, the rising sun fills the new summer day. May I, in a fullness of silence, a silence that leaves no room for fear, be one with you.

period of silent prayer or meditation

May my personal prayer be one with the prayer of your children Israel on this the Sabbath day. May my prayer rise like incense along with all prayers address-ed to you, the God of Abraham and Sarah.

a psalm, spiritual reading or personal prayer

Your love, O God, has been my tent this past night. As this new day begins in that love, may I taste your tenderness and care. Full-bodied and green are the leaves of trees that know no five-day week. Their labors ceaselessly create oxygen as a free gift for all, so that life might abound on this small green planet. May I also labor tirelessly to create a world of peace and harmony so that life may abound. I pray now for these intentions: _____.

Whatever this day holds for me, may I embrace it as sacra-ment and gift. In play or work, may I ever travel the pilgrim's path to you, O God. Restrain my desire to rush eagerly from one task to another. Slow me down that I may not miss the mysteries of your presence hidden in this warm summer day.

I bow before you, Divine Father, Holy Mother,
    Eternal Source of my existence.
    Your heart is my home,
    from you I have come
    and to you I journey this day.

sacred gesture

SATURDAY EVENING PRAYER

sacred gesture

O you who are Life—my very being, my peace and my
joy—you who are my hope, my wealth and my
strength, I bow before you as this week of seven days
concludes. Our daystar is disappearing as I again turn
outward to view a starscape of such vastness that it is
beyond the grasp of my mind. You are my home, my
place of rest, my heaven, my salvation. You are the
source of all the work of my hands and all the gifts of
this week now ending. I pause to recall from my
memory the days of this week. . . .

O Divine Magnet who draws me ever to yourself, make my
heart still and overflowing with gratitude at the
memories of these past seven days, as I now enter into the prayer of silence.

period of silent prayer or meditation

O you who hear all sounds as one sound, all songs as one
song, listen now as I sing of my love for you.

a psalm, spiritual reading or personal prayer

How quickly has this week passed, the days and nights now
fused as one. Just so quickly will my life reach its
fullness, like ripe fruit upon the vine, heavy upon the
limb.

I prayerfully place before you these intentions: _____.
I also pray for those who labor this night that the rest
of us may be secure and may relax and enjoy the
pleasures of life. May they know that their labors help
make possible the divine gift of joy for all who are at
leisure.

Warm Saturday night, electric with music and play,
feasting and celebration, may you praise the God of
joy who delights in the loves and pleasures of our
lives.

I bow before you, Divine Father, Holy Mother,
Eternal Source of my existence.
Your heart is my home,
from you I have come
and to you I journey this night.

sacred gesture

The Moon

THE SEASON
OF AUTUMN

AN AUTUMN EQUINOX RITUAL

For thousands of years we planetary pilgrims have welcomed the sacred event of the autumn equinox with fires, songs and celebrations. Day equals night and light balances darkness, as on this feast a season of completion and contentment begins. This is the harvest season; the fruits of summer are stored for the coming winter. Full barns, overflowing granaries and stocked cupboards give cause for rejoicing and feasting.

In spring, our ancestors bowed in expectant wonder before a fertile mother earth about to become the rich womb out of which would rise a harvest of life. But in fall maiden earth becomes an old woman, withered and spent by summer's growth. Our primal parents' celebration of yellowed autumn's harvest was tinged with fear. In their anxiety they wondered if their food supplies would last through the long winter. Might evil spirits, envious of their warm comfort and well-stocked cupboards, come and attack them? The sacred fires of this season were to purge away evil, to banish the fears of winter hidden behind the horizon.

Yet Old Woman Autumn held the secret of life even in withered old age. The last sheaf of grain to be harvested from the field contained her ageless spirit. It was carried into the home so that the old woman of vegetation, the grandmother of green energy, might live through the dreaded winter months. The season of colorful leaves, autumn is a time for thanksgiving. Annual celebrations of the Jewish Sukkoth, the Moslem Ramadan and Thanksgiving are among the feasts that decorate autumn with sacredness.

Autumn, you celebration of the harvest and the crowning of human achievement, rich textbook of wisdom, teach me to not take anything for granted but to be grateful for all. Wise Old Woman, teach me to take stock of the darkness within me and to acknowledge the great store of good that is also within. Teach me to balance the light and the dark as our earth now is a balance of day and night.

A RITUAL OF AUTUMN WELCOMING

In its annual pilgrimage around our star, the sun, the earth starts to cool after the autumn equinox. The tilt on the earth's axis is then away from the sun, lowering the angle of the sun's rays. In the northern hemisphere the season of autumn begins around September 23. It marks the time when leaves and fruit start to "fall" from northern trees and vines. While we rejoice in this harvest season of fullness and thanksgiving, our brothers and sisters in the southern hemisphere welcome the season of spring.

this prayer could be said at the door of your home after night has arrived

Welcome, Autumn, arms full of summer's blessings,
    carrying the seeds of life for next year's planting.
Come, enter my home with your golden wisdom;
    be my guest and share my table.

Welcome, Old Wise One,
    may I be your student in the school of gratitude.
Guide me in reflecting upon the summer now gone,
    that I might give thanks for all the many gifts
    that have enriched me in that season of growth.

I greet you, spirits of darkness
    that dwell in the night and within me.
While you are frightening, you are also a source of power;
    may I not fear you
    but learn to live in holy harmony with you;
    you are not evil unless you dominate me.
Night within me, I welcome you as well;
    may all your spirits that reside in me
    live in harmony with the Spirit of the Holy.

Amen+

AUTUMN EQUINOX BLESSING

this prayer could be said over a meal, a glass of wine or cider or while eating some autumn fruit or earthen food

My heart is the home of a banquet,
    and so I sing a song of thanks
    for all the gifts, talents, blessings and treasures
    that fill my life to the fullest.

My life is a feast
    that overflows with the delights of your presence.
In thanksgiving, I rejoice in that river of gifts
    that flows from taste, smell, touch and sight.
May my life be an endless song of gratitude.

May this, my life song, be a magnet
    that draws me ever closer to you, O Divine One,
    who has whispered in the silent spaces of my heart
    words that speak the gift of gifts:
    "You are my beloved."

Amen+

AUTUMN EQUINOX PRAYER

I unite myself with ancient memories that sleep within:
ancestors of long ago
whose fears have left their fingerprints upon me,
remind me of my holy communion
with that river of humanity flowing through my soul.
May this flame be my autumn sacred fire.

a fire or a candle may be lighted

I greet you, child of night, my anger;
may I live with you in a creative way.
Be fuel for the prophet within me
to speak and act against the darkness of injustice.

I greet you, daughter of the dark, my sexual needs;
may I always dance with you in creative, selfless ways.
May I live with you in openness and without fear.

I greet you, sons of darkness, envy and the need to be noticed;
I fear you not,
for you can teach me how I must love myself fully
if I am to love others and my God with all my heart.

I greet you, night-spirit of aggression;
may you be a powerful force for good in my life.
You are the energy that can impel me to achieve great deeds,
to heal the earth of brokenness;
may I live in healthiness with you.

And may all my friends of the dark
be in harmony with the spirits of light within me,
living together under the loving eye of God.

Amen+

AUTUMN EQUINOX FIRE PRAYER

a fire or candle may be lit

Dance with delight, O flame of autumn fire,
    as the earth, spinning and leaning away from the sun,
    begins to cool from the summer heat,
    and speak to me of the promise
    hidden in this season of autumn.
For spring is seeded in this season of completion,
    just as the giant oak exists within the acorn.

Autumn fire, orange and yellow sacrament of the sun,
    light up the darkness with your dancing.
Your power is seeded in the ripeness
    of the fruit and grain of this harvest season.
Great is God, whose heart is the shrine
    wherein lives this whole universe;
    great is your heart, my Beloved,
    greater still is your unceasing love for me.
May my love for you enflame my every word of thanksgiving
    to reflect the golden beauty of autumn
    that the earth dons once again.

Amen+

SUNDAY MORNING PRAYER

sacred gesture

As our planet earth whirls eastward toward the sun-star, I arise on this autumn morning refreshed by sleep. I greet the mellowness of this fall day with gratitude. As trees and plants acknowledge the death segment of their yearly cycle, I take hope in this morning that echoes the resurrection of your son Jesus. On this first day of the week, I enter into my heart to be one with you, my Sacred Guest, as I pray in silence.

period of silent prayer or meditation

I unite myself with all your children who on this day gather for prayer and worship of you. One with all the disciples of the Risen and Cosmic Christ, I now sing of my love for you.

a psalm, spiritual reading or personal prayer

May I greet every gift of this day with a song of gratitude. May my heart be full and content, like a harvest festival, as I enjoy this day of rest and re-creation. Guide me, O God, to spend it in a spirit of holy rest, free from the clock and its deadlines, free from the need to be useful.

Blessed are you, O God, who takes delight in the play and leisure of this first day of the week. I ask that these sacred elements of Sunday in which I engage will be worship and prayer, a holy communion with you who also played and rested on the seventh day of creation.

I begin my day as I place before you these intentions for my family and friends: _____. May these prayers be a communion ritual of love with them. I pray as well for all who are in need of your presence: _____. Grant your servant the grace of worship, as I fashion this day and every gift that it holds into the music of my continuous song of gratitude. I take up the challenge of this day one with you, my God, as I bow in adoration.

Blessed are you, O Harvest of my heart,
    Sacred Source of all life,
    Delight of my days.

sacred gesture

SUNDAY EVENING PRAYER

sacred gesture

Holy Mother, Divine Father, you who are beyond all images, this first day of the week is coming to a close. I
thank you for all it has held for me, the pleasure and
pain, joy and sorrow, each moment rich with a lesson
for my pilgrimage home to you. Sleep, death's sister,
is near at hand. But before I release control of this
day, I desire to enter into holy communion with you.
One with all the earth, one with all who pray as the
book of this day is closed, I enter into silence.

period of silent prayer or meditation

In the darkness of my heart, crowded with the memories of
this day and my plans for tomorrow, I have sat in
stillness with you, my Beloved. One with the harmony
of the moon and stars, I now sing of my love for you,
as I pray.

a psalm, spiritual reading or personal prayer

A new week of seven days has begun. Many will be the
demands upon me and many are my needs. So I place
before you, Divine Beloved, these intentions: _____.
I am mindful also of those who are in need, the
helpless and the oppressed, victims of violence and injustice. Be with them this night. I pray as well for the
needs of my family and friends: _____. Be as close
to them as you now are to me.

Once again, this planet's perpetual path around the sun has
come to the shrine of autumn. A year has passed so
quickly since last we visited here. Remind me by this
season of completion that soon my life will come
round full course. As I now open the doorway of sleep
with confidence, may I do the same, when the time
comes, with the doorway of death.

With a full heart and my soul at peace, I surrender to the
sleep of this night, as I bow before you.

Blessed are you, O Harvest of my heart,
    Sacred Source of all life,
    Ever-watchful Guardian of my sleep.

sacred gesture

MONDAY MORNING PRAYER

sacred gesture

Once again the earth has completed its 24-hour turnaround and again has come to face the brilliance of our sun-star. As its light floods the darkness of space, may the Spirit that sings its ageless song continuously in the cave of my heart now flood my heart with the rays of light eternal. Encircled in that light, I enter now into silence.

period of silent prayer or meditation

As the sounds of life begin on this Monday, may my voice be one with the chorus of all creation which rejoices in the ripeness of autumn. May this morning prayer echo through my every deed of this new day.

a psalm, spiritual reading or personal prayer

O Giver of all gifts, who has so enriched my life, I have many needs this day. Grant me the gift of patience so that I may live in harmony with all. Grant me the grace of compassion so that I may not bypass anyone in need. And give me enthusiasm for the tasks of this autumn day so that I may invest it with your love and life. I pray for the following intentions: _____.

Although alone at the moment, I embrace the mystery that I do not pray privately but am one with all the earth and all your children. I place within your heart these needs of the other members of the sacred family to which I belong: _____.

I ask you, my hidden God, who has filled heaven and earth with your glory, to help me to make my hands into your hands, so that your will may be done by me this day. Form my words into your words to affirm the faint-hearted, to support the faltering and to encourage the poor of spirit. Fill up all that is lacking in me, so that I may be your humble servant, a co-creator in your endless drama of creation.

I begin this day as I bow before you.

Blessed are you, O Harvest of my heart,
>   Sacred Source of all life,
>   Delight of my days.

sacred gesture

MONDAY EVENING PRAYER

sacred gesture

As this autumn day draws to a close, I marvel that this
earth has been spinning at over a thousand miles an
hour. Quickly indeed, for so massive a planet, has one
complete revolution finished since this time last evening. As the nighttime view of space opens before me,
filled with the splendor of sparkling stars, I pause to
be consciously one with you, the loving creator of this
whole universe. Wrap me in wonder and awe as I now
enter into silent communion with you.

period of silent prayer or meditation

This autumn evening, whose wind carries songs of harvest
gratitude, is part of the prayer my heart lifts up to you
with love and thanksgiving.

a psalm, spiritual reading or personal prayer

Oh how easily, my beloved God, do I believe that I am in
charge of my life, that this day has succeeded because
of my efforts. With humility I acknowledge that you
have been at the sacred source of the good that I have
done and the evil I have avoided. To raise that
awareness, I now ask your gracious assistance in my
life as I pray for the following intentions: _____.
May my prayers for those I love weave ever more
strongly the web that unites us, as I now lift up their
needs: _____.

Tired of body but full of gratitude, I prepare to enter into
the healing embrace of sleep. May this night be salve
for both body and soul; may it fill me with energy and
grant rest to my mind. I am mindful that I sleep
secure while many are homeless, aliens in a strange
land or separated from those they love. Cover them in
the tent of your holy presence and give them hope, as
I now surrender in love my day, my life and my very
being unto you, my Beloved.

Blessed are you, O Harvest of my heart,
Sacred Source of all life,
Ever-watchful Guardian of my sleep.

sacred gesture

TUESDAY MORNING PRAYER

sacred gesture

A new autumn day is dawning, as the earth turns around once again to view the majesty of our sun-star. While with each autumn day we lean further away from the rays of its great heat, the sun continues to warm creation as it embraces this season of completion. This fall day holds a great challenge as it calls me to toil for the harvest of justice and peace. Without you, Sacred Source of all energy, what success can I hope for from the work of my hands. So I now enter into holy union with you in a prayer of stillness.

period of silent prayer or meditation

With gratitude for the gift of speech, I add my voice to those of all your children who greet the dawn of this day with prayer and worship of you.

a psalm, spiritual reading or personal prayer

As the hours of daylight shorten, I give thanks that you are a luminous and loving God. You, my God, who are so Light-hearted, make my heart like yours. As a disciple of your son Jesus, may I be a light this day for those who are still in the darkness of night. As the light of the sun-star warms this planet after a nighttime of facing into the icy darkness of space, may I give warmth and light to all I meet. I pause to pray for my daily needs and for the graces necessary for this day: _____. Be mindful as well, O God, of the special needs of: _____.

May I see your holiness in the golden beauty of this day. May I touch with reverence all things, since everything is saturated with the sacred, is a tabernacle of your presence. Broaden the boundaries of my heart that it may encompass more than it did yesterday, as I begin this day one with you.

Blessed are you, O Harvest of my heart,
  Sacred Source of all life,
  Delight of my days.

sacred gesture

TUESDAY EVENING PRAYER

sacred gesture

Another day is ending as I put away the work of this
autumn Tuesday. I come before the doors of the holy
to seek and knock. Open to me, O God, the mystery
of your presence, for I rap with reverence, firm in the
faith that you open to all who knock at your door. All
about you, Most High, angels swarm and saints are
robed in blinding light. While my eyes are blind to
this reality, open my heart to the splendor of your
luminous presence.

period of silent prayer or meditation

Touch my restless heart which finds silence difficult. Affirm
within me the knowledge that you judge prayer only
by the heart's hunger to be one in you. One with all
your children, I now sing of my love for you.

a psalm, spiritual reading or personal prayer

Blessed are you who have made the entire universe your
holy temple, spread out in the autumn evening sky.
Sacred are the mountains and valleys, prairies and
fields of this planet. Holy are the forests and
meadows, the canyons and oceans deep, the cities and
villages—all your sacred space. All who dwell upon
this planet walk on holy ground, are priestly stewards
of your earthly shrine. Aware of that priestly dignity,
I now pray for the special needs of all the earth:
_____. I pray also for the needs of my family and
friends: _____. Pour forth through me the renewing
grace of your pardon as, in communion with you, I
now forgive all who have injured me.

May all the earth share the peace of my heart as I close my
eyes to this day of life and slip into sleep, filled with
confidence that I shall wake in the splendor of your
presence. Tomorrow as the earth again spins around
our sun-star, I shall return to my place of prayer to
sing of my love for you. Make of my sleep a prayer of
rest in you.

Blessed are you, O Harvest of my heart,
Sacred Source of all life,
Ever-watchful Guardian of my sleep.

sacred gesture

WEDNESDAY MORNING PRAYER

sacred gesture

With a silent thunderous roar, the sun-star of this planet is once again visible. The moon has reflected its light like a mirror this past night, but now our sun explodes in flaming beauty to warm this autumntide day. Make of my heart a mirror, O God, a new mystic moon to reflect your splendor, as I now enter into silence.

period of silent prayer or meditation

Aware of my spiritual poverty, my hands are upraised and cupped like a beggar's, as I ask you to fill my heart with your Spirit. Grant that this prayer will spread through my being like a forest fire driven by the wind of your Spirit. Then the flames of devotion will leap from word to word, causing each one to burst into flame, till all is fire, till all is love.

a psalm, spiritual reading or personal prayer

O Divine Beloved, how richly you have seeded your creation with the mystery of life. You are not a stingy God, for you allow the sun to shine on good and bad alike. You daily pour forth a torrent of beauty for all on this earth. Aware of your endless generosity, I now offer to you the following intentions: _____. Lean close and hear my prayers as I remember my family and all those I hold dear: _____.

Drenched in the shower of your gifts, I am amazed that every year two million tons of cosmic dust fall upon this small planet. I marvel that my body is dust from stars whose blazing beauty is now silent. May my body which is composed of star dust, blaze anew with light this day, as I seek to do all out of love for you.

May your justice shine in my deeds, your truth in my words, your love in my acts of compassion, as I begin this day one with you.

Blessed are you, O Harvest of my heart,
Sacred Source of all life,
Delight of my days.

sacred gesture

WEDNESDAY EVENING PRAYER

sacred gesture

The magnetic power of this planet's gravity makes walking on the surface of the earth effortless and also holds in place the atmosphere of life that encircles us. That magnetic force further holds the autumn moon in obedient orbit about the earth. May the mystic magnet of your love now draw me into the shrine of my heart and ever closer to you, as I enter now into sacred silence.

period of silent prayer or meditation

How rich a gift is this holy communion with you. It is the deep well of peace, the eternal fountain of creativity and womb of endless life. In this season of gratitude and fullness, I join the chorus of chants from midnight vigils and the praise rising up from temples, pagodas and mosques all over the world, as I now pray.

a psalm, spiritual reading or personal prayer

O Compassionate One, who knows my every need and hastens to provide whatever is lacking in my life, I place before you my intentions. May this prayer remind me of my poverty in your sight and that every gift comes from your generous heart. I pray for the needs of those I love: _____. Great is my family, spread far and wide across this planet. I pray tonight for those who are imprisoned, for those who are in fear and for all who suffer from injustice. Call all your children to live in peace, their hands empty of weapons, their hearts free of hatred and discrimination.

While I am quiet and still of body, I realize that, one with the earth, sun and planets, I am traveling 43,000 miles an hour toward our mysterious destiny in the uncharted starscape of space. As I prepare to surrender to sleep, remind me that I am indeed a planetary pilgrim, homeward bound to you. As this planet is encircled in our atmosphere's ocean of life, surround me with your peace and presence as I sleep.

Blessed are you, O Harvest of my heart,
    Sacred Source of all life,
    Ever-watchful Guardian of my sleep.

sacred gesture

THURSDAY MORNING PRAYER

sacred gesture

The darkness of outer space retreats as the earth turns full-face toward the sun-star, the flaming heart of our solar family. Having risen from sleep, my daily shadow of death, I greet this new autumn day in the joy of the resurrection. Blessed are you, Holy Parent, who awakens your children to light. Fill my heart with light as I now enter the shrine of my heart to be one with you, my God.

period of silent prayer or meditation

Like a parent who delights in a child's stumbling speech, receive my feeble efforts to pray, as I lift up my heart in gratitude and love to you.

a psalm, spiritual reading or personal prayer

Open my eyes this day to the splendor of your creation, now dressed in autumn colors. Enflame my imagination as you peel back the scabs of cynicism from my eyes, so that I might see your holiness ablaze at the tip of every branch and alive in every autumn leaf. Grant to me this day the heart of a child, holding within it the secret path that leads to you.

With a child's confidence, I place before you, my Beloved, these personal needs: _____. I also ask of you these favors for those who are dear to my heart: _____. And may the work of my hands and the journey of this day bring your age of justice and peace closer to realization.

As I prepare to meet the challenges and conflicts of this Thursday, grant me the constant advice of the Paraclete, your Spirit. So counseled, I will choose wisely those words and deeds that will make your ancient dream unfold in this time and place.

Blessed are you, O Harvest of my heart,
Sacred Source of all life,
Delight of my days.

sacred gesture

THURSDAY EVENING PRAYER

sacred gesture

Blazing in beauty, hovering full on the horizon, was our sun-star, as this autumn day ended. This part of our planet has turned its view from the sun and is now draped in darkness. Each night the dark beauty of space comes earlier as the starlight hours of our sun shrink. I lift up my heart in gratitude for the numerous gifts of this day. I pause now to be mindful of how I have been blessed on this Thursday. . . .

My heart wrapped in thanksgiving, I enter now into oneness with you as I pray without words.

period of silent prayer or meditation

Beyond all comprehension are you, O Divine Mystery. You are holiness, light and love in their fullness, yet you love me and delight in my childlike words of affection and praise. I lift up, as a gratitude gift, this prayer to you.

a psalm, spiritual reading or personal prayer

Hear, O God, these prayers for the special needs of my friends and family: _____. May the needs of my brothers and sisters who share this planet with me also be my needs. I pray for those who are without proper medical care, for those who must go to sleep hungry or homeless and for those who are without employment that gives them a sense of dignity and purpose in life. For these and for all who are helpless this night, I pray.

And for myself, I ask for the gift to truly appreciate all that I have been given, all my talents, blessings and gifts.

As I travel outward this night into the mystery of space, one with the earth, the planets and the sun, I soon will lay aside my consciousness in sleep. Grant a peaceful night to this pilgrim, who has sought this day to be faithful to the Way that leads to you.

Blessed are you, O Harvest of my heart,
　　　Sacred Source of all life,
　　　Ever-watchful Guardian of my sleep.

sacred gesture

FRIDAY MORNING PRAYER

As this new autumn day dawns, fresh with promise and abundant opportunities, the peoples on this side of the earth once again greet the gift of our sun-star and greet you, my God. While dawn has come to this hemisphere, I realize that on the other side of this earth, more than 7,000 miles away, night now enfolds my sisters and brothers in the East. O you who hear morning and night prayers with equal delight, as one song of love, receive my prayer of silence.

period of silent prayer or meditation

On this day, O Holy One, your children of Islam praise you as the one God, the only God. O you of countless names yet beyond all names, may my prayer now be one with all your earthly children as I lift up my heart to you.

a psalm, spiritual reading or personal prayer

May this prayer and all I do this day be in holy harmony with Tibetan prayer wheels that spin in sacred praise of you, with oblations in Hindu temples, fasting of Indian ascetics and the sacred offerings of all peoples. May the untold sacrifices of lovers and saints and parents for their children invest my day with beauty before your eyes. As I rejoice in this cosmic communion, I pray for these personal needs: _____, and the needs of those who are dear to my heart: _____.

The mystic guides of Islam teach that "a person who has put a foot to the holy path must be content to travel like a turtle." For me at least, O God, this seems so true. Grant me patience, then, as I plod slowly toward wholeness and holiness. But also, make me eager to achieve a largeness of heart, a generosity of giving and a greater depth of humble service.

The whisper of winter and of death is upon the autumn wind; let me not delay my enjoyment of this day nor the wise use of what little time I have in this life.

Blessed are you, O Harvest of my heart,
Sacred Source of all life,
Delight of my days.

sacred gesture

FRIDAY EVENING PRAYER

sacred gesture

The darkness of this autumn night is lit by holy fire as
candles flicker on Shabbat tables to welcome Saturday, the Sabbath, as Israel's Bride. I hear the night
wind's echo of far-off cries from minarets, as the
faithful of Allah are called to prayer. A holy night, an
evening of prayer, is this Friday, and I add to these
prayers of your Jewish and Islamic children, my prayer
of the heart.

period of silent prayer or meditation

May my heart pulse in rhythm with the drum beats of Hopi
Indians, with Hindu flutes that delight in Krishna and
the chimes of Buddhist temple bells, as I also praise
you, my God.

a psalm, spiritual reading or personal prayer

Holy Father and Mother of the children of this earth, hear
the many prayers that flood this autumn night. Mindful of the wondrous unity of the chorus of your devoted
lovers, I humbly ask you for these favors: _____.
When I pray for others, they are in my heart. So in an
act of holy communion, I pray for the needs of those
who are dear to me: _____. And I make my own the
needs of those who are trapped in poverty and ig-
norance, those whose life span is cut short by a lack
of food or medicine and those for whom this day has
been a heavy burden.

In this autumn season of gratitude for the fruits of this
earth, I give you thanks for the gifts of this Friday.
Full of thanksgiving, I seek to overflow with pardon
for all who may have caused delay or disturbance,
pain or injury on this fall day.

Lean near and close my eyes with your compassionate
touch so that I can sleep this night as I hope to sleep
in death: anointed in your love and at peace with all.

Blessed are you, O Harvest of my heart,
    Sacred Source of all life,
    Ever-watchful Guardian of my sleep.

sacred gesture

SATURDAY MORNING PRAYER

sacred gesture

This Saturday is saturated with the sacred. It is a day holy to all of Israel, set aside to remember the liberation from slavery and the completion of creation. I greet this day in a union with my Jewish brothers and sisters and with everyone who anoints the coming of dawn's light with prayer. One with all those I love, one with all those whom you, O God, love, I enter into the cave of my heart to sit in silence with you.

period of silent prayer or meditation

Generous are you, O Holy One, to overlook the wanderings of my mind as I try to center it in you. The Hasidic masters teach that "Every breath shall praise God," that every breath is a prayer. May each breath of my silent prayer be a morning benediction, one with the breath of heaven. To the prayer of my breath I add these words. It is my desire that each letter of my every word be filled with a fire of devotion for you.

a psalm, spiritual reading or personal prayer

May all my words and deeds this day be rooted in this time of prayerful communion with you, my God. May my worship extend to all I do this day, as I now ask these favors for those I love: _____. Grant me this day all I need to be a pilgrim, whether I am at play or at prayer, in work or at rest.

The brilliance of our one star, the sun, has hidden in daytime brightness the unfolding splendor of the millions of stars that light up our galaxy. To look upon a star so close, a mere 93 million miles away, is blinding. May I walk the pilgrim's path this day, aware that many other wonders may be hidden from my view, both near and far. Grant me the gift of worship on this autumn Saturday, the grace to live in perpetual wonder. May I treat all that is given me this day as gift.

Blessed are you, O Harvest of my heart,
Sacred Source of all life,
Delight of my days.

sacred gesture

SATURDAY EVENING PRAYER

Seven holy flames dance atop the days of this week whose
conclusion I celebrate this night. Each day has been
holy, as has this Sabbath. On this day that remembers
the creation of this planet, I rejoice that in an awakening of ecstasy you made your human creatures to be
your lovers. One with all the earth, the sun and moon
and with all those who love you, I enter into the
prayer of silence.

period of silent prayer or meditation

I thank you that it is not a drab world that you created, but
rather one of endless variety, color and form. I thank
you for all the beauty you have bestowed upon this
planet, so small in the vastness of the universe. May
gratitude enflame every word I now pray.

a psalm, spiritual reading or personal prayer

I marvel at how my pilgrim path this day, while passing
through the common and ordinary, has been filled
with the extra-ordinary wonders which you have woven
into your creation. I am humbled that you, my God,
have watched over me and so richly gifted me this
day. In trust as well as gratitude, I also ask these
favors for those I love: _____. For myself, I only ask
that my senses may be opened ever wider to the
magnificent mystery of your presence in all that you
have created. I place into your compassionate care the
needs of those who this night are alone and lonely,
who feel the sharp knife of separation, who are dying
or mourn the loss of one they loved. May you who
never sleep be at their side and at mine this night.

This autumn night, the windshield of the sky, reveals stars
whose number and size stun my small mind. One star
is awesome, but a million times a million stars,
gathered in galaxies like gems in a necklace, is
beyond my comprehension. I bow in humble adoration
before you, O God, and the grandeur of your universe.

Blessed are you, O Harvest of my heart,
    Sacred Source of all life,
    Ever-watchful Guardian of my sleep.

sacred gesture

The Moon

THE SEASON
OF WINTER

A WINTER SOLSTICE CELEBRATION

For us earthbound inhabitants, unable from our vantage point to see the curve of our planet's circumference, the earth appears flat. And we flatlanders do not perceive that our home planet is revolving in space around the sun; rather we watch our daystar, the sun, and the other planets and stars move across the sky and revolve around us. Contrary to the truth of Galileo Galilei's famous statement, "eppur si muvoe (but it does move)," our sun seems on this first day of winter, to have halted in its long southerly journey. It seems to have paused, deciding whether to continue moving away from earth, lessening in its light. It is as if it were contemplating a headlong plunge outward into darkness.

The prospect of such a decision terrified our ancient ancestors and so gave birth to one of the primal holy days—or rather holy nights—the winter solstice. We know today what they did not know: that there is a 23½ degree tilt to the axis of our planet—from a line perpendicular to the path of its year-long pilgrimage around our glorious daystar—which accounts for this season of darkness. The night of December 21st has the longest hours of darkness for those in the northern hemisphere.

Fearful that darkness and death would rule over the earth, our ancient forebears circled sacred fires built on hilltops and in holy places. Roaring prayers of red and yellow flames petitioned the gods to bring back the sun. On the winter solstice, the Old Ones danced about fires and chanted hymns to the sun's glory. They wanted to awaken the sun, lest they and all creation die in the freezing darkness of an endless winter.

Watching and waiting are the ritual activities of the winter solstice. It is a sacred night, full of echoes. If you listen carefully, you can hear upon the wind century-old chants from Egypt and Syria, "The Virgin has brought forth! The Light is growing." They saw, in this cosmic event, the death of an old sun and the birth of an infant sun.

Wrapped in December darkness, those in the northern hemisphere also have made it a vigil feast of the birth of the Son of God, the Light of Lights, the Prince of Peace. Those in the southern hemisphere begin the season of summer as they celebrate the birth of the Son of God. It is an equally appropriate time to celebrate the longest hours of sunlight, which speaks of the promise of the one who came to be the Light of the World in its fullest.

The following rituals invite you to be one with the Old Ones who have gone before you, to be in communion with the earth at this sacred moment of the changing of seasons. Citizens of the 21st century, often held comfortable prisoners by the marvels of technology, can easily be out of touch with Mother Earth and her seasons. Life then becomes an endless production line, devoid of communion with cosmic realities.

Like all the rituals in this book, they invite you to adapt them and to rework the basic elements of the solstice celebration: fire and feasting, hope and promise, darkness and light. Creatively add your own gestures and words to personalize the rituals and to initiate the arrival of a new yet ageless season, winter.

WINTER SOLSTICE FIRE RITUALS

A special fire can be lit in a fireplace, or even outdoors, to welcome the winter solstice, or a candle can be used in place of an actual fire. But because it wards off primal fears of darkness, the winter solstice is one feast that should not be celebrated alone. Join with family or community to mark this feast, one of the oldest of the human family. Invite your friends or neighbors if you live alone, or at least be in communion with all who at present or in past ages have gathered to put primal fears to flight.

Each guest could be invited to bring a piece of firewood, a small stick or even a piece of paper to add to the communal fire pile if a fireplace or outdoor fire is used. As this feast signals the end of one season and the beginning of a new one, a period of silence could be provided for each guest to invest his or her piece of wood with an old habit or undesirable pattern of thought or behavior to be consumed in this holy fire of the winter solstice.

The following ritual is intended to take place indoors, around the dining room table; it can, however, easily be adapted. It was an ancient custom to give a gift of light to all who attended. And so an unlit candle may be given out before the ritual begins. Again, this ritual can be adapted if candles are not available.

A RITUAL OF THE WINTER SOLSTICE FIRE

Leader: Let us take into our hands a solstice candle.
or
Let us light the sacred solstice fire.

We pray on this night of ancient fear,
when those who have gone before us were fearful
of what lurked outside the ring of fire of light and warmth.
They feared all that prowled in the darkness:
evil, disease, death, beasts that might destroy them
and the hidden dangers of winter.

fire is lighted

As we light this fire,
we ask that God who is the fullness of light
would protect each of us on this night
from what we fear most.

*a silent pause for reflection, then the leader walks around the dining room table with
a lighted candle, saying:*

May we all be encircled by the magic of fire,
by the warmth of the light and love of God
and the flame of our friendship with one another.
May we who sit at this table be protected
from all harm and disease, all evil and wickedness.

On this holy night that welcomes the season of winter,
it was the ancient custom to exchange gifts of light,
symbolic of the gift of the new light of the sun.

*candles are exchanged and perhaps the greeting, "Light be with you"; then all are
seated at the festive table*

A BLESSING OF THE SOLSTICE FEAST

As our great star, the sun,
    graciously shares light, warmth and energy with us,
    may we, as children of the earth and the sun,
    share with one another the life and joy of this meal.
We acknowledge that the food and drink before us
    is sun-soaked and filled with star energy.
In this food and drink is the taste of the heavens;
    may we partake of it in peace
    with each other and with all the earth.
A winter solstice toast to the sun
    and to the joys of this winter season.

food and drink are now shared in an evening of friendship, entertainment and enjoyment

CONCLUDING PRAYER AFTER THE SOLSTICE FEAST

Tonight we stand at the threshold of the feast of Christmas,
    the birth of the Son of God.

May tonight's celebration be in harmony
    with that most holy day of our tradition.
May it help us to truly rejoice
    in the birth of the Light of the World.

May this our winter solstice celebration
    bring us into communion
    with all those who prepare to celebrate
    the feast of the Nativity of Jesus Christ.
May we also be in communion
    with our Jewish brothers and sisters
    who in this time of darkness
    celebrate their holy feast of light, Hanukkah.

All respond: Amen *or* Amen, let there be light!

Lighted candles in the windows of various rooms of your home can add a great deal to the mood of this celebration. Guests may take home the candles used in the celebration. Even flashlights may be used as gifts and ritual objects of this feast.

AN OPTIONAL CONCLUDING PRAYER

The dark shadow of space leans over us
 as we conclude this festival.
We are mindful that the darkness of greed,
 of exploitation and hate
 also lengthens its shadow
 over our small planet Earth.
As our ancestors feared death and evil
 and all the dark powers of winter,
 we fear that the darkness of war,
 of discrimination and selfishness
 may doom us and our planet to an eternal winter.

May we find hope
 in the lights we have kindled on this sacred night,
 hope in one another and in all who form the web-work
 of peace and justice that spans the world.

In the heart of every person on this earth
 burns the spark of luminous goodness;
 in no heart is there total darkness.
May we who have celebrated this winter solstice,
 by our lives and service, by our prayers and love,
 call forth from one another the light and the love
 that is hidden in every heart.

All respond: Amen *or* Amen, let there be light!

SUNDAY MORNING PRAYER

sacred gesture

I lift up my heart to you, Creator God of heaven and earth and of all seasons. In your cyclic design the earth now leans away from the fire of the sun in this season we call winter.

Although the sun's light weakens as the earth tilts away, I ask in this time alone with you that your light not lessen within me. May I, with your assistance, not turn away from the truth when it visits me, even the truth about myself. I desire rather that I turn toward the light in all I say and do, in all I think and dream. Guided by your light I now enter the cave of my heart to be alone with you in stillness.

period of silent prayer or meditation

I rejoice, O Blessed One, that you have placed within my small heart not only your divine seed but the essence of all that you have created. I now express my joy in your being, as I invest these words with love for you.

a psalm, spiritual reading or personal prayer

Today, Sunday, is a day of prayer and worship for your children who follow Christ. May my morning prayer be in harmony with all the prayers, songs and acts of devotion that rise up to you from churches and places of worship.

May I also be one with all who fail to worship you, with all who reject you and your dream because those of us who profess to be Jesus' disciples have failed to be living examples of your love and justice. Instill in me this Sunday the fiery heat of the sun—and of the Son—so that ablaze with devotion for you, I may enflesh your love and kindness in all I do and with everyone I meet on this first day of the week.

Mindful of the needs of those I love, I pause to lift up into your sacred heart the special intentions of: _____.
Care for them and for all the children of this planet as it journeys through the winter of endless space.

> Blessed and beautiful are you, my God.
> May your light be my sun this winter day.

sacred gesture

SUNDAY EVENING PRAYER

sacred gesture

I bow before you this night, Beloved One, my heart
overflowing with gratitude for all that this first day of
the week has held for me. May the thanksgiving of my
heart give glory to you and enrich this time of silent
prayer. One with the far distant stars of the winter
night sky, one with all the earth, I now enter into
silence.

period of silent prayer or meditation

Holy is this night, holy is the earth and the heavens, for all
is filled with your glory. May my prayer glisten with a
star's brilliance as I now proclaim my love for you.

a psalm, spiritual reading or personal prayer

As I prepare for sleep, may I join the seeds of plants that
sleep in the long night of winter as they await the
sunrise of spring. May I let go of this day with faith, in
the conviction that with unconditional love you watch
over all that you have created. May I enter into sleep
in a lover's surrender to your will, mindful that you
embrace all living beings with a mother's love.

I lift up to you who never sleeps, the special needs of my
family and friends: _____. May those who will pass
this night through the doorway of death be reunited
with you for whom their hearts have hungered
throughout their lives.

May the hunger in my heart for goodness, for truth and for
love remind me that you, and you alone, are the Feast
that satisfies. As I soon will let go of this day and will
surrender to sleep, may I fall asleep by falling into
you.

> O Guardian of galaxies,
> Mother of the cosmos and
> Father of stars beyond counting,
> may I sleep in you tonight.

sacred gesture

MONDAY MORNING PRAYER

sacred gesture

O Creator of day and night, I begin this first day of the workweek with gratitude for the gifts that have come to me over the weekend. May my gratitude for being renewed through resting from my usual tasks help me to begin this week of work with a desire to remember what truly is the work of my life.

I have come from you and to you I return. And so as I journey home to you, my work is to become one with you. I desire to do your will and so become your love and compassion in the midst of a busy world.

May this prayer of the heart, my striving to sit in silence—quieting my ever-restless mind by returning again and again to you—inspire me to imitate you in all that I do. Come, Beloved, sit beside me now as I enter into the prayer of meditation.

period of silent prayer or meditation

O you who search all hearts, we both know that my words fall short of what I feel in my heart, but allow these words that I am about to pray to become love-filled vessels of my devotion for you.

a psalm, spiritual reading or personal prayer

The time has come, my Beloved who lives outside of time, to leave this time of prayer and to invest myself in the activities of this first workday of the week. As I do, I ask that you be with all who are in need of you this day: _____. I pray as well for all the earth, all her children and for all life on this planet.

> Blessed and beautiful are you, my God.
> May your light be my sun this winter day.

sacred gesture

MONDAY EVENING PRAYER

sacred gesture

Our earth has turned once again toward the endless limits of space, as a thousand stars come out to play. I come before you in adoration and in wonder at the vastness of your creation which spans thousands of billions of miles. I descend now with devotion into the tiny cave of my heart to be one with you in silent prayer.

period of silent prayer or meditation

O Beloved, your song of love is a silent one, heard only by the ears of the heart. Look with compassion upon my feeble efforts to still my ever-restless heart and my desire to listen to your eternal whisper. Look with affection upon my words, as I now proclaim my love for you.

a psalm, spiritual reading or personal prayer

I pray to you, aware that my prayer is never private, even if I pray alone. For my prayer is but a single thread in the great weaving of this world's prayers which rise up to you from every part of this planet.

My friends and my family are dear to me, and so I ask that you care for them this night. In your providence especially watch over: _____. Care for and protect those who on this winter night are without lodging and food. And grant that the children of this earth may look upon all who are in need as their brothers and sisters.

Grant a peaceful night, O God, not only to my body but also to my mind and soul. May the sacrament of sleep refresh my whole being this night.

> O Guardian of galaxies,
> Mother of the cosmos and
> Father of stars beyond counting,
> may I sleep in you tonight.

sacred gesture

TUESDAY MORNING PRAYER

sacred gesture

I greet you with affection, my Beloved One, as this new winter day begins. The weather weaves a chilly spell around me, as I seek to keep warm and dry. May this my morning prayer awaken me to the needs of others, to all the needs I will encounter this day.

While my body naturally responds to the winter wind with a shiver, may my heart respond with a warm wave of love as I seek to make my heart aflame like yours. Make me one with the earth as it makes its journey through this season of winter. Make me one as well with all those who lift up their hearts to you at this early hour, as, through the doorway of silent prayer, I seek to enter your compassionate heart.

period of silent prayer or meditation

One in stillness with you, I have also sat in the stillness of creation wrapped in winter sleep. On behalf of creation that slumbers till spring, in harmony with all earth's children, I now lift up my heart in prayer.

a psalm, spiritual reading or personal prayer

O Merciful God, you who held me in the palm of your hand as I slept, hold me in your love and providence as I begin this new day. May I not fear the challenges of this day but rather see them as opportunities to live out my beliefs in non-violence, compassion and justice.

May my work this day be a continuous prayer of praise to you. I ask your loving care for all those who are in need, especially for: _____. I lift up to you all who begin this day frozen without hope or empty of purpose and meaning.

I bow before you, O Beloved Source of my life, you from whom I have come and to whom I return.

> Blessed and beautiful are you, my God.
> May your light be my sun this winter day.

sacred gesture

TUESDAY EVENING PRAYER

sacred gesture

O you for whom my heart hungers, the night sky is arched over me like a winter window that looks outward onto the vastness of space. Earth, her sister planets and their moons and our great daystar are on an eternal voyage toward a cosmic mysterious destination. I too journey toward a lover's rendezvous with you. May this time of silent prayer be but a foretaste of that eternal encounter.

period of silent prayer or meditation

Invisible Lover, I know that you are here even if my senses do not experience your presence. I thank you for being at my side every minute of this day that is now concluding. I sing of my gratitude for your abiding presence, as I now pray.

a psalm, spiritual reading or personal prayer

May the hours of sleep into which I shall sink, grant me the divine gift of elasticity. May I know the gift of new wine skins, which are able to embrace the new and the untried. When I awake tomorrow I will need such flexibility to flow with the changes in my life and in the world. Such a gift is a necessity if I am to be a faithful steward of the Spirit in these times of great transition.

I pray now for those who live in my heart, my family and my friends: _____. I pray as well for all the citizens of this earth, men and women of all races and creeds, of various political beliefs. I ask that you gift us all with elasticity of mind and heart, so that we might create a new earth according to the design of your son Jesus' new age.

But for now, I let go of my quest for peace and justice and surrender myself into your loving nighttime embrace.

> O Guardian of galaxies,
> Mother of the cosmos and
> Father of stars beyond counting,
> may I sleep in you tonight.

sacred gesture

WEDNESDAY MORNING PRAYER

sacred gesture

The part of this earthen planet in which I live is wrapped in winter as this new day dawns for me. The winter earth leans away from the sun, and I miss its light and warmth. How easily do I lean away from you, Beloved God, and your warmth. How readily I lean toward other things and so find the cold touch of winter upon my words and deeds. How often I forget you, who formed my being and who shaped the cosmos, sending spinning suns by the billions into the winter wasteland of empty space.

I dedicate this winter day to you, as I now enter into the chapel of my heart to sit in stillness with you. May I leave outside the circle of silence all my worries and concerns for this day, as I enter into prayer.

period of silent prayer or meditation

O Weaver of oneness and Reader of hearts, I know you need no spoken words to tell you of my affection for you. But may these words of prayer be sacraments of my love.

a psalm, spiritual reading or personal prayer

I pray for the needs of all those across this small planet who are in great need this day, and especially for: _____. I am mindful of all those who suffer because of the winter weather, of all who suffer because they experience on this Wednesday the winter of war, of those who know the cold winds of oppression and violence. May all who suffer this day experience your compassion through their brothers and sisters.

May this morning prayer awaken me to turn the needs of all who ask me for help this day into my personal needs. May this brief time of prayer make me aware that the needs of those whom I assist are really your needs. Grant me the grace to see you in all whom I meet and serve. With that sacred vision this prayer of communion with you will have no end.

Blessed and beautiful are you, my God.
May your light be my sun this winter day.

sacred gesture

WEDNESDAY EVENING PRAYER

sacred gesture

O Clever Creator of all life, just as you have created your
children as male and female, so you have created time
as day and night. Our whirling planet has turned me
around again toward the perpetual winter of outer
space as I come before you to conclude my day. All
this day I have tried to be in prayerful communion
with you. May this act of devotion, as I enter into the
silence of my inner space, be but the final note of this
Wednesday's song of love.

period of silent prayer or meditation

As I come out of silent prayer, I open my eyes to the small
world of my home. May the following prayer open my
heart to all peoples in the larger world around me. I
knock at the door of your heart, O Fountain of mercy
and Source of all blessings: open to your beloved.

a psalm, spiritual reading or personal prayer

Through the open door of your divine heart may blessings
pour forth in great abundance to those I love: _____.
I pray for those who are prisoners of fear or hate and
for the intentions of all the peoples of this planet, in
particular this night for: _____. May those who find
it impossible to pray, who are burdened with cares or
lost in the desert of loneliness, be touched by your
gentle healing and find peace this night.

As this part of the earth and her children look out upon
the freezing darkness of unknown space, may we find
comfort in the marvelous order and design of all that
you have created. Pitch above my bed the tent of your
peace and your presence, as with confidence and
without regrets I now close the cover of this day.

> O Guardian of galaxies,
> Mother of the cosmos and
> Father of stars beyond counting,
> may I sleep in you tonight.

sacred gesture

THURSDAY MORNING PRAYER

sacred gesture

As this winter day begins, O God, I realize that while I have
risen from sleep, I must also be awakened in my
heart. Your son Jesus has called me to live each day
awake, for I know not the hour or the day when you
will knock at my door to call me home.

Open the eyes of my heart, stir the seat of my soul and
awaken it to the mystery of your presence in every
corner of this day. Send forth your Spirit, and ignite
the embers of my heart that it may come alive with
compassion, devotion and zeal.

As I enter into silence, I proclaim the mystery of my faith,
that you dwell perpetually within my heart.

period of silent prayer or meditation

O Loving God, prevent me from judging this time of
prayer. Remind me that only you read hearts, that
regardless of how poorly I have prayed, how many
were the distractions or wanderings of my mind, that
you take delight in my desire to be with you in
stillness.

As the numerous duties of this winter day call to me, I take
time to put into words my affection and devotion for
you, as I now pray.

a psalm, spiritual reading or personal prayer

I pause before I begin my day to be mindful now of the
needs of all who struggle for peace and justice, of
all who refuse to return violence for violence and
for those who labor to lift the burdens of all who
suffer in mind or body. I remember in particular the
needs of: _____.

The clock calls me, my Beloved: my day is about to begin.
May this time of prayer be the design of my day; may
everything I do be done in, with and through you.

> Blessed and beautiful are you, my God.
> May your light be my sun this winter day.

sacred gesture

THURSDAY EVENING PRAYER

sacred gesture

O Gracious God, the season of winter wraps much of this part of our planet with long dark nights. Our daystar, the sun, seems to have turned its face away, as we feel the cold of winter upon us. The warmth of this winter must come from within. So stoke with your Spirit the dying embers of my heart, that my meditation may be afire with love. Send your Spirit to guide me down the passageway to the innermost temple of my heart where you dwell in luminous splendor, as I now enter into the prayer of silence.

period of silent prayer or meditation

As the sounds of the winter wind rattle about, I join my prayer to the sacred wind of heaven, the Holy Spirit, so that it may become one with the aspirations of all those who love and adore you this night. I join this my winter night prayer to the prayers of my brothers and sisters on the other side of our planet who rejoice in the warm glories of summer. From north and south, east and west, may the wind of heaven sweep up all acts of devotion into a single song of love, as I now pray.

a psalm, spiritual reading or personal prayer

I pray this night for those who are sick and dying, for those yoked by heavy debts or poverty, for those in the midst of divorce and separation and for all who face this night in great need. I lift up to you the special intentions of those I love, especially the needs of: _____.

My trust is buoyed by the touch of your presence. I now prepare, without fear or dread, to close my eyes in sleep. Grant me the grace to also close my eyes at the moment of my death with the same peacefulness and confidence.

O Guardian of galaxies,
Mother of the cosmos and
Father of stars beyond counting,
may I sleep in you tonight.

sacred gesture

FRIDAY MORNING PRAYER

sacred gesture

The touch of winter has made much of the earth seem like the moon: cold and barren. But as the first gray light of dawn creeps across the earth, I ask that my heart will not be a chilled chapel, but rather a torrid temple, filled with the fire of love. In that desire I now anoint this new day with my prayer of silence.

period of silent prayer or meditation

The night has ended and day begins. I likewise long for the night of winter to be over and for spring to dawn upon us. I seek not so much to grow in virtue this day as to grow in likeness of you, O Compassionate One. As one of your priestly people, may the following prayer express my care for all peoples and all of creation.

a psalm, spiritual reading or personal prayer

May this time of prayer awaken me, Gracious God, to all the hidden gifts of your life that are secretly contained in this day. I ask to be awakened to the wisdom within the words of your son Buddha who, guided by your Spirit, said, "Wakefulness is the way of life, the fool sleeps as if already dead but the saint is awake and lives forever."

Send me frequent wake-up calls this day, that I might become aware of the true purpose of life. May I be awake to life as a gift from you that is intended to be enjoyed and experienced with delight. Remove from me ruts of habit that prevent me from truly seeing, hearing and tasting your presence in this winter day.

May wakefulness be my watchword as I dedicate my desire to be mindful of your glory for the intentions of all who are in need this day, and especially for:_____.
May my prayer on this Friday morning be one with all the prayers that rise up from mosques on this sacred day of Islam. May it join the great chorus of praise that rises up from all those who love you.

> Blessed and beautiful are you, my God.
> May your light be my sun this winter day.

sacred gesture

FRIDAY EVENING PRAYER

sacred gesture

God of all creation, who lives in one eternal season, this
season of winter seems the longest of the four.
Perhaps it is the chill and dampness or the short
hours of daylight, but part of me longs for spring.
Soon the hearts of birds will ring with a call to make
their migratory journeys homeward. Awaken my heart
to journey inward to you, the source of my life's
migration as well as its destination. May your Spirit
lead me into prayer, as I now enter the innermost
chamber of my heart.

period of silent prayer or meditation

O Ever-patient One, the affairs of this day often felt like
magnets that pulled me away from the still point of
your presence. Forgive any lack of zeal in my prayer
and fuel me with fervor as I now pray.

a psalm, spiritual reading or personal prayer

I acknowledge that my prayers are threads within a web of
worship that spans this earthen planet. I reach out
across the miles to touch with prayer and love those
who are dear to me; in particular this night I pray
for: _____. I remember as well those who have
tasted the bitterness of loneliness and defeat this day
and those whose hearts are empty of faith in
themselves and in you. I pray too for my sisters and
brothers who are called the national enemies of my
country, and for all who work for disarmament and
peace.

As this day rapidly comes to a conclusion, I ask that you
would encircle me with the Spirit of the Holy and with
the abiding presence of your son Jesus Christ. Bless
my home on this winter night. Bless too my sleep and
my dreams. May Mary, the Blessed Mother, watch by
my bed this night that I may sleep in peace.

O Guardian of galaxies,
Mother of the cosmos and
Father of stars beyond counting,
may I sleep in you tonight.

sacred gesture

SATURDAY MORNING PRAYER

sacred gesture

How quickly, O Creator of wintry ice and snow, has this
week passed. May any chill within my heart be melted
by your Spirit, as a summer sun would melt a field of
snow. I begin this morning prayer mindful that my life
passes as quickly as the days of this winter week. This
morning the temple of my body rises from sleep,
seeking to enter into prayer. May I do so in communion with all who pray to you this Saturday in
synagogues and who worship by study of the Torah. In
that unity, I now descend into the bottomless well of
your presence within the cave of my heart.

period of silent prayer or meditation

As all lovers long to sing the praises of their beloved, I
desire to express my love for you. May I fill each of
these words with my very self. May each letter of each
word dance with devotion, so that this prayer will be
pleasing to you, Yahweh, my God.

a psalm, spiritual reading or personal prayer

As this winter day begins, may I see your glory in the
heavens and in all the earth. Grant, O Blessed One,
that I may look with love upon every person, object
and event that I will encounter this Saturday.

Long ago you called Moses to spend this day in restful
pleasure in your presence. May I use whatever this day
holds for me to refresh my body and rest my soul,
and so give great pleasure to you. I pray for all who
must work this day as well as those who have no work
and must struggle for the bare essentials of life. Look
with favor upon the needs of all who petition you in
their need, especially: _____. May this day lead me
to trust more fully in your great care for all the earth
and her children. And may I grow in the capacity to
care as you do.

> Blessed and beautiful are you, my God.
> May your light be my sun this winter day.

sacred gesture

SATURDAY EVENING PRAYER

O my Beloved, your heart is wider than the whole universe whose great black starlit eye stares down on me this winter night. I bow before you, whose glory fills the heavens and all the earth. Tonight is a sacred wedding night that unites the Sabbaths of the first and second testaments and makes all peoples chosen.

As a bride and groom long for their wedding night, I long to be joined with you, as I now enter the shrine of my heart to begin my silent prayer.

period of silent prayer or meditation

Awesome and full of power are you, my God, who finds delight not in poetic words or long hours of vigil, but only in the passion of love that prompts your children to pray. May your Spirit, who prays continuously within my heart, now fan the flames of devotion into a living fire in the words of this prayer.

a psalm, spiritual reading or personal prayer

How quickly have these past seven winter days slipped through my fingers. I pause now to recall in gratitude all the numerous gifts of this week that you have given me. . . .

My heart overflowing with thanksgiving, I ask another gift from you. Watch over those I love, especially: _____. Smile upon all who relax and enjoy themselves on this Saturday night after a long week of work. And bless our earth and all who dwell upon it.

Tomorrow, Sunday, is the memorial of the resurrection of your Son. May my sleep this night be filled with hope in the fullness of life that has been given to me through him. And when death closes my eyes in a final sleep, may I awaken to the splendor of an eternal Sunday, my resurrection and eternal life in you.

> O Guardian of galaxies,
> Mother of the cosmos and
> Father of stars beyond counting,
> may I sleep in you tonight.

sacred gesture

The Lagoon Nebula in Sagittarius

PRAYERS BEFORE
AND AFTER PRAYING

A DEDICATION OF A PRAYER TIME

Gracious and Beloved One,
    at the beginning of this time of prayer,
    I lift up to you
    my heart overflowing with gratitude
    for the many gifts and blessings
    that you have given me.

I dedicate this time of worship and prayer,
    and the graceful energy that shall flow
    outward from the altar of my heart
    as an offering for the welfare, good health
    and personal needs of: _____.

As your priestly servant and friend,
    I ask that all those persons who are in need this day,
    especially those who are close to my heart,
    may also be refreshed and strengthened
    by the rivers of grace that shall flow
    in all four directions from this place of prayer.

I also lift up all those who are oppressed or living in fear,
    who are without hope or devoid of dreams,
    into your divine heart.

As I hold these prayerful intentions,
    may your Holy Spirit take me by the hand
    and lead me deep into the center of my heart,
    into your Holy of Holies.

Amen+

A VESTING PRAYER BEFORE PRAYER

The wearing of vestments, sacred clothing, for times of prayer and worship is part of our human religious tradition that dates back to the gift given to our primal parents, Adam and Eve.

I come to your altar-shrine, O God of Holiness,
> to offer you the pleasing sacrifice of prayer.
Cleanse my hands of all those works
>> that might have divided rather than united,
>> of all that blocks my way
>> through the narrow gates of the Kingdom.
Cleanse to the core these hands
>> that they truly might be priestly hands
>> that will be your instruments of service
>> by which praise is lifted up to you
>> and peace passed on to those I meet this day.

a silent ritual of hand-washing might take place at this point

Vest me with the linen robe of a seeker of truth;
>> holy is the one who comes in your name
>> and who finds your love in every atom,
>> in every activity and every person.
Tie the apron of simple service around my waist;
>> adorn it with signs of humble deeds
>> performed with great love.
May that sacred vestment
>> awaken me to serve you, my God,
>> by helping the person near me
>> and the stranger on the street.

Cover my head with the mantle of fire and light,
>> which shows the presence of your Holy Spirit,
>> that I might pray with great passion and devotion.
May this mystic mantle be like the stars
>> that grace the prayer shawl of night,
>> covering all the earth in luminous light.
Robed in the splendor of your Spirit,
>> may my prayer give peace to all the world.

Finally, Gracious God,
>> anoint me with the glad oil of joyful gratitude
>> that I may worship you with all my heart,
>> with all my mind, body and soul.

I ask this in the name of Christ, the eternal high priest
>> according to the order of Melchizedek.

Amen+

A PRAYER BEFORE SILENT PRAYER

Divine and Hidden Friend,
  I often feel that I fail at prayer,
  but I rejoice that your Spirit
  prays ceaselessly in the cellar of my heart.

Grant me the grace to sit still
  that I may hear the Spirit's silent song,
  ever flowing like a river deep within,
  singing my love for you.

Quiet my restless heart,
  calm my roving, runaway mind,
  as now, in communion with all the earth
  and her many-colored children,
  I enter into the song of love,
  the prayer of stillness.

Amen+

A PRAYER BEFORE READING SCRIPTURE
ON A RAINY DAY

Your wet words of life
    in thousands of thin sentences
    saturate my meditation
    as I lift up my heart to you,
    O God of rain-gifts.

The earth, like an ear,
    soaks up your words.
Oh, that my heart
    would do the same.

Soften my heart,
    O God of living waters,
    that the shower of Scripture
    I am about to read
    may enrich the soil of my soul.

Rain down your wisdom
    in sacred streams
    to carry me like an upturned leaf
    through the currents of this gray day.

Amen+

A PRAYER FOR ZEAL

Implant within my heart, O God,
    the fiery zeal of a Jeremiah,
    the conviction of a Ruth or Rebecca
    and the zest of a Francis of Assisi.

Stir my slumbering soul,
    that it might sing a song of passion and devotion,
    drunk with dancing joy and desire for you,
    my divine and loving Friend.

May my heart be as hot as the heart of Moses
    for all your children burdened by slavery,
    for all who feel oppression's steely heel
    or suffer rejection in an alien land.

May I, like your son Jesus,
    be consumed with zeal for you, Divine Beloved,
    for life, for justice and for peace;
    for all that I know in faith.

Fill me with zeal, O God.

Amen+

A PRAYER FOR LIGHTING
INCENSE FOR WORSHIP

The use of incense as an ally at times of prayer is a global sacrament. The aroma of incense allows the nose to pray and so invites more of the whole person—body, soul, heart and mind—into our prayer. Visually, the small but aromatic streams of incense smoke are external signs of the beauty of ascending prayer that is deeply devotional, that is on fire from within. The act of lighting incense can be a ritual of devotion, an opportunity for awakening the aroma of prayer.

As I light this incense,
    I ask that I might ignite a burning desire
    and a great love for you, my Gracious God.

May my prayer
    be like pleasing incense before your presence,
    you who desire not long prayers
    but rather love-filled prayers.

Remind me that you measure prayer
    not with a clock but with a thermometer.
They are fools who believe
    that you are pleased by clock worship,
    for you desire all my time and all my heart.

May the light clouds of incense smoke
    that softly billow up to you
    soften my heart and lighten my spirit
    in my sacred journey home to you.

May this incense prayer arising to you
    teach me to rise beyond time and space
    and to rest only in you.
As this incense burns before me,
    so may every letter of every word of my prayer
    burn with the fierce fire
    of my love for you.

Come, Cosmic Lover,
    and set my heart aflame.

Amen+

A PRAYER FOR THE RITE OF INCENSE
AT A TIME OF WORSHIP

O Divine Guest within,
    all is ready for my time of prayer.
I now prepare what is the most important,
    the shrine of my heart.

a stick of incense is lit, or incense is placed on a burning charcoal

May this incense which I now enkindle
    be a smoking sacrament of my desire
    for the thoughts, words and actions
    of this time of prayer
    to become sacred gestures,
    on fire with a love for you.

Grant me a devotional zeal,
    that my body may become a living vessel,
    a sacrament of incense pleasing to you,
    a delight in your sight.

As this incense is consumed by fire,
    may my life become fuel for your blazing love,
    that the offering of my heart may give forth
    the pleasing aroma of selfless service
    and a love for all the world.

As this incense arises on high,
    so may my prayer, empty of myself and my needs,
    rise effortlessly in silent salutation to you,
    that it might be prayer for all the world.

May this prayer reach you through your Holy Spirit,
    who prays continuously within me
    and dwells eternally with you and your Son.

Amen+

A BENEDICTION AT THE END OF A PRAYER TIME

O God of kindness and compassion,
    I have come to the conclusion
    of this time of prayer and worship,
    mindful of my position as your priestly servant.

I throw wide open the windows of my heart
    so that the peace of your presence
    may pour out in all four directions,
    showering its blessing upon all the earth.

May this benediction heal the wounds of war,
    bind up the bitterness of painful divisions
    and mend broken hearts and failed friendships.

As the blessing of your presence encircles the earth,
    may it awaken in all people
    a great desire to serve one another
    in humble and loving ways.
May it call proud hearts to gentleness
    and awaken the child in those
    who seek to hold power over others.

Inflame those hearts that have grown cold;
    reawaken within the weary of soul
    your spirits of youthfulness and joy.
Stir up your breath of freshness and enthusiasm
    that slumbers in tired hearts.

May this blessing flow forth from my heart,
    in your holy and infinite Name,
    in the redeeming name of your Son
    and in the living presence of the Holy Spirit.

Amen+

A PRAYER AFTER SILENT PRAYER

My time of prayer is finished,
    trailing its ashes like an incense stick
    burned to the end.
Quiet my mind
    before it passes judgement on this prayer,
    my gift of time to you.
How can I judge its worth—
    this struggle to still my mind in you,
    my efforts to feel your presence in my prayer?

Only you can judge the simple song of love
    sung in the noisy chambers of my heart,
    often drowned by the wail of fear
    or the sweaty shouts of work that must be done.

You, my hidden Friend, waited in patience
    as memories called from the past
    and future prospects clamored for attention,
    filling my mind with yesterdays and tomorrows,
    stealing my sense of your presence.

As I prepare to go about my work today,
    may my intention to live in your present moment
    be the pattern for this day and my life.
With your help, may I forever do
    only one thing at a time—
    always in communion with you, my Beloved,
    with all my heart and mind and soul.

Amen+

The Barred Spiral Galaxy

PSALMS FOR
THE 21st CENTURY

The dictionary defines a psalm as a sacred song or hymn. It comes from the Greek "psalmos," whose mother was the Hebrew word "miznor." Jews and Christians have prayed the 150 psalms of the Bible for thousands of years. These ancient prayers, traditionally attributed to King David, were originally sung or chanted.

David's life prepared him well to be God's pen, a composer of prayer. He was versed in music, and his song was sweet enough to soothe a savage beast, to calm the often disturbed and moody King Saul. The psalms have a cosmopolitan breath. They reach well beyond David's own nation and historical age. Hasidic masters throughout the ages have prescribed reading the entire Book of Psalms without interruption to alleviate all kinds of distress. And the psalms have been the bedrock of Christian monastic prayer for centuries. Their universality springs from their composer's humanity. David was both shepherd and king. He experienced the full range of human passions: lust and love, infidelity and nobility, rage and tenderness, remorse and forgiveness, intense devotion and utter despair.

Those who want their prayers to be all peace and love often censor, or at least skip over, the bloody sections of the psalms which speak about bashing babies' heads against stone walls or delighting in the death of an enemy. But all prayer is human encounter with God, which means it should always be "whole" prayer, involving the full spectrum of our human energies. Such "catholic" prayer does not allow us to slip out of the skin of our humanity. To be part of the human family is to share in a corporate reality composed of both saints and sinners, peacemakers and war-makers, the exploited and exploiters, believers and unbelievers, those who are good and those who are evil.

The psalms of David remind us of a fact that we would love to forget. Within you and me are the darkest and ugliest of powers and ungodly emotions, even if well chained to the basement walls of our subconscious. Only after having embraced the nonviolent and creative energies within us are such dark powers allowed to live upstairs with our virtues.

The daily prayers in this book have a space set aside for a spiritual reading or a psalm. The psalms of David are ideal at these times. They are like King Solomon's fabled mines whose 150 tunnels are never-ending sources of inspiration. Those willing to pray them slowly and with devotion—willing to dig into them with sacred shovels—are never disappointed.

This book also contains some new psalm prayers created for planetary pilgrims who, despite the date on your calendar, already have entered the 21st century. The prayers are called psalms not only because they reflect the style of King David but also to build on the thousands-of-years-old tradition of lovers of God praying psalms at the sacred hours of morning and evening. They also are intended to awaken the psalm writer in you. They call you to compose, as did David, when life visits you as a seed-laden spring breeze or a raging winter storm.

The seasonal prayers in this book have been written with the hope that you can use them even if you live, or are traveling, through parts of our planet other than the center of the United States. But winter in Canada is very different from winter in South Florida, just as autumn in the deserts of the Southwest is different from autumn in the New England states. And so as a way of seasoning your daily prayer, you may find it of value to use the section of Seasonal Psalms. Also, since it would be impossible to include psalms to fit the uniqueness of each season in each of the various parts of this planet, you are encouraged to rewrite the psalms in this book or to create your own seasonal psalms.

Besides the four seasons of the year, Christians celebrate the sacred seasons of Advent and Lent. You can season your daily prayers with new psalms for these sacred seasons which you will find listed in the table of contents. There are also Psalms of Solidarity, which are intended to assist your praying in union with those who suffer from a lack of justice and peace, as well as those who suffer for justice and peace. And finally there is a section of psalm prayers for various occasions or for no particular occasion. In their variety, these prayers speak to the human condition of planetary pilgrims on a journey not only outward into space but also into the great mysterious cosmos of inner space.

SEASONAL PSALMS

SPRINGTIME OVERTURE

God of all seasons,
    with artistic splendor
    you have given us an overture
    to the resurrection of your Son
    in the resurrection of spring
    from the cold tomb of winter.

With joy I greet
    the coming of flowers
    and the return of birds,
    as I eagerly await
    the feast of the resurrection of Christ.

Remove from my heart
    on this holy day
    any division or discrimination
    that keeps me frozen
    in separation from others.
And make me one
    with all creation
    that sings the song of springtime.

PSALM TO VIRGIN SPRING

Drawn upward by some hidden power,
    life is cracking the crust of earth
    and bursting forth from limb and stem.
Your aroma, O Life-giver,
    is upon the springtime wind,
    and I feel its power
    stirring deep within me.

Green is your color, O God,
    the green of new life
    that lovingly transfigures earth's dreariness,
    long held prisoner
    by the icy web of winter's cold.

Green up my heart with hope,
    in your perpetual promise of life.
Send forth from my soul
    new shoots, fresh buds
    eager to grow in your divine image.

May this year's visit of virgin Spring
    make my heart a virgin once again
    intoxicated with wild love for you,
    whom I discover in all things
    and in everyone.

A SEED PSALM

Awaken, you buried seeds
    asleep in your earthen tombs!
Rise up with joy to break forth
    the hard coffins of your shells!

Your Eastertime has come;
    the song of the dove
    is heard over the softening land.
Winter has hidden,
    and Spring now dances on your graves
    to waken the dead.

Awaken, seeds of holiness
    buried deep within me.
Rise up to fulfill your destiny
    whose time has come.

For sanctity is scribbled
    bold within my blood and brain.
Onward and beyond
    have I been called
    even before I felt the sun
    or knew the earth around me.

May spring enchant the saint,
    shy and hesitant within me,
    and set the rhythm for my sluggish feet
    in a dance of holy yearning.

PSALM TO THE SPRINGTIME SUN

O Sun of spring, wrap us all
    in your fiery lover's embrace.
Long enough has frosty Earth
    been host to winter's cold.

Like mourners at Lazarus' wake,
    we shout with joy that Earth
    is free of her shroud of snow.
Obedient to her God,
    according to her primal pattern,
    she rises once again from winter's grave,
    seeking her bright lover
    in the gleaming sky.

O beautiful springtime Sun,
    daily as Earth soaks up your warmth,
    call forth to resurrection
    all who sleep in caves
    lingering half-awake in lifeless mud,
    all who await your quickening call.

May your caressing warmth,
    which brings green resurrection to the earth,
    be a sacrament and sign,
    that I too shall be touched by fire,
    awakening from my earthen hibernation
    to live in endless light
    in an eternal spring.

A PSALM OF THE SHRINE OF SPRING

O Spirit of Life,
    not that long ago the trees around me
    looked like upside-down roots
    dangling in the wind.
Today it looks like great, green clouds had come
    to nest in their longing limbs.

The spring breeze that plays in the branches
    is full of the song of birds, recently returned.
As flowers lure bees and insects
    by their beauty and perfume,
    so I am drawn out-of-doors
    to smell and feel your presence.

What cathedral made by human hands
    could contain the awesome majesty
    of your springtime splendor?
And Bach or Handel would be humbled
    by the music of this season's sounds,
    blended in harmony by your baton.

O you who delight in children at play,
    may I not be ashamed to bow in wonder
    as I offer, this day, my prayer and adoration
    in your sacred springtime shrine.

A PSALM OF SPRING'S ENCORE

Each day I take delight, Creator God,
      as did my great-grandparents Adam and Eve,
      in enjoying the garden of Eden called earth,
      which each spring graciously grants
      an encore of your first act, creation.

I stand and applaud with all earth's audience
      and cry out with gratitude,
      "Again, again, please do it again."
And you smile and return to center stage
      to repeat the song you sang so long ago.

And blades of grass shoot up through crusted soil,
      as seductive flowers sway in the breeze
      and young, green leaves
      belly-dance on the tips of twigs,
      while soft, gray clouds pour down liquid life
      to make all the earth come alive.

Like the primal parents of paradise,
      part of me longs to stand naked once again,
      stripped of the symbols of society
      which so easily separate me
      from my flesh, which is dust,
      and from my bone, which is stone,
      to once again walk in the cool of the garden
      in naked innocence with you, my God.

A SUMMER PSALM OF FREEDOM

O God of all seasons,
    it's summer—the season I dreamed about
    throughout winter's long, dreary days.
Now is the time of leisure,
    time to be out-of-doors-and-walls.
But so often I feel like an over-civilized child
    of this century of convenience and comfort.

Six months ago, it was snow and ice
    that screened me in from earth's delights.
Now it's a television screen that too often
    massages my mind, weary from work,
    that screens me in
    from shaman summer's healing touch.

And even if I flick that dead-window off
    and go outside on the porch,
    I'm still screened in or carefully protected,
    lest bugs and flies disturb my comfort
    by bringing nature far too close.

Grant me, O never-tiring Miracle Worker,
    the freedom of my childhood
    to run and play with abandon,
    without thought of comfort, bugs or flies,
    in summer's great vacationland.

A PSALM OF SUMMER'S SIREN

I salute you, God of rest and vacations,
    who laid down the law
    that every seventh day must be free.
No work for beast, man or woman
    was your legal word.

On this summer day, when my heart longs for leisure,
    my head tells me, "It's time to go to work."
I wish I had an extra sabbath
    to enjoy your gift of liberty and peace.

Part of me is so grown-up,
    and knows how to be productive,
    to be responsible and to achieve.
I have learned to listen to that inner adult
    and how to successfully silence
    the echoes of childhood's play.

I may know and possess more, but I've lost something
    in being a repeat offender, O God,
    in breaking your law of Seventh Day Vacations.
I have forgotten how to vacate my work,
    to come out of my head and go out-of-doors,
    to play with you in the summer sun.

A SUMMERTIME PRISONER'S PSALM

O Summer, zenith of the year,
    I praise your robust life, your hot blood.
You are a liberator who calls us out-of-doors
    into your desert-like sun and heat,
    just as the God of Moses and Aaron
    called the children of Israel
    out of the brickyards of Egypt.

Those who work in the warmth of this day
    are blessed to be outside,
    while others are stuck in buildings built of brick,
    constructed with concrete and glass.
Chilled-but-artificial air
    blows upon the new slaves
    of electric Egypt's indoor brickyards.

Fortunate are those children who play today
    under the great yellow face
    of our giant daystar, the sun.
Free to jump through sprinkler sprays
    or ride their bikes in the free flight
    of real air-conditioned coolness.
Corporate giants in their stainless steel skyscrapers
    dream of their treehouse days
    when every kid was truly a millionaire.

O Liberator God, who called your children
    away from the Nile's sweaty slavery,
    lead me, this day, into the glorious freedom
    of which the spirit of summer sings.

A SUMMER SUNSET PSALM

O Beloved Friend and Earth Designer,
    this day's light is seeping away,
    and dark night crouches
    beneath the amber horizon.
I am tired from the work of this warm day,
    but not so weary that I can forget
    this day's rich harvest of gifts.

I lift up my heart to you,
    singing a sunset song of gratitude.
I praise you for the blessings that fill my life,
    for the gifts I can recall
    and for treasures I take for granted.

Gently refresh me now
    with your evergreen pardon
    for my failure to drink deeply of your love,
    hidden cleverly in each gift
    that has come my way today.

Forgive my rushing past
    the countless visions of you, unique to this day,
    held so tenderly in the beauty of your love.
Forgive my absent-mindedness, the deafness of my ears,
    my senses blinded by my busyness today.

Blessed are you, Holy Parent,
    who will soon wrap me in sleep
    and cradle me in the womb of your peace.

A PSALM OF THE PROPHET SUMMER

O Sacred Creator of heaven and earth,
    like a loving parent with a choice Christmas gift,
    you keep your present of paradise
    hidden away from my sight.

Your son Jesus said that eye has not seen nor ear heard
    what you have dreamed up for us
    when we finally come home to you.
But I wonder: are there seasons in heaven
    just as there are on earth?

Or have you chosen one of earth's four as your favorite,
    one unending, changeless season of bliss
    for those who love you?
If so, I'd bet that you selected summer,
    with its picnics and leisurely pace,
    with its fun and play and whole-hearted zest.

I'd lay odds that you set apart summer,
    the season of vacations—
    children's favorite free-time,
    when both young and old
    drink in the enjoyment of life—
    to be the work-free environment
    of your heavenly paradise.

May I, by your grace, taste your eternal sabbath
    in the warm pleasures of this summer day,
    and slowly savor the flavor of your reward
    in the nectar of this summer night.

A SUMMER PSALM OF VISITATION RIGHTS

O Divine Parent, you who are forever One,
    I don't remember the divorce:
    it happened long before I was born.
You yourself performed the marriage;
    Civilization and Creation were wedded,
    and what God has joined together
    let no one put asunder.

But it wasn't a happy marriage, I guess:
    Father Civilization spent more and more time
    away from home; "Busy at work," he said.
He walked all over Mother Earth and treated her badly,
    showing less and less affection
    as the years went on.

He has custody of me, most of the year;
    I walk only on leather or concrete
    and stay indoors most of the time.
I'm told not to play in Mother's dirt,
    to keep clean and not walk on her grass.
I've grown accustomed to the divorce,
    but at times I long to be with my Mother, Creation.

I rejoice in these summer days and nights
    when I'm free to visit her again,
    to take delight in her earthy embrace,
    to feel the touch of her warm, soft skin,
    to know that I'm still her child
    as well as being a child of Civilization.

AUTUMN PSALM OF CONTENTMENT

O sacred season of Autumn, be my teacher,
    for I wish to learn the virtue of contentment.
As I gaze upon your full-colored beauty,
    I sense all about you
    an at-homeness with your amber riches.

You are the season of retirement,
    of full barns and harvested fields.
The cycle of growth has ceased,
    and the busy work of giving life
    is now completed.
I sense in you no regrets:
    you've lived a full life.

I live in a society that is ever-restless,
    always eager for more mountains to climb,
    seeking happiness through more and more possessions.
As a child of my culture,
    I am seldom truly at peace with what I have.
Teach me to take stock of what I have given and received;
    may I know that it's enough,
    that my striving can cease
    in the abundance of God's grace.
May I know the contentment
    that allows the totality of my energies
    to come to full flower.
May I know that like you I am rich beyond measure.

As you, O Autumn, take pleasure in your great bounty,
    let me also take delight
    in the abundance of the simple things of life
    which are the true source of joy.
With the golden glow of peaceful contentment
    may I truly appreciate this autumn day.

AUTUMN PSALM OF FEARLESSNESS

I am surrounded by a peaceful ebbing,
    as creation bows to the mystery of life;
    all that grows and lives must give up life,
    yet it does not really die.
As plants surrender their life,
    bending, brown and wrinkled,
    and yellow leaves of trees
    float to my lawn like parachute troops,
    they do so in a sea of serenity.

I hear no fearful cries from creation,
    no screams of terror,
    as death daily devours
    once-green and growing life.
Peaceful and calm is autumn's swan song,
    for she understands
    that hidden in winter's death-grip
    is spring's openhanded,
    full-brimmed breath of life.

It is not a death rattle that sounds
    over fields and backyard fences;
    rather I hear a lullaby
    softly swaying upon the autumn wind.
Sleep in peace, all that lives;
    slumber secure, all that is dying,
    for in every fall there is the rise
    whose sister's name is spring.

PSALM OF AUTUMN HOMECOMING

Brisk is the breeze of autumntide
    which sweeps in its path
    crowds of leaves from countless trees,
    collecting them in amber-colored communities
    to share bright memories of the summer sun.

Fall is homecoming time,
    a reunion and return to remember
    and so to re-member what has been dis-membered
    by the choice of different pathways,
    or severed by the sharp knife of time.

"Dust we are and to dust we shall return,"
    sing orange-brown leaves,
    as they circle-dance and cluster
    in colonies of the dead.
Crumbled and crushed in time's crucible,
    stroked and soaked by rain's wet fingers,
    we shall once again become rich soil,
    the stuff of earth's dark flesh.

Autumn wind, dance master of fallen leaves,
    sing to me of my reunion,
    my re-memberment and great homecoming,
    my return into the luminous flesh of God.

PSALM OF THE FEAST OF AUTUMN

Tinted orange and yellow is the sunlight
    that pours through the stained glass window webwork
    of the countless gothic tree branches,
    as God's cosmic temple
    celebrates the feast of autumn.

The aroma of burning leaves
    fills every one of my pores,
    as blue-gray clouds of autumn incense rise,
    amidst the tall, tree pillars
    of basilica earth.
"Holy, holy, holy are you, God of Creation,
    heaven and earth are full of your glory,
    holy, holy, holy are you."

In sacred dance, great hosts of brown leaves
    circle-turn before earth's altar,
    whirling round like brown-robed sufis,
    lost in the ecstasy of God.
Their voices whisper ancient chants of God's secret name:
    "Ahhh, so beautiful!"
    "Ahhh, so breathtaking!"
    "Ahhh, yes, ahhh!"—whispering the name of God.

I come like a pagan, unbaptized,
    a gentile outsider standing on holy ground,
    with shoes still on, yearning to be converted
    to this most primal worship,
    the awesome adoration of the feast of autumn.
O God, grant me the gift of conversion.

WINTER PSALM OF A PRAYERFUL PYROMANIAC

O Winter, from your wide mouth
 come the wild winds of arctic cold
 that swirl about my home.
You come stalking in the snow,
 like a giant prehistoric beast,
 to pound upon my roof with icy claws.

In less technological times,
 before the days of central heating,
 earth's children gathered around a blazing fire
 to find warmth from your icy breath.
They found around those flames of fire
 another gift, the great blessing of family,
 the warmth of the circle of companionship,
 a never-dying firebrand
 that frightens away the worst beasts
 that haunt the human heart.

May the family feasts of this wintertide,
 the holidays and parties,
 and the festivals of inner fire
 be carnivals of community for me.
May my merrymaking be family-making
 and so be God-making for me.

God of thermostats and tinderboxes,
 make of me, during this cold winter season,
 your faithful friend and fire-maker.

A WINTER WONDERLAND PSALM

The ancient psalmist plucked his strings
    and sang a sentence sprung from you:
    "Be still and know that I am God."
Be still, my soul, like a winter landscape
    which is wrapped in the white prayer shawl
    of silent snow fringed with icy threads.
Sit still, O my body, like an icy pond
    frozen at attention, at rest yet alert.

Be still, my gypsy mind,
    from your whirling like a perpetual gyroscope,
    constantly restless, ever on the move.
Endlessly you rove on a nomadic quest,
    roaming the roads of my Egoland,
    visiting its likes and dislikes,
    a Disneyland of distorted discriminations.
Ceaselessly you visit its sacred shrines
    of self-righteous beliefs
    and its numerous forts of fears.

Be still, my being,
    so that, like Lewis Carroll's Alice,
    you may, with grace, find the tiny, hidden doorway
    that leads to Wonderland.
Be still so that you can discover slowly, day by day,
    that God and you are one,
    to know in that Wonder-of-Wonderlands
    who you really are.

A PSALM OF ICY AWARENESS

The earth around my home
    is now locked in a winter wrap
    of bone-chilling snow and ice.
Water, once clear and liquid,
    a joyous, flowing community,
    is now frozen into crystals of ice.

Recently in humanity's long history
    there has arisen an isolation,
    a separation of those who share
    common human flesh and bone.
While once upon a time we gathered joyfully
    in families, tribes and clans,
    we now so often live divorced
    from earth and from each other,
    with loneliness as our only company.

All isolation is ice-olation,
    frigid to human flesh,
    cold and lifeless to the touch,
    untrue to our most basic unity, comm-unity.
And whenever I act single-handedly,
    apart from an awareness of my sisters and brothers,
    I become a deformed divine disciple.

And tribeless, O God, how can I tread the Path
    which you have designed as a companion course?
Ah, the wisdom, so divine,
    in your Genesis words,
    spoken to perfectly made, fully automated Adam,
    "It is not good for one to be alone."

A WINTER PSALM

The earth is rigid like a corpse,
    locked in the snow and ice
    of this winter day.
Silent and stiff, it lies in state.

The trees are bare,
    and the songs of birds have left;
    gone too the chanting of insects.
Only the winter wind raises her voice
    in chilling canticles of praise.

Wrapped in her burial shroud of snow,
    the earth patiently awaits
    the warm touch of your Spirit, O God,
    to rouse her from the sleep of death,
    calling her to rise and come forth
    from today's tomb of winter.

I proclaim the mystery of my faith
    that spring will follow winter,
    that life will follow death
    and that one day
    all the tombs of death's white season
    will be transformed into the green of spring,
    who is the sister of your Spirit.

May my trust in the coming of spring
    on this cold winter day
    be a sign of my faith
    in the resurrection of all life,
    the fulfillment of your promise
    that we all will share
    in the new life and eternal spring
    of your son Jesus Christ.

Come, but only in due season,
    O glorious spring.
And, until then,
    may I live in the promise
    of your life-giving touch.

PSALMS FOR
SACRED SEASONS

AN ADVENT PSALM

Awaken, my heart,
    God's reign is near;
    the Peaceable Kingdom
    is in my hands.
If the wolf can be the guest of the lamb,
    and the bear and cow be friends,
    then no injury or hate can be a guest
    within the kingdom of my heart.
Eden's peace and harmony will only return
    when first, in my heart,
    there hides no harm or ruin,
    for the Peaceable Kingdom is in my hands.

Isaiah's dream became Jesus' vision:
    "Come, follow me," Emmanuel's echo rings.
    "Reform your life, recover Eden's peace,"
    for only then will salvation appear.
For Advent's dream is the healing of earth,
    when the eagle and bear become friends,
    the child and the serpent playmates.
Arise, awaken, my heart,
    the Peaceable Kingdom
    is in your hands.

PSALM OF AN ADVENT EAR

With prayerful pleas
    and Advent songs of longing,
    I await the birth of God's Anointed One.
Come, O Gift of heaven's harmony,
    and attune my third ear,
    the ear of my heart,
    so that I may hear,
    just as Mary, faithful woman of Israel, heard.

O God, the time is short,
    these days are too few
    as I prepare for the feast
    of the birth of Mary's son.
Busy days, crowded to the brim,
    with long lists of gifts to buy
    and things that must be done.

Show to me, also your highly favored child,
    how to guard my heart
    from noise and hurry's whirl,
    so that I might hear your voice
    calling my heart to create an empty space
    that might be pregnant with heaven's fire.

Quiet me within,
    clothe my body in peacefulness,
    that your Word
    once again may take flesh—
    this time, within me—
    as once it did in holy Mary,
    long Advent days ago.

AN ADVENT SHOWER PSALM

Isaiah of old prayed,
    "Let the earth open wide her mouth;
    as justice descends, O heavens,
    like the dew from above,
    like gentle showers,
    let salvation fall from the skies;
    let justice spring up
    and salvation bud forth."

Come gentle rain of Advent-tide,
    soak deep into my heart,
    calling forth signs of an early spring.
Make buds appear on my heart's barren rosebush
    and blooms on its dried flower stalks.

Come showers of silence and wet my soul;
    soak deeply with your fertile fingers,
    dripping heaven's dew.
May I come forth from my times of prayer
    as from a bath:
    dripping wet from a sacred soaking,
    refreshed, renewed, revitalized.

Advent prayer of December stillness,
    dampen my dry soul,
    coax forth green leaves of the Spirit
    and bring forth buds of bright flowers
    as green trees flicker with magic lights
    and green wreath circles
    whirl on front doors,
    red-bowed in festive joy.

May soggy souls ooze out awesome gifts,
    for Emmanuel, God-among-us,
    is awakened from a yearlong slumber
    by gentle mists of Advent longing
    and is eager to give gifts of love,
    presents of your presence.

Radiant Rain God,
    make me your brimful cloud,
    ready to shower down Emmanuel's justice and peace
    upon all I meet.

ADVENT PEACE PSALM

*based on chapter thirty-one of the **Tao Te Ching***

O Prince of Peace,
>   whose advent we seek in our lives,
>   come this day and show us
>   how to beat our swords into plowshares,
>   tools of life instead of instruments of fear.

May your love strip us naked
>   of all weapons and strategies of conquest,
>   which are not the tools of lovers,
>   wise ones and God's children.

Let us not lust for power
>   but rather strive for the insight
>   to be guided on the Way of Peace.

Let us not yearn for a victory
>   that requires a sister's sorrow
>   or a brother's shamefaced defeat.

With tears, black suits and dresses
>   and tolling funeral bells,
>   let us attend life's victory parties
>   that are won at such a cost.

Let us be Advent adventurers and peacemakers,
>   hammering swords into shovels,
>   filling holes and leveling peaks.

Let us be disarmed and vulnerable,
>   for only through such open hands and hearts
>   can Emmanuel come.

PSALM OF AN EMERGING EMMANUEL

"O Come, O Come, Emmanuel,"
    I pray with upraised eyes.
Drop down, O Dew of Heaven,
    that God might walk and talk on earth,
    might heal and feed our sin-soaked world.

O Come, O Come, Emmanuel,
    my prayers like searchlights
    comb the starry winter skies.
Descend from the black hole of some neighboring galaxy
    to green with your grace
    our barren earth.

Such an Advent waiting prayer
    can be a lifelong profession of patient longing,
    unless I know, with all my heart,
    that Emmanuel not only comes down
    but also comes forth and emerges.

O Come, O Come, Emmanuel,
    come forth from deep within me
    with Christmas luminous beauty.
For my heart has become the sacred crib,
    the birthing place of God-among-us.

Peace on earth and justice for all
    will only become manifest in our lives
    when enough of your sons and daughters
    awaken to your divine design
    that has made each of us
    an emerging Emmanuel.

A CHRISTMAS CARD PSALM

O you who showered sacred stars
    on the tiny town of Bethlehem,
    I thank you for guiding artists' brushes
    to create cards of beauty,
    bursting with blessings
    and filled with love and greetings from friends.
I lift up my heart in gratitude
    for these beautiful yearly bridges
    that bind us together in love,
    we who are often too busy
    for keeping up with friendship's needs.

My cards of Christmas past are now precious relics,
    and like the bones of saints
    they hold great power,
    and so I hate to bury them
    or see them burn.

Opened Christmas cards
    hum to me the hymn of love
    and teach me the sacrament of correspondence.
Tie about the finger of my mind, Beloved One,
    a reminder that without reminders
    friendship fades from the failure
    to express words of love and appreciation
    to one another.

May these twelve magical days of Christmas
    inspire me to celebrate
    the un-holidays of the year,
    the feasts of no-occasions,
    with love notes to friends who are far away.

Sacred season of the twelve days of Christmas,
    gift me with the magic power to stop the clock,
    so as to keep God alive within the world.
For if God is love, then God may be found
    in the mystery of love exchanged.
May I be a holy messenger of that mystery.

A CHRISTMAS PSALM

O Blessed One,
>it is said that Christmas is for children.

Indeed, I agree:
>it's only a feast for the young of heart,
>a feast for finding beneath the tree
>gifts to surprise and delight the eternal child.

Peel back the scabs of cynicism from my eyes
>so that this calloused and aging child,
>may see holiness blazing at the tip of every branch,
>may see every tree as a Christmas tree.

Let me not be ashamed to dance with delight
>at hidden gifts wrapped in shimmering paper
>with bows of rainbow-colored ribbon.

But also grant me the youthful and wide-eyed wonder
>to recognize, and even to expect,
>life-giving miracles on every street corner,
>miracles of kindness and generosity and care.

Gift my all-too-calculating heart
>with the excitement of anticipation
>to truly receive the gifts of life,
>the capacity to feast and rejoice.

Give birth within me to a spaciousness of heart
>that can celebrate this feast
>of the birth of Christ, the Child,
>as a child.

A PSALM FOR THE TWELVE DAYS OF CHRISTMAS

O timeless and ever-youthful God,
    I thank you for these twelve days of Christmas.
And I ask the gift of an endless encore
    of this feast of the birth of your Son.

Though I am grown now
    beyond the age of childhood toys,
    gift me with the playful tool
    of how to treat each day
    as a Christmas gifting day.

Grant me within these twelve days of Christmas,
    the bottomless gift
    of the heart of a child:
    enthusiastic with the excitement of expectation,
    unashamed to play and dance with delight
    and filled with a faith in elves and fairies.

Place upon my feet
    shoes of lead
    that I may be slow to put away
    the electric stars that have hung
    like clusters of constellations
    upon my Christmas tree.
They have nightly spoken to me
    of what a child's eyes
    can see in every tree.

Turn to concrete my Christmas consciousness,
    that I may continue to greet
    hassled clerks in crowded stores
    and nameless strangers on the street
    with blessings and joyful wishes.

And so by living the whole year
    in the quality of Christmastide,
    your Word may endlessly become flesh
    in me, your Christmas child.

A PSALM FOR A SECOND CHRISTMAS (DEC. 26)

As the Child of Bethlehem
      was showered with gifts
      by star-led magi kings,
      I too have been blessed royally.
I am grateful for all the gifts of love
      that have flooded into my life
      on this second Christmas Day.

I who have so much already
      now have more!
I look with awed eyes
      at all my new possessions,
      each a gift of love.

With holy wisdom,
      the feast of St. Stephen
      falls on December 26th.
St. Stephen, who was stoned to death,
      a deacon, servant of the poor,
      rides the tail of the Christmas star.

First martyr of the faith,
      you who died blessing those who gifted you
      with a shower of the stones of death,
      inspire me with the spirit of your feast
      to share some of my gifts with the poor.

Guide my hand to select a gift of love
      and make it sing again,
      for someone in need,
      love's melody of God made flesh.

Or coax me to my checkbook,
      to provide food, shelter or some special need
      to those who found slim their celebration
      of the birth of Love
      into an uncaring world.

LENTEN PSALM OF AWAKENING

Come, O Life-giving Creator,
    and rattle the door latch
    of my slumbering heart.
Awaken me as you breathe upon
    a winter-wrapped earth,
    gently calling to life virgin Spring.

Awaken in these fortified days
    of Lenten prayer and discipline
    my youthful dream of holiness.
Call me forth from the prison camp
    of my numerous past defeats
    and my narrow patterns of being
    to make my ordinary life extra-ordinarily alive,
    through the passion of my love.

Show to me during these Lenten days
    how to take the daily things of life
    and by submerging them in the sacred,
    to infuse them with a great love
    for you, O God, and for others.
Guide me to perform simple acts of love and prayer,
    the real works of reform and renewal
    of this overture to the spring of the Spirit.

O Father of Jesus, Mother of Christ,
    help me not to waste
    these precious Lenten days
    of my soul's spiritual springtime.

LENTEN PSALM OF LONGING

I thank you, O God,
>for the warming of the winds
>that brings a melting of the snow,
>for daylight hours that daily grow longer
>and richer in the aroma of hope.

Spring lingers beneath the horizon
>as approaching echoes of Easter
>ring in my ears.

I lift up my heart to you, Beloved,
>in this season of Lent
>that gently sweeps across
>my sluggish and sleeping heart,
>awakening me
>to a deeper love for you.

May the wind of the Spirit
>that drove Jesus into the desert,
>into the furnace of prayer,
>also drive me with a passion
>during this Lenten season
>to enkindle the fire of my devotion
>in the desert of Lenten love.

Birds above, on migratory wings,
>signal me to an inner migration,
>a message that draws me homeward bound
>on Spirit's wings
>to the heart of my Beloved.

May I earnestly use this Lenten season
>to answer the inner urge
>to return.

LENTEN PSALM OF THE ROYAL ROAD

Lenten road,
    four-laned royal way,
    lead me to my Beloved
    in these forty days
    of prayerful pilgrimage.

Royal and rich is the roadway
    of earnest prayer and worship,
    and blessed are those who travel it.
They will find in the cave of their hearts
    the One whom they seek.

Royal and treasure-filled
    is the lane of study and reading,
    hours spent in feeding the soul
    with food of knowledge,
    insights into the divine nature.

Royal and compassionate
    is the avenue of alms-giving
    and of working for the poor.
Twice-blessed are those
    who give of self and treasure
    as a Lenten work of worship.

Royal and fertile with life is the lane
    of discipline, fast and abstinence
    which makes all disciples aware of their dependence
    on the truest ground of being,
    carrying every pilgrim
    homeward bound.

Spirit of holiness, come to my aid,
    that I might walk with prayerful passion
    during these forty days
    on all four lanes
    of heaven's Lenten royal road.

PRIESTLY PSALM OF LENTEN SACRIFICE

O God of all worshipers,
　　I offer you a Lenten prayer.
Ordained in my mother's womb,
　　anointed by the Spirit
　　before the sun burned bright,
　　I am a priest as was your son Jesus,
　　according to the order of old Melchizedek
　　upon whom no one laid hands.

"This is my body, this is my blood."
　　I silently say these words with a priestly heart,
　　in each act of holy sacrifice
　　poured forth with love this day
　　for family and friends,
　　for stranger and foreigner.

Awaken me during this Lent
　　to my sacred calling to the priesthood,
　　that by sacrificial gift,
　　I have the power to lift up a fallen world
　　and to bring to fullness your divine dream
　　of a whole, united and healed cosmos.

Like precious jewels upon a cord,
　　I link my crosses this day,
　　my sufferings and self-denials,
　　with those of your countless other lovers, O God.
And I join these millions of gifts of love
　　with the one great sacrifice
　　of the holy priest of Nazareth
　　who surrendered upon his timeless tree of the cross
　　that our old and beloved world
　　might be healed and cleansed of sin and division,
　　might come to wholeness and oneness in you.

PSALM OF MY CROSS

With wisdom deeper than the oceans,
    you have fashioned with great love
    a special cross for each of us.

May my Lenten gift this year
    be to more clearly see
    my cross as a Jacob's ladder,
    rising to you
    out of my painful, troubled sea.

I place my hand with trust,
    into the hand of my Gethsemani Guide,
    so that I might joyfully embrace
    everything that I would gladly prefer
    to discard as disgrace
    everything that makes up my cross,
    my way to you, Beloved God.

Open my heart this day
    that I may see with eyes of truth
    whether the painful cross I bear as mine,
    claiming it as holy burden,
    does indeed come from you, my God—
    or if by chance my cross
    is one of my own creation.

Teach me this day
    not to carry my cross
    but rather the Jacob's ladder of your will.
Guide me as I seek with all my heart
    to climb it daily as a sacred spiral staircase,
    spiraling in sacrificial splendor,
    winding ever wider, ever higher,
    opening me more and more
    to your wisdom and will,
    to becoming one in you.

AN EASTER PSALM

"Christ is risen, Alleluia!"
      cries out the chorus of creation.
"Christ is risen, Alleluia!"
      sing the supple winds of spring.
"Christ is risen, Alleluia!"
      ring out lilies in silent splendor.

The feast of feasts,
      the festival of hope,
      the mother of all Sundays,
      luminous in the full moon of spring,
      radiant in the rising of the sun,
      Easter dances upon my rooftop
      and plays like a newborn child
      in the cradle of my heart.

I rejoice like all of creation,
      sailing on springtime's seed-bearing breezes,
      and like the lily's trumpet,
      I open wide my throat and my heart
      to join with all of heaven and earth
      in singing out the symphony of joy
      at Easter's annual return.

I take hope in Christ's victory over death,
      hope that, one with him,
      I will also have my Easter morning
      when I will be freed from the prison,
      the decaying dusty tomb,
      of my narrow and stony spirit.
I trust that I too will spring-like arise
      to a fullness of living and loving,
      to a life beyond all time and space,
      to a life one with you, my God.

"Christ is risen, Alleluia!"
      I soon will be next,
      Alleluia, Alleluia!

A PSALM OF THE RESURRECTION

Before dawn,
    the great Seder celebration having passed,
    his empty cross awaiting death's next meal,
    into the darkness of his lifeless body
    the finger of God's Spirit
    stirred in slowly spiraling circles
    as once it had moved
    over the deep and empty waters
    about to be pregnant with creation.

From the blast of the birthing
    of ten thousand galaxies,
    Jesus, son of Joseph and Mary
    and son of God,
    exploded outward from his tomb
    in radiant light and love
    to fill the earth and the whole cosmos
    with the fullness of divine life.

Paul of Tarsus penned it well
    in a letter to his Ephesian friends:
    "God has put all things under Christ's feet
    and made him head of the Church, his body:
    the fullness of him
    who fills the universe in all its parts."

I look up into the Easter sky,
    beyond the limits of this small galaxy—
    far beyond the boundaries of my mind—
    into the billions of galaxies that glow
    like flaming Easter flowers
    filling the garden of the universe.

Light travels 5,787 trillion miles a year;
    and to cross, just once at the speed of light,
    this universe whose every starry body
    contains the fullness of the Risen Christ
    would take all of twenty billion years.

Oh, beyond comprehension,
    too vast for my little mind,
    is the mystery of the Resurrection,
    is the wonder of the Easter nighttime sky,
    the body of the Risen Christ,
    the whole and holy Church to which I belong.

A PSALM OF E=MC² EASTER

Brother Einstein's Easter Law
    delights my hopeful heart
    which wishes to never die.
For that quantum equation maintains
    that matter taken to the speed of light squared
    is turned into pure energy again.

My body, so subject to sickness,
    to aging and death's cold bite,
    is a companion human body of Christ
    who encountered the kiss of death
    upon Good Friday's consecrated cross.

The lifeless matter of his once vibrant body
    was carried away to the grave,
    condemned to become a worm's decaying dinner.
Yet, you who are Life could not stand to see
    your beloved's body decay,
    so you carried out once again
    your first and awesome act of creation.

You reanimated the matter of his body
    and moved its molecules
    at more than the speed of light,
    and it was again transformed
    into the Light of Lights,
    into pure eternal energy.
In your infinite design
    nothing dies;
    it only changes form,
    until it finally and forever changes
    into your form,
    into the energy of the light of love divine.

Take hope, my heart,
    be firm, my feeble faith,
    for the matter of the flesh and bone I call me
    will also become an Einstein Easter Event.

AN EMMAUS PSALM

How easily, O Christ,
    do I long for a firsthand touch
    from you, my friend and savior,
    risen and glorious, victorious over death,
    radiant with luminous life.

Oh, how easily does my yearning arise
    to have been one of those in the upper room
    when you returned in resurrected form.
I know that my faith would be strong
    if, like Mary in the garden,
    I had reached out to hug your living presence
    on Easter morning.
I do not doubt the quality of my zeal
    had I broken bread with you
    at the sunset inn on the Emmaus road.

It's not easy to be among the living faithful
    fed by second-hand accounts
    of your resurrection visits,
    even though they have been passed on with loving care
    for milleniums mouth-to-mouth.

But I take hope today, in this Easter season,
    that I too can taste and feel
    your fulfilled promise:
    "I am with you always, even to the end."

Every time I break bread with friends or strangers
    or encounter kindness on my daily byroads,
    when I am visited by you
    even though my inner doors are locked in fear,
    let my heart be as open as the horizon
    for the feast of an Easter visit
    from you, my Risen Savior.

A PSALM TO THE WIND OF HEAVEN

O wind that blows when and where it will,
 teach me to reverence the Wind of Heaven.
O mover of tree tops and tall grasses,
 you who are the servant of no other forces,
 open me up to the mysterious Breath of God.

O Divine Wind, blowing with the Spirit's sweetness
 through a chant-filled mosque in Arabia,
 or causing a silent heart to dance
 in a hidden hermit's cave high in the Himalayas,
 or caressing with compassion
 an abandoned packing crate in an urban slum,
 wherein sleeps a homeless drifter;
 let me feel your loving touch.

Lift me up above my selfish interests,
 spreading my concerns wider than myself.
Exhale a gale of your grace into me
 and set me under full sail
 as your servant of life and of love.

Remind me with your every movement
 that history has shown clearly
 how you are the private property of none,
 how great and passionate movements
 have lost touch with your breath of life
 and so have become empty of their youthful zeal.

Wind of Inspiration, Creative Spirit of God,
 teach me not to forget
 that you come always as gift.
Remind me always to be ready
 to receive and romance and dance with joy
 wherever and whenever you visit,
 or risk that you may move on without me.
May I ever be sensitive to your gentle breezes
 and willing to soar with your wild winds.

A PSALM FOR CREATING SACRED WIND

O winds of this planet earth,
    you are the children of the sun's passion.
As the heat of our daystar
    strikes the equator of our small planet,
    warm air rises up and peels backwards,
    spiraling toward the two polar regions.

Swirling northward and southward,
    they become the air currents of North America
    and the winds of the outback in Australia.
Children of the sun's fire,
    offspring of the uneven heating
    of our planet's atmosphere,
    let me learn your secret.

Unless my prayers possess a hot equator,
    a great devotion in my love for God,
    unless there is a passion in my love
    for my work, my hopes and dreams
    as well as for all those I hold dear,
    how can I expect to give rise
    to the Sacred Wind in my life.

May I practice the secrets of the four winds
    and intensify my love for life,
    for the literature and art of ages past,
    for music, dance, food and drink,
    for my family and friends
    and for all that comes my way.
For only by such an overflow of passion
    shall I feel the romance of the Spirit,
    heaven's wind of fire,
    filling my love for you, my Beloved.

A PSALM OF NEW WINE SKINS

Comfortable and well-worn are my daily paths
    whose edges have grown gray
    with constant use.
My daily speech is a collection of old words
    worn down at the heels
    by repeated use.
My language and deeds, addicted to habit,
    prefer the taste of old wine,
    the feel of weathered skin.

Come and awaken me, Spirit of the new.
Come and refresh me, Creator of green life.
Come and inspire me, Risen Son,
    you who make all things new:
    I am too young to be dead,
    to be stagnant in spirit.

High are the walls that guard the old,
    the tried and secure ways of yesterday
    that protect me from the dreaded plague,
    the feared heresy of change.
For all change is a danger to the trusted order,
    the threadbare traditions that are maintained
    by the narrow ruts of rituals.

Yet how can an everlastingly new covenant
    retain its freshness and vitality
    without injections of the new,
    the daring and the untried?

Come, O you who are ever-new,
    wrap my heart in new skin,
    ever flexible to be reformed by your Spirit.
Set my feet to fresh paths this day:
    inspire me to speak original and life-giving words
    and to creatively give shape to the new.

Come and teach me how to dance with delight
    whenever you send a new melody my way.

A FEAST DAY PSALM

O Blessed One who created calendars and clocks,
    today is a feast day.
Come and show me how to make each hour a feast.

May the meals I share today
    be true adventures of taste.
Let me delight in every flavor
    as a special gift of the moment.

May this day be a feast for my eyes
    as I drink in the vast range
    of the colors, forms and textures
    of all the things I see.
Gift me, on this day of celebration,
    with fresh-cleansed eyes,
    open to beauty and alive with wonder.

On this feast day
    may my ears feast as well.
Unplug them of habit—the deafness of routine—
    that the whisper of the wind,
    the soft sounds of gentleness,
    the magic of human speech
    and the healing laughter of mirth
    may enter my mind and heart.

On this feast (of _____)
    may I also feast as never before
    in the joy of those I love
    and with whom I share my life.
May this feast day be a holiday of love
    for my community of family and friends.

In these and in all ways,
    may this day, created by you,
    be truly a feast day.

PSALMS FOR PERSONAL SEASONS OF CHANGE

PSALM OF A WAKE FOR A CHANGING BODY

Wakes are for the dead;
    even the term leaves me cold.
I usually prefer to deny my death,
    which comes by inches,
    but comes relentlessly all the same.

Another signal from my body,
    another sign of age,
    has visited me, with its foreboding forecast
    that I'm growing older.

I look with envy at the young
    and am often tempted to try
    a wizard's wonder herb
    to restore my aging body
    to its former age of agility
    that was free of aches and pains.

Today I must mourn,
    aware that those who hold enough wakes
    die with dignity
    and even dance with death
    in a Chronos childhood play.

To wake with great love each small death and loss
    and then move on to what life offers next:
    it is thus that I can honestly rejoice
    at another's youthful beauty.

I sense that by observing enough wakes
    I'll awaken, to my surprise,
    to a new, mature magnetic beauty
    that radiates from those
    whom time has tanned into a handsome hybrid
    of the eternal youth.

A PSALM AT SIGNS OF AGING

I see you,
    time's messenger of maturing,
    a hair grown gray.
You signal the ending
    of my season of youthfulness.

I'm tempted to tone you
    back to your original shade,
    or to silence your prophecy
    by pulling you out.
But I know too well
    that you are only the first
    of many gray messengers to come.

I sadly receive the turning of the seasons
    and tend to reject the painful truth
    that time is taking its toll!
Quietly, I rage within,
    that my skin, with age,
    begins to fold and crease,
    no longer as resilient or tight
    or as elastic with the yeast of youth.

I shall hold a wake, yes, and lament,
    weeping within my heart at the passing
    of the springtime and the summer of my short life,
    so that I may embrace the autumn of age.

O Ever-youthful God,
    make clear to me the ancient truth
    that like the billion-year-old universe
    I too grow younger each day as I grow older.
Within me, that which is beyond
    the corroding clock of time—
    at the core of my being—can implode,
    traveling backwards to the beginning,
    to the inner space that's forever young.

PSALM OF CHANGING WORK

In this erratic era of change,
    this earthquake season of transition
    which causes the crumbling and collapse
    of social structures and traditions,
    I personally am a victim of the upheaval
    and must seek a new direction.
I am challenged to rise up out of the rubble,
    not a victim but a victor.

Social scientists, like weather forecasters of the future,
    predict in these tempest times
    that career changes will occur
    perhaps ten times within a lifetime.
But every sweeping storm of change
    is so strenuous and fraught with fears,
    so threatening at my age,
    to begin afresh again.

O God of creations and transformations,
    who constantly begets new beginnings,
    inspire me by your perpetual creativity.
Call me to change,
    to dig deeply within myself,
    to find the uncultivated capabilities,
    the undiscovered diamonds and reserves of resources
    that you buried deep within.

And as I step out on the edge,
    afraid and doubtful of my abilities,
    come and support me with your hand
    as my mother took me by the hand
    to my first day of school,
    and like my father's hand under my arm
    as I sat upon my first bicycle,
    that menacing machine of balance.

With your belief in me
    and your great hand to support me,
    all things are possible
    as I seek once again to balance myself
    and to learn something new.

A PSALM OF LOSS BY DEATH OR DIVORCE

Part of me is gone:
> what years of love and affection
> had fused in me as one
> has now been cut away.
I stand now on a single leg,
> and work with only one arm.

Every divorce is a death,
> every death a divorce.
My heart has been split
> by the stripping
> of what I've learned to feel
> as an integral part of my being.
By the surgery of separation
> I've become an amputee,
> disabled by my death-divorce.

O Divine Healer of hearts,
> remind me daily not to expect
> a miracle of quick recovery.
Guide me as I stumble,
> blinded by my tears,
> limping along from the loss
> of the one I have loved.

Teach me that even cripples
> can again learn to dance.
Enlighten me to see
> that in my vault of memories
> lies the healing herb
> that renders pain less deadly:
> the remembering and reliving
> of my rosary of our many moments of love.
And grace me with your regenerating presence
> so that I can begin again.

PSALM DURING A MENSTRUAL CYCLE

O Divine One,
    Loving Source of sacred cycles,
    Life-force of the rising and setting sun,
    of the waxing and waning moon,
    help me to celebrate the cycles
    that are present within my own body.
May I listen to my bodily rhythms
    and embrace my menstrual cycle
    which I am experiencing today.

These are sacred days of the month:
    as I welcome and accept the life-blood
    which is flowing from within me,
    may I also respect the full range of my feelings
    and honor the difficulty of these days,
    the low physical energy and deep sensitivity
    during this time of my menstrual cycle.

Help me to create space during these days
    for reflection, for quiet and dreaming,
    realizing how thin at this sacred time
    is the veil between you and me.

O Endless Fountain of all life,
    may I embrace this time of my monthly cycle
    with awareness and sensitivity,
    reverencing the life-force
    that is flowing through me.

PSALM FOR A WOMAN WHO NO LONGER BLEEDS

O Divine One,
    Source of the feminine life-force,
    I thank you this day
    for your life-energy within my body,
    for the order of its rhythm and cycles.

Even though I no longer have
    my blood time to mark my cycles,
    teach me to listen with my inner ear
    to the other cycles and patterns
    of my body.

As I listen with attentiveness and respect,
    may I daily grow in understanding
    of how to care for my body
    with gentleness and love.

May I always remember
    that my femininity
    is an integral part of me,
    regardless of whether I am fertile or not.

And as I listen with greater reverence
    to that rhythm of your life within me,
    may I allow the special gifts
    of this stage of my life to emerge,
    creating space for the wise woman within me
    to find fuller expression in my life.

PSALM DURING PREGNANCY

I knew at once that something new had happened,
    a feeble, fleeting flutter of awareness.
I am now not I, but we; someone's deep within me,
    part of me but not me.
O Sacred Source of all, I am in awe at this new life within me,
    and I pray for the grace to carry it well,
    to honor the rhythms and seasons of the birthing cycle.

May I respect the morning sickness
    that comes to me even at sunset
    and the inner dance that keeps me awake
    through half-sleepless nights.
As I am sensitive to the changing contours of my body
    which are now beyond my ability to control—
    I wonder if my husband will still find me lovely—
    may I celebrate this season of change
    and the energy to provide for the needs
    of this growing life within me
    that these changes make possible.

Teach me the art of patient waiting,
    especially at those times when I wish
    that I could just take a peek inside
    to find out who this little person is
    who's tap dancing on my ribs while I try to sleep.
I want so much to be a good mother,
    to care for and nourish this new life.
Help me to gift this child with all the love I can,
    now during this time of pregnancy
    and also at each stage of life when I am called
    to set my baby free into fuller life.

O Holy Womb of Life, help me, for I am frightened;
    I do not feel ready for this awesome task.
Free me from my fear of a painful delivery;
    may it be a holy, harmonious experience for us both.
Free me from my fear of inadequacy
    about raising this child into maturity and holiness.
Please help me, Holy Parent,
    to protect my child who's yours as well;
    bring this baby safely through this birthing
    and the many other birthings in life.

PSALMS OF SOLIDARITY

PSALM OF A MAIN STREET MADONNA

No Raphael will paint me:
    a mother with child,
    but without a husband,
    clutching a welfare check
    with a babe in my arm.

No Bottichelli background
    behind this mother and child;
    the bleak walls of public housing
    rather than a hidden, luminous light.
No singing angels cluster
    around my head.

Half-a-home, half-a-wife
    and less than half-a-life:
    a poor single parent
    who holds in her lap
    a condemned child.

Yes, condemned to live
    an entire life in poverty,
    so too my grandchildren
    and great grandchildren,
    forever prisoners
    of the lowest class.

No Michelangelo will carve me
    holding the dead body of my son:
    shot by police,
    dead of drugs,
    a victim of a gang war.

I am the sorrowful Madonna.

PSALM OF THE HOMELESS

Adrift, abandoned cargo
>of a civilization that races headlong
>on success' interstate.
Dirty clothes, dirty body,
>unlike you who speed by,
>I have no bathroom,
>not to mention a home of my own.

I'm your rent-a-family member,
>part of your Christmas gift family
>or a Thanksgiving meal relative:
>those special times
>when you recall my plight.
But today's an ordinary day,
>the more habitual occasion
>when I'm the forgotten one.

The Gospel Mission kitchen preacher said
>that Jesus had nowhere to lay his head,
>but he wore a real live halo
>and rested in its light.
I've got no halo,
>and a packing crate
>or a dirty doorway's
>the place I call home.

You're afraid of me
>and avoid my glance,
>fearful that my arm will extend with a "please"
>to become a panhandle.
And I'm also afraid, I constantly live in fear
>of freezing to death,
>of being beaten or killed
>by some half-crazed alley hunter.

Look kindly on me, for I'm a ragged refugee,
>a wanderer in the exodus of economics,
>a hungry, hunted, homeless hobo,
>a cousin of Jesus
>with nowhere to lay my head.

PSALM OF THE JOBLESS

I'm naked, so please don't look:
   I've been stripped of my identity
   by the loss of my work.
I've been disrobed of my dignity,
   of my purpose for rising from bed.

My life has lost its compass point,
   for work gave order to my days.
Weekends were something to look forward to;
   now every day is a hollow holiday,
   a sad Sunday of idleness.

I stand in line and scan the want ads;
   I stand in line and wait,
   only to be met with a tinfoil smile
   and "Sorry, check back again!"

I want what seems beyond my grasp,
   a job, some decent work to do.
I want my dignity back, my purpose;
   I want my children, my family,
   to hold me in respect.
It's more than money that I need—
   it's a return of my self-esteem.

God did not create us to be the styrofoam slaves
   of the keepers of Dow and Jones,
   who when the corporate world is finished with us
   can cast us aside
   like once-used coffee cups.

Who cares . . . who cares:
   I'm no longer a useful cog in the machine
   but only a percentile person.
I'm only one of the faceless idle millions
   of the economy's kidnaped victims,
   a statistic on the evening news.

PSALM OF THE DISEASE OF POVERTY

Unclean! Unclean!
>Stand well upwind;
>that my disease is easily caught
>is among your greatest fears.
My soul is covered with repulsive sores:
>there is no cure,
>there is no cure.

You turn away to see no evil;
>you are blind and deaf
>to the plague of poverty.
Did you know that 85%
>are only three paychecks away
>from my lethal leprosy?

You hide from the fact
>that you live so close to the edge
>and could so easily
>become homeless and hungry
>for compassion's understanding.
You too so easily
>could become infected
>and quarantined in poverty's ward.

You too could become
>one of the invisible ones,
>never seen, never heard, abandoned,
>jettisoned as useless baggage,
>excommunicated from the flow
>of the Good Life.

Stay upwind,
>keep your distance,
>for your immune system lacks an adequate defense
>for my disease.

PSALM OF THE POOR

I understand that God said,
    "This is the fasting that I desire:
    releasing those bound unjustly,
    sharing your bread with the hungry,
    sheltering the oppressed,
    the homeless ones,
    not turning your back on your own."

I guess I'm not one of your own
    but rather an alien from another world;
    exiled here on earth
    but not really one of your own
    since you so easily
    turn your back or look away.

It's mostly hand-to-mouth
    and day-to-day
    that I not so much live as exist,
    forever exiled to the state of poverty,
    a prisoner without much hope
    of a governor's reprieve,
    no eleventh hour pardon
    from my sentence of life in poverty.

My prison walls
    are too high to scale,
    towering above the reach
    of my oh so limited
    reading, writing and arithmetic.
You see, I'm chained and bound
    by my lack of marketable skills
    and wear only lead shoes of despair.

What was it that God said?
Those words seem like a faint murmur
    from a far-distant land.

AN ALIEN'S PSALM

I wear the mark of your disapproval
    and your often unspoken words
    pierce straight to my soul,
    "Why didn't you stay where you belong?"
I feel the icy stare that says,
    "Keep your distance, you foreigner,
    with your different-colored skin
    and your strange-sounding speech,
    with your culture, food, religion and clothing
    that are inferior to my own."

I'm an immigrant, a wetback, an alien,
    an outsider operating a sweatshop sewing machine;
    cheap labor: unwanted or dirty jobs
    are mine for the taking;
    I'm one of the countless invisible ones
    who puts fresh vegetables on your plate
    or stitches the fashion dresses and shirts
    that you buy in your stylish stores.

As Moses of old once said,
    "Remember, you were once aliens
    in the land of Egypt,"
    remember that your grandfathers and grandmothers
    were immigrant-unwanteds,
    were exploited cheap labor,
    second-class citizens,
    uneducated and poor,
    used and abused,
    ignored or looked down upon
    for their foreign religion, speech and food.

The White House,
    first house of this great land,
    says it well:
    white is this land of promise;
    no room for other colors or creeds.
Someday we'll paint the first house
    in rainbow colors—
    someday, not long from now.

A PRISONER'S PSALM

I'm your caged brother/sister/friend:
    a criminal, yes,
    a prisoner since my youth.
I've lived in many prisons:
    a broken home,
    a narrow neighborhood,
    the prison of my mind.

You've sent me to this walled hospital
    where you say that I'll be cured,
    but this is no place of healing
    or even rehabilitation,
    but rather a guarded schoolhouse
    whose crowded classroom cells
    teach a wild wisdom
    that you and I both know
    is poison to the touch.

You've excommunicated me for life
    into a warehouse of unwanteds
    and branded the center of my forehead
    with an indelible red X:
    X-con,
    X-citizen,
    X-rated brother/sister.

You'll never really trust me
    or give me a second chance,
    even if I graduate and "pay my dues,"
    I'll forever wear the brand.
Forgiveness, seventy-times-seven
    is your supposed creed,
    but not for those of my breed.

In here, my brother/sister,
    know that the sun of hope never shines;
    no light at the end of the tunnel,
    escape-proof my permanent prison,
    the place where I was born,
    the place where I will die.

PSALM OF THE STARVING

I am one of 700 million
    and so am easily lost from your view.
There are so many of us—
    mostly third-world and non-white,
    the disposable people.
Put us together from far and near
    and we amount to more
    than the whole population of the western hemisphere
    of our once-fertile Mother Earth.

While you abound in affluence
    and play in the luxury of her lap,
    her breasts here are dry as dust:
    there is no food,
    there is no food.

I wander with the rest,
    like swarms of hungry locusts
    from camp to camp
    when word spreads that there's food.
A handful of grain is given to me,
    to a body that has learned
    by months of hunger to ration it,
    and so prolong the play of death.

They say you're on a special diet,
    are selective about what you're served,
    prefer whole-grain health food
    and watch your weight.
I dream nightly of the feast
    that's given to your garbage can,
    could dine like a prince
    on your leftover scraps.

Thank you for listening to my psalm;
    I know that you would care
    if I came to your door
    with my skinny bones and sunken eyes.
I know you would care—
    at least I would care
    if I were you.

PSALM OF A POLITICAL PRISONER

I'm a prisoner, though not your ordinary kind;
  my crime was to stand up for justice,
  to think and speak the truth.

I'm cut off and isolated,
  lost to my family and friends;
  a hostage of hatred,
  now only the political plaything
  of my sadistic keepers
  before whom I hang naked
  so that they can play
  with their crude toys of torture.
Scarred are my wrists and my back,
  pierced is my skin and muddy my mind.

Who knows my whereabouts,
  does anyone care?
What difference does it make
  in a world inundated with injustice,
  where lies are only loosely wrapped,
  tissue papered to look like truth:
  such thoughts torture me too.

But the most terrible torment comes at the hands
  of the one whose fiendish fingers nightly slip sinister
  into my last safe place, my mind,
  and who whispers in a serpent's hiss,
  "Was it worth all of this pain,
  to simply speak the truth?
  Why did you not keep silent like all the rest;
  you could have been sleeping
  in a comfortable bed this night,
  secure with your family around you."

My God, if you are out there,
  why have you forsaken me too?
I have prayed for the end of this —
  there are times when I'd even welcome death,
  but it seems you are deaf!

I hear footsteps in the hall: it's my turn again,
  back to the devil's playground.

PSALM OF THE MEDICALLY DEPRIVED

A Catholic pope declared, Paul VI his name,
    that it's an intolerable scandal,
    when so many of us are hungry;
    with hospitals, clinics and classrooms
    needing to be built,
    with states or individuals
    squandering money on ostentation!
A scandal, when so many are sick and dying,
    when so many are in such great need,
    to spend billions upon billions on weapons of war.

Ah, but that was long, long ago,
    back in 1967,
    two dear, and now dead, children ago—
    and good Pope Paul, he's also dead—
    and this sick child of mine,
    will also soon be dead.
Dying in my arms,
    her once blue eyes
    now are the color of pain.
There's no doctor in our village,
    no medicine or health care for miles.

My poor country's pocketbook
    is now bone-bare for medical care
    and we're heavily in debt.
No money for medicine,
    or doctors to train or hire;
    our resources used
    to buy from your credit catalogs
    more machines for war.
Why are weapons, agents of death,
    more necessary for peace
    than food, shelter and medicine,
    agents of life?

No answer!
    Nor do I have one,
    and, see, my child's dead:
    please forget that I even dared to speak.

THE PASSION AND DEATH OF JESUS CHRIST ACCORDING TO ST. THOMAS

I'm called "Doubting Thomas." But of all of them, I was the only one who proposed, "Come, let us go up to Jerusalem and die with him." But it was long ago, a thousand yesterdays, when I who could be called "Thomas the Brave" proposed a communal Calvary.

Today I come to you—yes, you—and say, "Look out your windshield or into the window of your television, and let us go up to Neon Jerusalem and die with him. Come along with me to the city park of Gethsemane, where Jesus suffers the sweaty-palm agony of the sick and those dying of the deadly diseases, AIDS and cancer. Tomorrow is their Good Friday; tonight their lonesome vigil. Come, let us go and die with him.

"Come and look—stare if you like—Jesus is stripped of his clothing, exposed to shame in those stripped of their jobs, naked by the loss of their homes and possessions, disrobed of their dignity.

"Come, stand and watch, helpless by habit, as Jesus is mocked and ridiculed by the centurions of society, in being the butt of crude minority jokes and tongue-cutting, clever discrimination humor. Join the crowd and let your silence or laughter lash away at him.

"Don't turn away from the pain; see the crown of thorns upon his head in the form of each one who is mentally ill, their foreheads pierced by deep depression. There he is as a bag lady muttering to herself, or, there, see him sitting and staring out the window of a ward.

"See the crowd press closer, and you can view him being scourged by physical or mental abuse. Watch, don't turn away your prudish eyes: see him sexually abused in a confused and forever crippled little child. Genuflect if you like, or bow in reverence.

"Turn your head, we're passing a prison; behind those walls and bars sits Jesus as an innocent man or woman—even in those guilty of some crime. Jesus—in the person of one unjustly tried and condemned, lacking a clever lawyer, or a victim crippled by poverty or a broken home—is caged in a crowded cell.

"Come with me up Main Street of Neon Jerusalem; watch Jesus go by in all disabled persons carrying their crosses in the daily passion parade and in those back-bent with the heavy burdens of life. Where is a Simon from Cyrene, Texas or Minnesota, who will lift a hand to raise a wheelchair, open a door or lift with compassion the crosses they bear. Ah, how quickly he has passed.

"Come with me, let us go up the trashy hill of 10,000 Calvarys, look how in the body of the needy they have nailed him secure for life to the icy cold cross of poverty. Stand with me at the foot of millions of crosses shouldered in the midday darkness of hopelessness. Listen to that piercing cry riding on the wind of a year of Good Fridays, 'My God, why, why have you abandoned me?'

"Come, let us go up to Neon Jerusalem and die with him—suffer with him, be shamed with him, be imprisoned with him, feel the lash of laughter, be mocked for a lack of money, sweat blood with him in a slow painful death and hold out our hands to be nailed for life."

You're late, have pressing matters to attend to, oh yes. You don't want to get involved, obedient to your culture's commandment, "Mind your own business." I understand—I, of all, understand. I too was afraid to get involved; the risk, you know was really great. I understand: brave words come easy, it's defeat and shame that test convictions. Remember, I'm Doubting Thomas, even to this day. I'm your patron. Can he . . . he be dying of AIDS? Can he really sit in the chair of an electric cross and die: aren't only criminals condemned? O doubting disciples who turn away from ugliness and brokenness, saying to yourselves: "Surely this is not the Chosen of our God." Take consolation, I know your thoughts.

I doubt today, as long ago, but I doubt that you really believe that he is risen and among us. I doubt seriously that if on meeting someone homeless or broken on Main Street of Neon Jerusalem, you would say, "My Lord and my God."

PSALMS FOR
ALL OCCASIONS

A MORNING PSALM

Show me, O Ever-new One,
    at the beginning of this new day,
    that I am no master at the art of living
    or in spending the gift of these new hours of life.

I'm no expert, even though I've lived a thousand days
    like this gift-day, so brightly wrapped in sunrise.
Give me, O my Creator, a beginner's mind
    to play with this new day that has dawned.

With a beginner's mind, fresh and open,
    I can see countless ways to explore
    the promise these hours hold,
    as gift from you.

May I approach the tasks
    and unknown challenges that await me
    as if it were the first time.
Grace me with your insight as I use this time
    to explore new ways to live this day.

pause for reflection

May the experiments I have considered
    make this day rich in an abundant harvest
    of the fruits of kindness and love
    that you, with infinite patience, desire from me.

Grant me also the generous spirit
    of your servant son, Albert Schweitzer, who said,
    "Even if it's a little thing,
    do something for others—
    something for which you get no pay
    but the privilege of doing it."

AN EVENING PSALM OF INVENTORY

As Earth turns outward into space
    and the light fades into turquoise,
    I step aside to inventory
    the thoughts, words and deeds of my day.

I carefully scan today in the light
    of the far-flung dimensions of the universe.
Have I failed this day by shrinking its vastness
    to the narrow limits
    of my life, my needs and desires?
Has the smallness of that space
    caused my heart to contract as well?

Have I failed to view my work
    against the cosmic background of my mission
    as a co-explorer and co-creator with God?
Has my limited view of the scope of life
    given me permission to fill my time
    with negative thoughts and careless assumptions?
Have I judged as insignificant
    the needs of other members of our earth-ship crew?

Guided by a wider vision of my responsibilities,
    as well as our common duties and destination,
    I now take inventory of this completed day
    assisted by your Spirit, O God.

pause for silent reflection

Mindful that you have already forgiven and pardoned me
    the very moment I had forgotten who I am,
    the moment I had forgotten who we are
    and where we are traveling together,
    I give you thanks, O Sacred Mystery,
    Gracious God who forgives so unconditionally.

A SUNSET PSALM OF TURNING

Slowly we are turning once again
      to look into the dark, star-sprinkled space
      through which our planet is traveling.
All life is aware of the approaching view,
      and the sunset beauty of this day's end
      is an overture to the awesome grandeur
      of the eternal vision that awaits us.

As the earth turns outward,
      may my thoughts turn inward
      to the Sacred Mystery that dwells in my heart.
At the end of this day
      I sing a song of thanksgiving
      for the wonder of life.
I lift up my voice in gratitude
      for all this day has held for me
      as I turn my memory to its flood of gifts.

pause for recollection of blessings and gifts

Blessed are you, Divine Mystery,
      who has chosen to dwell within me
      and has enriched this day
      with zestful life, beauty, love
      and the discipline of my trials and temptations.

Blessed are you, O God,
      most blessed are you.

PSALM FOR A SOGGY DAY

The sky has disappeared,
    and shapeless clouds hang low.
Dripping water leaks into my life
    as I listlessly begin this dull day.

The electric blue of the sky is gone,
    as is the yellow song of the sun,
    which spurs enthusiasm,
    spreads smiles
    and breaks depression's grip.

Dear and Faithful Friend,
    who created both blue and gray,
    both sun and rain,
    show me the gift of this dull day.

Expand my spirit outward,
    before this sulky day
    drags me under like a tide
    into the basement of my soul,
    drowning me in gloom.

Help me turn the tide of depression
    and lighten my heavy body
    by the recollection of your love.
May my smile be sunlight for others,
    my zest the blue sky,
    my hope like towering white thunderheads,
    swollen with the promise
    of your presence.

A PSALM OF LONGING

My spirit hungers for your love,
    O Divine Maker of hearts,
    for the taste of your joy
    and the aroma of your peace.

May this time of prayer
    fill me with the whisper of your presence
    and let me feel the touch
    of your hand upon my heart.

How I long for the depths of your love,
    to know your quiet constancy,
    the feast of your friendship
    that feeds me without end.

Oh, how my soul longs for you.
You elude all names we give you
    and dwell beyond the grasp of brilliant minds.
Your essence pulses within every atom
    yet extends beyond the far frontiers of space,
    unscanned by the strongest telescopes.
Awaken me to your presence,
    now, this moment,
    in my heart.

PSALM FOR A STALLED HEART

My heart is cold today, O God,
    I feel no burning desire,
    no zeal to pray or be with you.
My heart is frozen by the chill of emptiness—
    sluggish and stalled.

Send forth your Spirit
    to revive my heart.
Spark it with a relish for service,
    with a longing to pray.

Take me beyond the need to feel
    the reassurance of a lover's heart.
May I seek to love and serve you,
    even when my wintry heart
    declines to dance
    with springtime grace.

Remind me of the ageless truth
    that we become what we pretend to be.
And as this long day passes,
    may I begin to glimpse a growing warmth
    beyond my words and deeds,
    the marriage of what I would be
    and what I am.

And may my desire
    to be your flame of warmth and love
    spark other stalled souls
    to come alive, aflame in you.

May this be so, O God, may this be so.

A PSALM OF ANGER

O God, I am so angry:
    my small heart is filled
    with as much energy
    as a nuclear power plant,
    and just as dangerous.

I fear the effects of the radiation
    that surely leak outward
    to all living things that surround me,
    invisible energy of destruction
    that leaves in its wake
    the residue of death.

O Merciful One,
    plunge my soul's raging inferno
    into your cool, purifying water
    to still the savage storm
    that boils beyond control
    with the heat of hell.

Calm my heart by filling it with peace;
    filter all the way into the core,
    to transform its deadly energies
    into creative power,
    into the light of love.

Come, O God,
    for without your help
    the danger to the life-force around me
    may be beyond repair.

A PSALM OF PARDON

Pardon is your name,
    Forgiveness your eternal title,
    by "Mercy as vast as the universe" are you known.
Grant me, O Gracious One,
    your great gift of pardon.

I have searched for it
    in every pocket and hiding place;
    I cannot find it, your gift of Self.
I know it is here,
    buried beneath my pain,
    somewhere in a back corner of my heart:
    but for now it is lost.

Make me your messenger
    of the good news I cannot now speak.
Give to me words of forgiveness,
    the healing touch of pardon,
    the love that weds two as one.

I know that to forgive is divine,
    but I am no deity,
    and I fear I will be a demon,
    who, by failing to forgive,
    will spread the kingdom of darkness.

Remind me ten times and more
    of all that you have forgiven me—
    without even waiting for my sorrow,
    the very instant that I slipped and sinned.
Remind me ten thousand times and more
    of your endless absolution,
    not even sorrow required on my part,
    so broad the bounty of your love.

Yes, I can—I will—forgive
    as you have forgiven me.

A PSALM WHEN PARDON IS IMPOSSIBLE

It feels impossible, O God,
  totally beyond my reach,
  to forgive what has been done to me.
You know my pain,
  you know the hurt I hold.

Surely you, O God—
  who in a moment of anger
  swept away all the earth in one great flood,
  leaving only old Noah and his boatload of refugees
  safe from your rain-soaked rage—
  surely you know the storm within my heart.

But I'm doubly caught in this bind,
  snagged on the sacred fence
  of my friendship with your son Jesus,
  who has told me that I **must** forgive,
  seven times seventy times,
  those who injure me,
  who cause me pain.

Caught between pain and pardon,
  I wish to choose his way of pardon.
Nailed by pain to his cross,
  covered by the spit of scorners
  and whipped by his torturers,
  he prayed the impossible prayer.
This prayer is one I now desire to make mine:
  "Father, forgive him, her, them,
  for they know not what they do."

O Infinite Sea of Mercy,
  make this unworthy servant
  the channel of your gift of pardon,
  that I also may be healed
  as your forgiveness passes through me to others.

PSALM OF THE RAZOR'S EDGE

The path we walk to you, O God, is narrow,
 as narrow as a razor's edge.
The Way is only as wide as a human hair,
 and many are those who lose their balance
 on such a thin and uncertain edge.

Each day, like a circus aerialist,
 I walk the tightrope of the command,
 "Come, follow me."
Who can stride safely on such a narrow bridge
 which swings between heaven and earth?

Downward is the pull of self;
 it tugs at me: "for me, for me . . . me."
Heavy the gravity of the urge:
 "I want, I want, I want."

The Way is narrow and high:
 holy and brave are those
 who climb upon the razor's edge,
 swaying from left to right or right to left,
 straining too hard or relaxing too much.

Holy are those who fall
 but rise again
 and climb back upon the narrow edge
 and begin again
 and again.

The Way is narrow and high,
 and high are those who walk it,
 one small step at a time,
 intoxicated by the risk,
 joyous at the fine balancing line
 of the razor's edge.

A PSALM OF MY WHERENESS

The question "Where have I come from?"
    rises up and haunts me;
    lingering, it floats like a flower
    in the backwaters of my mind.

From somewhere deeper than I know,
    in the place where I am held to the divine breast,
    the voice of God echoes in reply:
    "You, my beloved little one,
    were hidden in my heart
    before your sun burned bright.
You were the dream of my delight
    before the earth was born
    of the dust of long-dead stars.
Before I shaped a single star,
    I nursed you for endless ages,
    feeding you with the essence of my life.

"In my great lap I played with your infinite childlike form
    and gazed with love upon your original face,
    the mirror form of my own image.
I laughed with delight at the marvel of your being,
    the flesh of my flesh and bone of my bone.

"And you laughed with glee as I winked,
    as the four winds sprang to life
    and suns like dandelions
    lit up the dark lawn of space.

"Where did you come from? O my child,
    you in whom live all my hopes and loves,
    you came from me."

A RAINY DAY PSALM

I greet you, Pilgrim Rain, mystic, ancient traveler,
    visiting me today, washing over our land,
    soaking the earth and enriching it,
    nourishing growth with greening gifts of life.
But you are only passing by,
    briefly streaming past my door
    on your pilgrimage to the sea.

You are a pilgrim who blesses all you touch;
    O gentle yet powerful pilgrim,
    stone-carver and sand-maker,
    what hidden gift do you have for me?

"I teach you about illusions;
    like brief bubbles riding tiny trickles
    are your ideas that you control your life:
    flick a switch and you create light,
    turn a key and power fires,
    just twist a dial and music plays.
You live in an illusion of control.

"But I, by my downpour descending from the sky
    and flowing past your door,
    have altered your life today:
    your outdoor plans now rearranged,
    your neat agendas put on hold.
Learn of me how little you control in your life;
    yet, by changing your present plans,
    I offer you entrance to a timeless reality,
    a chance to listen and be present
    to the One who is always beyond."

Thank you, Pilgrim Rain:
    it's a small but beautiful gift
    to be reminded of the reality of life.
Soon the fireball of my daystar sun
    will pierce with long yellow fingers
    your mobile home of gray clouds,
    and the wind will push them onward
    to send you on your restless way again.

Thank you for your holy pilgrim's gift:
    may I live like you, always on the move,
    my home the endless journey, sacred-sea-bound.
May I live like you, falling and rising;
    nourishing always, till I ascend, once and for all.

SACRED HEART PSALM

O Divine Beloved,
    so often I am casual and half-hearted
    in my love for you, my God.
Come and set my heart ablaze
    with the fire of your love.
Inflame my heart and prayers
    as you did for your chosen son Jesus.
His holy heart was constantly on fire
    with a consuming love for you, his God.

Envelop me in your flaming Spirit,
    that my lukewarm prayers and acts
    may spring alive with the fire of faith.
Make my heart, like the heart of Christ,
    burn with compassion for the outcast,
    with comfort for the lonely
    and all who are in need.

May my heart thus formed
    in the pattern of his Sacred Heart
    become a fiery furnace
    where the Kingdom will be forged,
    the age of peace and justice.

Grant this prayer
    in the name of your Son,
    who dwells with you and the Holy Spirit,
    One God, forever and ever.

THE PSALM OF THE GREAT AMEN

When I finish praying apart from others,
    as the final word of prayer
    drifts away beyond reach of ears,
    I listen for the Great Amen.

Like silent thunder
    it comes rolling back.
Or it leaps across the roof tops,
    racing madly through the leaves of trees,
    whipping wildly over electrical wires
    linking pole to pole,
    and with the surge of a cosmic sea wave
    it crashes upon my shore:
    "Amen."

From all creation comes the chorus,
    from snow-swept glaciers
    and ever-extending deserts,
    from dark-brown jungle rivers
    and majestic mountain ranges,
    from vast redwood forests
    and endless rolling prairies,
    from flocks of flying birds
    and herds of wild animals,
    from swarms of monarch butterflies
    and schools of fish in the ocean deep:
    to each of my prayers
    comes the Great Amen.

From God's great family, one and all,
    rainbow-colored in skin and faith,
    from those of every compass point,
    from country, town and urban slum,
    it comes, it always comes.

From heaven's host in splendor wrapped,
    angels and archangels,
    saints and mystics all,
    it slowly swells and rises;
    then rushes cascading into the cave of my heart:
    "AMEN, AMEN, AMEN."

A LOVER'S PSALM

O Ever-present Beloved,
    my soul sings and my body rejoices
    that you are the flesh and bone of my life.
You are the ever-youthful life-seed
    at the core of all that grows.
I bow before you, Gracious God,
    that while you are greater than this vast universe,
    you are also the innermost essence of every being.

I delight that you are the fiery force
    that gives the flowers their beauty;
    you are the life-giving wetness of water
    and the warmth of the sun;
    you are the breath of all living things
    and the fertile soil out of which
    all things draw their life-nourishment.

The blood in my veins races madly,
    and my heart drum-beats like thunder
    at the very hint of your holy voice.
I hear you in the song of birds,
    in the gurgle of flowing water,
    in the rush or the whisper of the wind.
You are here,
    with me and in me
    and all around me.

O Intimate Presence, my Beloved,
    I am drunk with a love for you.

A PILGRIM'S COMPANION PSALM

The road home, O God, seems long
    and at times is difficult and painful.
Grant me a holy communion, a companionship with others,
    as I journey homeward to you.

I live in times of great trial:
    an age of change sits at my door.
Without a community with others
    I can so easily loose the way,
    can be led astray by illusions of holiness,
    misguided by my ego's desires.

Open my eyes to your precious gift
    of the Church's Communion of Saints.
"Saint" is a name I would never call myself,
    but the treasury of my faith
    teaches me about my holy birthright,
    that I am part of the web of sacred communion,
    uniting me with all other home-bound pilgrims
    and with all who now rejoice
    at their homecoming in you.

May I feed this day upon the food
    of this mystic, holy communion
    with those friends and fellow pilgrims
    with whom I share this planet earth,
    as well as those saints now fully one with you.

May this awareness of my companion journey
    with all the saints
    deepen my life of prayer
    and fertilize my faith in you, my Beloved.
By this communion of holy ones
    may I be daily challenged
    to greater compassion and charity
    as I walk the way of the pilgrim.

A PSALM OF COSMIC COMMUNION

May I join you, cosmic congregation of galaxies,
    as you dance with delight before our God.
You spin and leap with brilliant bursts of light,
    never tiring of your sacred circle-play.

May I join you, star-children of countless constellations,
    in the worship of our common Creator
    in your rotating rituals of nuclear energy
    as you sing cosmic chants of divine fire.

May I join you, I who find my times of devotion
    so often flat and fireless,
    bound by routine and uninspired,
    stagnant due to their lack of zeal.

May I join you, so that my prayers
    may also spin with sparkling splendor,
    spawning long tails of luminous devotion
    to carry my praise and adoration
    straight to the heart of my Beloved God.

A PSALM OF FREEDOM

O you who are eternally free,
  you who dwell within all yet beyond all,
  listen to my heart's song.

I long to escape the inner prisons
  that limit my liberty;
  to flee the wardens of fear
  who daily double my chains.

Each second of my life
  seeps through the seams of my heart,
  slowly and surely slipping away,
  like the sands of an hourglass.
Now is the hour, this is the day,
  yet higher, ever higher,
  do my dull prison walls skyward rise.

Set my foot to the ladder,
  glue my eyes upon you.
Call loudly and clearly,
  and I will follow.
For in your voice, O Divine Beloved,
  is the grace to be free.

Free Spirit who roams the galaxies,
  unrestrained as the prairie wind,
  in you is Life.

A PSALM OF FLEXIBILITY

O Spirit of God's eternal springtime heart,
    grant me the virtue of elasticity.
Make my heart as boundless as my Beloved's heart,
    which at this moment is creating
    new galaxies and infant suns.

Make me pliable and playful with your Spirit
    as you teach me the alchemist's recipe
    of how to keep my heart's skin
    like baby's skin, ever-expansive,
    able to hold the wildest of wines.

Stir my mind well with your sacred spoon
    to awaken the fermentation of ideas
    stilled by the ten thousand little compromises
    required of me by the stiffness
    of the old leathered skins of society and religion.

Gift me with elastic frontiers of heart and mind,
    so I can see before my eyes,
    both in the heavens and on earth,
    how old and ever-new are those partners
    passionately dancing together
    in the perpetual birthing of your universe.

A PSALM FOR THE DYING

Relatives and friends, I am about to leave;
     my last breath does not say "goodbye,"
     for my love for you is truly timeless,
     beyond the touch of boney death.
I leave myself not to the undertaker,
     for decoration in his house of the dead,
     but to your memory, with love.

I leave my thoughts, my laughter, my dreams
     to you whom I have treasured
     beyond gold and precious gems.
I give you what no thief can steal,
     the memories of our times together:
     the tender, love-filled moments,
     the successes we have shared,
     the hard times that brought us closer together
     and the roads we have walked side by side.

I also leave you a solemn promise
     that after I am home in the bosom of God,
     I will still be present,
     whenever and wherever you call on me.
My energy will be drawn to you
     by the magnet of our love.
Whenever you are in need, call me;
     I will come to you,
     with my arms full of wisdom and light
     to open up your blocked paths,
     to untangle your knots
     and to be your avenue to God.

And all I take with me as I leave
     is your love and the millions of memories
     of all that we have shared.
So I truly enter my new life
     as a millionaire.

Fear not nor grieve at my departure,
     you whom I have loved so much,
     for my roots and yours
     are forever intertwined.

A PSALM BEFORE BEGINNING WORK

To you, O Divine One, from whose hands
    comes the work of creation, so artfully designed,
    I pray that this work I am about to do
    may be done in companionship with you.

May the work that I will soon begin
    sing praise to you
    as songbirds do.

May the work that I will soon begin
    add to the light of your presence
    because it is done with great love.

May the work that I will soon begin
    speak like a prophet of old
    of your dream of beauty and unity.

May the work that I will soon begin
    be a shimmering mirror of your handiwork
    in the excellence of its execution,
    in the joy of doing it for its own sake,
    in my poverty of ownership over it,
    in my openness to failure or success,
    in my invitation to others to share in it
    and in its bearing fruit for the world.
May I be aware that through this work
    I draw near you.

I come to you, Beloved,
    with ready hands.

A PSALM BEFORE BEGINNING WORK

My day begins, O Gracious God;
    let all my work be done as prayer
    as I do it one with you.
May I, like your son Jesus,
    be Emmanuel, "God among us,"
    here in this place of work.
May I carry your presence
    as I respond to all with kindness and warmth,
    with joy and humble service.
Grant me the grace to love Christ
    in all who will share my life this day.
O God, grant me this gift.

A PSALM OF OFFERING MY WORK

As one of your priestly people, O Gracious God,
    I offer up to you as my sacrifice
    all the irritations and interruptions
    that this day may contain.
I offer up the work of my hands
    as an act of sacrificial prayer
    performed in holy solidarity
    with all in need of your presence and help
    (especially today with: _____).
As this day begins, be at their side and at mine.

A PSALM BEFORE LEAVING WORK

My day ends here, O my Beloved,
  and I give you thanks for my employment
  when so many are jobless.
I thank you, my God, for your grace
  in the difficult moments of this day.
I am grateful for the gift of community
  with those who share this work.
Look with compassion upon any failure
  to treat each person I have met today,
  whether friend or stranger, as Christ.
With your holy help, tomorrow I will do better.
Blessed are you who gives me a share
  in the work of re-creating the world
  in love, justice and peace.

The Planet Earth

COSMOPOLITAN PRAYERS

The ancient Sanctus prayer of the Liturgy of the Holy Eucharist proclaims: "Holy, holy, holy are you, God of power and might. Heaven and earth are full of your glory." Being full of the divine glory, the cosmos is also God's dwelling place. And speaking through the lips of the prophet Isaiah, the Divine Mystery said, "My house shall be a house of prayer for all peoples." Thus to view the cosmos as a temple means to view the prayer and worship of all those who dwell on the planet Earth as the praise of the children of God. The following prayers that flow from some of the world's great religious traditions invite you into a cosmopolitan communion of prayer.

In the First Letter of Saint John is a truth that opens us to the great mystery that God does not show partiality because of creed or race: "Beloved, let us love one another because love is of God; everyone who loves is begotten of God and has knowledge of God."

In these cosmopolitan prayers is an invitation to the planetary pilgrim to find his or her path enriched by the knowledge of God found in the gifts of the Holy Spirit given to those of other religious traditions.

The early disciples of Christ called themselves "catholic," which means universal or all-embracing. We become catholic, regardless of our religious tradition, when our love becomes all-embracing, as wide as the cosmos. It is to be a cosmopolite, a citizen of the cosmos. As planetary pilgrims and true children of God, that is our birthright.

The author George Moore in *Hail and Farewell!* said, "Art must be parochial in the beginning to become cosmopolitan in the end." Likewise, the art of prayer must begin firmly rooted in one's spiritual tradition. As we descend deeper and deeper to the center of true prayer, we are paradoxically pushed past parochial frontiers into cosmic—truly catholic—prayer that embraces all that is true and holy.

The following prayers are intended for those who feel themselves drawn by God over their parochial fence and outward into the cosmos.

BUDDHIST TRADITION

We are what we think. What we are is
the result of our thoughts. With our thoughts
we make our world. Speak or act with an
impure mind and trouble will follow you as
the wheel follows the ox that draws the
cart. Speak or act with a pure mind and
happiness will follow you as unshakable
as your shadow.

> the Lord Buddha
> from the **Dhammapada**

How easily do I see myself, O gentle Divine Parent,
    as a victim of the evils of this world,
    a victim of the greed and injustice of others.
Yet in the wisdom of your son Buddha
    I come to understand that it is I
    who create my world with my thoughts.

I struggle to understand the mystery
    that my dark and negative thoughts
    weave about me a negative world
    of fear, evil and harm.
Is it true that my seemingly harmless thoughts
    are magnets that draw darkness to me
    as surely as iron bits are attracted to a magnet?

If so, then come and help me this day, O God,
    to strive to keep in my mind
    only pure, loving thoughts
    about others and life.
Your son Jesus taught in many ways
    that evil thoughts breed evil deeds,
    so let me banish such thoughts
    from my mind and heart
    the moment that I become aware
    of their destructive presence.

May I think only loving and kind thoughts toward others,
    even toward those who harm me,
    and so help create a compassionate world
    full of your glory and holiness,
    a world filled with happiness and joy.

They are true disciples who have trained
their hands, feet and speech to serve
others. They meditate deeply, are at
peace with themselves and live in joy.

the Lord Buddha
from the **Dhammapada**

As a potter shapes clay into a vessel,
    shape me, O Blessed One,
    into a true disciple of your Way.
Fill me with your grace
    that I may train my body this day
    to serve others.

May each act of my hands to assist others,
    even such simple acts of service
    as opening a door or passing a plate,
    train them to reach out
    with ever-greater generosity
    in humble service to anyone in need.

Let each step my feet take
    to answer a request for help,
    to visit the sick, to comfort a friend
    or go out of my way to assist another,
    train them to move with the grace
    of a true disciple.

I seek, this day, to train my tongue
    as your son Buddha instructed,
    to speak only words of kindness,
    to praise and encourage others,
    to defend those scorned or discriminated against,
    and, by speaking only the truth,
    to be a true disciple.

Awaken me as you did the Buddha, the Awakened One,
    to know that all expressions
    of my hands, feet and speech
    that serve others
    are prayers that are perfect
    in your holy sight.
Awaken me to know you deeply, to live in peace and joy.

TRADITION OF THE NATIVE INDIANS
OF THE AMERICAS

Oh, only for so short a while
have you loaned us to each other.
Because we take form in your act of drawing us,
and we breathe in your singing us.
But only for a short while
have you loaned us to each other.
Because even a drawing cut in
crystalline obsidian fades,
and the green feathers, the crown feathers,
of the Quetzal bird lose their color,
and even the sounds of the waterfall
die out in the dry season.
So, we too, because only for a short while
have you loaned us to each other.

Aztec prayer to God

O Divine Parent and Gift-giver,
let me not take those I love for granted,
failing to remember
that you have only loaned them to me
for a very short while.

Help me, this day, you who are absolute love,
to love those you have loaned to me,
as if tomorrow you would call them home to you.

Let me not take them for granted
or be blind to the marvel of their presence,
to the sound of their voices,
the joy of their companionship
or the beauty of their love.

May their minor faults and failings
which often cause me discomfort
be seen as trivial transgressions
compared to the marvel of the gift
that you have loaned to me
for only a short while.

When you arise in the morning, give
thanks for the morning light. Give
thanks for your life and your strength.
Give thanks for your food and give
thanks for the joy of living. And
if you see no reason for giving thanks,
rest assured the fault is in yourself.

Native American Sioux Indian

O Divine Gift-giver,
    I stand beneath the endless waterfall
    of your abundant gifts to me.
I thank you especially for the blessing of life,
    the most precious of all your gifts to me.
I thank you, Ever-generous One,
        for clothing to wear,
        for food and drink to nourish my body,
        for all the talents and skills
        that you have bestowed upon me.

I thank you for the many joys of my life,
        for family and friends,
        for work that gives to me a sense of purpose
        and invests my life with meaning.
I thank you as well
        for the sufferings and trials of my life,
        which are also gifts
        and which together with my mistakes
        are among my most important teachers.

Grant that I may never greet a new day
        without the awareness of some gift
        for which to give you thanks.
And may constant thanksgiving
        be my song of perpetual praise to you.

Father, a needy one stands before you,
I that sing am that one.

Native American Omaha Indian

O Blessed One,
    I take great pride in my independence,
    that by my work and effort
    I can supply all my needs.
I tend to look away from those who are in need
    or look down on them as weak.

It is not easy for me to expose my needs,
    to even let on that I too am needy.
I have learned from years of practice
    to mask well my many needs
    for love, affection and admiration.
So it is difficult for me
    to stand or kneel before you
    and admit my poverty.

Help me to become a blessed beggar
    who can stand tall beside the truth
    that I am indeed needy.
Gift me this day with the understanding
    that there is no shame
    in being a dependent child of yours.
Help me to realize, as did St. Paul,
    that in my weakness lies my greatest strength.

Open me wide to the reality
    that my impoverishment may day by day
    be removed by you, my God,
    as through the graced channel of others in my life
    you fill my beggar's bowl
    with love and attention,
    with recognition and appreciation.

O Holy Parent, like a small child
    I come to you, needy but not ashamed.

ISLAMIC TRADITION

We are born asleep and at death we awake.

the Prophet Mohammed
from the **Koran**

Your visionary son Mohammed
    reminds me this day, O God,
    that I am a sleepwalker
    who wanders through life
    with eyes closed to the glory of your presence.

Lift my drooping eyelids this day
    from the slumber of the unawakened,
    so that I might see you
    in the vastness of the universe,
    in the busy work of the ant,
    in the awesome beauty of the flower,
    in the ordered cycles of the seasons
    and in all I shall encounter.

Oh, that I might be awakened this day
    to how your glory fills all of heaven and earth,
    the temple where you have chosen to dwell.
May I treat with profound reverence
    each blade of grass and the earth beneath my feet,
    the food and drink that nourish me
    and every person whose path shall cross mine.
May I honor everything that lives and breathes.

Answer this prayer, as I bow before you,
    so that I need not wait until death
    to behold your divine face,
    to feel your embrace
    and to live in your blessed presence.
As your son, St. Benedict, once said,
    "It is time now for us to rise from sleep."

Don't make friends with an elephant trainer
unless you have room in your home
for an elephant.

saying of the Sufis,
Islamic mystics

O Blessed One, you whose voice calls me
to the sacred path of the pilgrim,
I wish to seek you with all my heart.
Yet I am often half-hearted in that desire
when I realize the cost of such a quest.

My life is rather comfortable and well-ordered
and fits me like an old shoe.
I fear the knowledge that if I romance you
I may lose what I hold dear.
Be compassionate with my hesitation,
as I measure the cost of loving you.

I have read in the holy books,
and know from the lives of the saints,
that you, my God, come as purifying fire
to burn away all that is not true.
I tremble at the thought
of you consuming those things that I love
and even my prized image of who I am.
Yet, I also want to know you more fully;
help me to embrace the awesome implications
of my inviting you to enter my life.

Enlarge my half-hearted love
with the ageless truth
that if I seek your kingdom first,
seek to be fully possessed by you,
everything I need shall be given me,
and happiness beyond my wildest dreams
shall be mine.

Come today, Creator of elephants and saints,
and be my friend.

Do not say, regarding anything,
"I am going to do that tomorrow,"
but say only, "God willing."

the prophet Mohammed
from the **Koran**

O Beloved One, for whom the future is always now,
    I am busy making plans for my tomorrows,
    what I shall do and where I shall go.
Am I not the captain of my ship,
    competent to chart its course
    through calm or stormy seas?

Teach me the foolishness of such thoughts,
    and place upon my lips this day
    the Arabic word *Inshallah*, "God willing."
May it remind me constantly
    that I cannot control today,
    let alone tomorrow.

God willing, I will be alive tomorrow;
    if God wills it, I shall be able
    to meet my commitments,
    arrive safely at my destination,
    complete the work that I have promised.

Inshallah, wondrous word which reveals to me
    that I must live day by day,
    always dependent upon God's providence.
May every plan and dream I propose
    be sealed with what God may dispose,
    and bear the mystic's motto,
    "God willing," *Inshallah*!

COSMOPOLITAN PRAYERS • 201

HINDU TRADITION

We are born into the world of nature;
our second birth is into the world of spirit.

the Lord Krishna
*from the **Bhagavad Gita***

Each year, O God, I celebrate my birthday,
    a feast to remember
    that special day when I was born.
With candles and cake, with parties and gifts,
    I celebrate my first birth.

While that first birth lasted
    only a matter of minutes or hours,
    my second birth into the world of spirit
    is a daily and ongoing feast.
Each day is a blessed birthday
    into a greater awareness of how this world—
    from the tiniest atom to the greatest mountain—
    is infused with your Spirit.

Each day, O God, I see more clearly
    into the world inside this world;
    not two worlds divorced
    but one world of spirit and matter,
    married eternally as one.
"And what God has joined together,
    let no one put asunder."

May I embrace the birth pains
    of my second, continuous birthing,
    with joy and hope.
Let me befriend every spirit guide, however humble,
    whom I meet upon my pilgrimage to you
    as a sacred midwife sent by you.

Grant, O God, that this ordinary day
    may become my birth day, a coming forth
    into that wider and more awesome world
    full of your glory and holiness.

Do what you do
but dedicate the fruit of your acts to me.

the Lord Krishna
*from the **Bhagavad Gita***

O Ever-understanding Lover,
    I have grown up in a world
    which is addicted to success,
    which places halos on those
    who achieve fame and fortune.
Free me, I pray, from this addiction.

Guide my hand to lift up to you
    all the harvest that may come
    from the labor of my hands this day.
Help me to dedicate to you
    the results of all I do.

And by offering to you the fruit of my labor,
    may the words of your servant, St. Paul,
    become a guiding compass for me:
    "Whatever you eat,
    whatever you drink,
    whatever you do at all,
    do it for the glory of God."

May I thus fully surrender
    the success or failure of my work;
    they now belong to you
    and to you alone.
May I find my pleasure not in the prize
    of my work's successful completion
    or my pain in the shame of its failure,
    for my joy is in toiling for your glory.

Fix my heart firmly only upon the work at hand
    and not upon the final product,
    whether it be victory or defeat.
Let my delight
    be only in the task before me,
    for to you, my God,
    I dedicate the fruits of all my acts.

JUDAIC TRADITION

You shall love God with all your heart,
and with all your soul,
and with all your mind.
And you shall love your neighbor
as yourself.

the Prophet Moses
from the Book of **Deuteronomy**

O my God, Creator of the universe,
you give to me an impossible task,
to love you with the totality of my being.
You desire that I love you
with a fullness of my heart,
with every ounce of my soul's power
and with all the strength
of my body and mind.

I know that with and through you
all things are possible,
and so I strive this day
to fulfill the great command
that you gave to your beloved Moses.

Today I shall, to the best of my ability,
try to make my love for you so encompassing
that it shall absorb me body and soul.
Look with compassion, Ever-merciful One,
upon my times of amnesia,
when I stumble in my striving
and give priority to things other than you.

And enlighten me each morning to the sacred knowledge
that in loving others as myself,
in loving this world and all you have made,
I am loving you.
Make me this day, I pray,
a passionate lover of you
and of all that is full of your glory.

God is my light and my salvation;
whom shall I fear?
God is the strength of my life;
of whom shall I be afraid?

Psalm 27

My Beloved One,
how easily do I allow fear
to be the soil of my life.
Ten thousand fears cluster at my door:
fears of death and of life,
fears of thieves and evil,
fears of sickness and old age,
fears of unemployment and war,
fears of being shamed and injured.

How easily do politicians and preachers,
merchants, militants and advertisers
feed off my countless hidden fears,
promising protection and salvation.
Yet in you and you alone
do I find sufficient strength
to live my life unafraid.

I firmly believe that you love me
with all my faults and failings,
and if I am in your embrace,
whom or what should I fear?
Teach me the wisdom of caution,
to live with a watchful eye,
and liberate me from all fear.

O Blessed One, you are my insurance and my pledge,
you are my defense and security, my ground,
in your love is my sole safety;
of whom shall I be afraid?

Do not think that the words of
prayer as you say them go up to God.
It is not the words themselves that
ascend; rather it is the burning
desire of your heart that rises like
smoke to heaven. If your prayer
consists only of words and letters,
but does not contain your heart's
desire, how can it rise up to God?

Hasidic tradition,
mystics of Judaism

Whenever I pray, O Blessed One,
    let my words be only the containers
    of my passionate love for you.
Free me from the false notion
    that any combination of letters,
    regardless of how poetic or pious,
    can make a prayer beautiful.

Unless the words I speak in prayer
    are aflame with my love for you,
    they fall from my lips
    to litter the floor of my place of prayer.
And the incense of my worship is held earthbound
    by the gravity created by my lukewarm heart.

If my prayer is to ascend to you,
    then I must move beyond mere words
    to the power of the heart
    that even the most humble speech may contain.
So let me have a poverty of words
    that each one may be filled with great richness.
And save me from the error of believing
    that you find delight in the length of my prayers
    instead of in the love with which I fill them.

TAOIST TRADITION

We are born gentle and weak.
At death we are hard and stiff.
Green plants are tender and filled
with sap. When they die they are
withered and dry. Therefore the
stiff and unbending are the disciples
of death. The gentle and yielding
are the disciples of life.

Lao Tzu
from the **Tao Te Ching**

Save your servant, O Sustainer of Life,
    from too early a death.
Free me of that affliction of believers
    who so easily become rigid of heart
    in their journeys to you.

Make my heart like the green willow tree,
    that easily bends in the wind,
    that bows gracefully before the storm
    only to raise its head again with renewed life
    when the angry clouds have moved on.

Fill me this day, I pray,
    with the strength of your Spirit,
    the strength to be flexible and ever-green.
Create within me the heart
    of a disciple of life,
    a heart that is gentle and meek.

Let me learn a lesson from your daughter water
    who seeks the lowest path,
    ever yielding and humble,
    yet wears down the strongest stones into sand.
In her I see the wisdom of the Tao:
    "The hard and strong will fall;
    the soft and meek shall overcome."

Learn the strength of man,
but keep a woman's care!
Become the stream of the universe!
And being so, ever true and unswerving,
become a child once more.

Lao Tzu
from the **Tao Te Ching**

O you who are beyond all names,
  yet whom we call Father and Mother,
  help me to balance power and compassion,
  a woman's gentleness
  with a man's strength,
  as I open wide the doors of my heart
  for the life of the universe to flow through.

I know that the gates of paradise,
  both here and there,
  swing open only to the child.
Instruct me this day
  in the art of perpetual childhood
  which truly knows
  both honor and humility.

Unfold for me your best kept secret:
  how by becoming the stream of the universe,
  I may learn to be playful, yet prayerful,
  ever-relaxed, yet constantly alert,
  always prepared, yet carefree as a child,
  and so achieve the harmony of heaven.

The Pleiades Cluster

The Comet West

RITUALS FOR
A PLANETARY PILGRIM

Worship involves both prayer and ritual. The term "ritual" usually means a prescribed order of religious ceremony. But life is full of rituals, those patterns of activity that we repeat time and again. Society has numerous rituals, from sporting events to dining. All rituals, even the most secular, speak of the presence of the holy. They remind us that what now seems totally secular was once, long ago, very sacred and religious. But all rituals call for caution; they can become behavioral prisons that enslave us or containers in which are embalmed a once-living experience. While this can be a danger, personal rituals may also hold the power to awaken us to the presence of the Divine Mystery in all our actions.

While ritual is something that is repeated, all rituals, like traditions, were once new and fresh. They were born out of experiences that had significance beyond the actions themselves. We should not be timid about beginning a tradition or initiating a ritual as a means of expressing what is important to us, as a way of praying with our bodies as well as our minds. We can also ritualize daily patterns, elevating them from the commonplace to the cosmic by using them as doorways to the divine.

The following rituals for a planetary pilgrim are adapted from some of the great religious traditions of the world, which recognize that when body and mind, head and heart, are united in sacred activity, the Way is made easier.

THE RITUAL OF HOUSE CLEANING

Cleaning our living space is a necessary chore in daily life. "O Soji" is the name of a Buddhist ritual of daily cleaning. It plays an important part in the life of monasteries and temples as well as private homes. O Soji is also part of the spiritual training of those who are seeking to be one with God.

The ritual involves sweeping and washing floors and the removal of dust and dirt from one's living environment. Ancient rituals hold more worth than meets the eye. Today science teaches us that ions or electrically charged particles in the air have a profound effect upon our lives and personal behavior.

Positive ions (surprisingly, from their name) make one feel tired, restless and depressed. Negative ions, on the other hand, create in us a sense of peace, good energy and cheerfulness. Dirt, dust and disorder absorb negative ions, creating an environment that is alive with positive ions.

It seems that water is able to absorb positive ions, and together with fresh air and sunlight, it can change our living and working spaces dramatically. When we clean our homes and rooms, we creatively care for that part of the world that is our responsibility as well as actually reshaping our atmosphere. Dr. Ronald Kotzsch, in his *Tao of Cleanliness*, quotes an old Zen proverb that expresses the result well: "To polish the floor is to polish one's soul."

THE RITUAL

Lighting a candle or vigil light can awaken you to the sacred nature of any activity in which you are engaged. Brooms, dust mops or rags become sacred ritual objects for cleaning the temple of your personal living space. Pause in silence before beginning, and remember that the space you are about to re-create in cleanliness is that part of the world for which you are personally responsible. Then with a bow to your prayer corner or to the four corners of the room, begin the ritual of cleaning or straightening the room with a cheerful heart.

This invocation may be used:

> May this work that I will begin
> be a prayerful re-creation of my world;
> may I bring order out of chaos
> as my Beloved Creator brought order
> on the first day of creation.

After the cleaning is finished and the tools used in the ritual have been put away, wash your hands as a sign of your own cleansing. Then, after a bow, blow out the lighted candle and breathe in deeply the freshness and cleanliness of your personal world.

A URINE RITUAL

The human body is wondrously designed. Our blood becomes filled with certain impurities which can result in our death if not removed. As a river of blood flows through a million tiny coiled tubes in our kidneys, the poisonous impurities are removed and enter a liquid called urine. Daily the body disposes of its deadly poisons in the urine.

We also acquire, many times unknowingly, angry and negative thoughts, judgements and assumptions about others that are equally poisonous. If these negative and hostile thoughts are not removed our hearts soon become poisoned. The following ritual is intended to remind us to constantly remove all such thoughts from our hearts.

The following prayer is meant to accompany that daily bodily ritual of discharging your impurity-filled urine.

> O God of all life, as my body
> now flushes out its physical impurities,
> grant that all negative,
> harmful and angry feelings within me
> may be flushed out as well.

THE RITUAL OF FINGERNAIL TRIMMING

Your fingernails and toenails are composed of hardened skin cells. It is the same material that makes up the claws of animals and birds. Each time you trim your fingernails you are involved in primitive arms-limitation, the earliest and most basic of all disarmament.

As often as our fingernails need trimming, so do our minds need to shed the perennial weapons of self-defense: words and deeds of anger, sarcasm, superiority and ridicule. The following ritual-prayer is intended to remind you of your sacred role as a peacemaker in this world.

> O Divine Friend, as I trim my fingernails,
> may I also transform my inner aggressions into love.
> May I, by your grace, seek to be a peacemaker
> in all my dealings and in who I am.

THE RITUAL OF LIGHTING CANDLES

Long ago, every act of making fire was considered sacred, since fire was a gift from the gods. With the invention of electric lighting, the lighting of candles and fires ceased to be a necessity and thus lost much of its awesome power. While we may not think of fire as sacred, we use it at special times in prayer, worship, at meals and on holidays. With their small tongues of fire, candles speak of warmth, love, celebration; God appeared as fire in many Old Testament stories.

The lighting of candles and vigil lights should be more than a means of decoration; it should awaken us to our vocation to be "the Light of the world." It can be a powerful sign of the presence of God in times of trouble, suffering, storm and inner darkness as well as times of celebration and great joy. The following rituals for lighting candles provide patterns for personal prayer using light, the most universal and ancient symbol for the mystery we call God.

RITUAL OF LIGHTING A CANDLE FOR PRAYER OR WORSHIP

As I now bring fire to this candle wick,
    making it glow with light,
    may I also bring the fire of love
    to this time of prayer and worship.

CANDLE PRAYER AT ANY TIME

Fire is your sacrament, O God, fire is sacred;
    as I light this candle may I be reminded
    that I am to burn with the same fire for you.
May I fill my life with that burning love.

CANDLE PRAYER FOR A DINNER CELEBRATION

May the warmth of fire and light
    that radiates from these candles
    reflect its glow on all who sit at this table,
    blessing this meal and our conversation.
May the memory of this gathering linger
    long after these candles have been extinguished.

CANDLE PRAYER AT A TIME OF ROMANCE AND LOVE

May the fire that dances lightly
    on the tip of these candles
    be a sign of the fire of love within our hearts.
May that fire burn as long as the stars shine.

CANDLE PRAYER AT A TIME OF DISTRESS

Beloved and Gracious God,
    I am in need of your presence in my life.
I know that you are hidden
    in the midst of my daily activities,
    but I need some sign
    that you are with me at this difficult hour.
You are the Light eternal;
    may this candle be a sacrament of your presence
    as I place myself totally in your loving arms.

CANDLE PRAYER AT A TIME OF DARKNESS

O Divine Wisdom, I am confused and unsure;
    it feels like I am lost in the darkness.
As I light this candle,
    let your light enter my heart
    that I may see the path before me.
May this holy light
    quiet the voices of fear that confuse my judgement
    and cloud my heart's true vision.
Grant me the gift of divine wisdom
    that I may step forward with faith and courage.

CANDLE PRAYER AT A TIME OF GREAT JOY

May this holy candle send forth dancing rays
    like sunrise on the most glorious morning.
May these rays of light encircle me and those I love,
    as I celebrate: _____.
I give you thanks, O God, for this happy moment
    and I ask that as I am one in this circle of light
    with all those who are dear to me,
    I may always be one with you
    in the circle of your loving presence.

CANDLE PRAYER AT A TIME OF
NEED FOR ANOTHER

O Gracious God who knows all our needs
    and who cares for us daily with such great love,
    be with: _____,
    who is in great need of your presence.
I light this candle of prayer
    and dedicate it for his/her needs.
May your light surround him/her;
    may your love be his/her support
    and may your life flow through him/her.
I dedicate the actions, prayers and duties of my day
    for his/her needs at this special time.

THE RITUAL OF WRITING

You, the owner of this book, are obviously able to read and write. We usually think nothing of this ability, but long ago those skills were a magical art known only to priests and scribes.

The Egyptians believed that Thoth, one of their gods, had invented writing, and they called it hieroglyphics, "the words of the god." To write a word was to be engaged in a sacred act, a ritual.

Christians call Jesus "the Word made flesh," a title which expresses the power of words to make the invisible come alive before us. When we write a letter to a friend by hand or by machine, we are making visible that great invisible reality of our affection, concern and love.

A hieroglyphic ritual can awaken us to the power we take for granted and alert us to the sacred quality of letters as incarnations of our friendship, love or gratitude. The following ritual is intended to encourage us to view this activity as holy and prayerful.

With the blank sheet of paper before you, with pen in hand or your fingers on the keys, pause and picture in your mind the person to whom you are writing. Encircle him or her with love and experience his or her presence.

Grant, O Divine Beloved, that as I write this letter,
    my words may carry my heart's feelings to: _____.
May this letter strengthen the mystical bridge between us,
    and by this experience
    may we both grow in love and unity.

RITUAL FOR WRITING A DIFFICULT LETTER

If it is necessary to write a letter that may cause pain to the one who will receive it, this prayer may be recited:

O Gracious and Loving God,
    the ancients believed that writing
    is a sacred gift from you.
Send me the gift of words
    so that I can say what must be said
    in a way that will cause as little pain as possible.
Inspire me with your wisdom
    and guide my hand as I write.

CONCLUDING RITUAL OF WRITING

After the letter has been written and sealed in its envelope, touch the envelope to your forehead or to your heart as you pray:

May these words be hallowed containers
    to carry my heart's deepest feelings.
May this letter be sealed in affection
    and bring the spirit of my presence to:_____.

The envelope then may be kissed or the sign of the cross made upon it.

RITUAL OF A TELEPHONE MESSAGE

Modern technology has provided us a means of communication that would have truly seemed divine to people in ancient times. To speak with a person who is countless miles away is truly a remarkable ability. The telephone is a machine, but just as a typewriter can be used for the sacred ritual of writing, so the telephone can be used in a sacred way, especially if our call is one of friendship or love.

Before picking up the phone, pause before you dial and be one in body and soul with the person you are calling. This brief prayer might preface your dialing:

Blessed are you, O God,
    who has filled our world with wonders.
I thank you for the gift of this instrument
    that will allow me to hear the voice of:_____
    and for him/her to hear mine.

May this call bind us even closer together
until we finally are one in you,
and one beyond all space and time.

When the call is completed, pause and rejoice in the communion you feel. Lift up the person with whom you have spoken into the heart of God. A brief closing prayer could be:

I lift up my heart to you in gratitude, O God,
for the gift of:_____,
and for the wondrous gift of this telephone
that has made our time together possible.

THANKSGIVING RITUALS

Perhaps our first experience of prayer as children was that of folding our hands and humming along with the rest of the family the prayer of grace before meals. While we may not have understood the words, it was obvious that something holy was going on and that we were a part of it. If our families were very pious, we also said a prayer of grace after meals.

We prayed before a meal to ask God to bless the food and those partaking of the meal. We also acknowledged that it was from the bounty of God that the mashed potatoes and bread came to us. It is strange that as children we never asked the logical question, "Why don't we pray grace before we do other things besides eating?"

The answer to that unasked question is that the prayer of grace before meals is the last survivor of a tradition of countless prayers of gratitude that Christians inherited from their Jewish mother-religion.

Jesus, as a devout Jew, would have prayed many different kinds of prayers of gratitude. They were very brief, no more than a sentence or two long. Before enjoying any gift of the five senses—tasting food or drink, smelling a flower or freshly baked bread, seeing something of great beauty or a natural phenomenon such as lightning, hearing good news or beautiful music, feeling the touch of a new garment or putting on clothing at the beginning of the day—all these actions were prefaced by short acts of thanksgiving. I say "acts" because it was necessary not only to "say" prayers but to follow the blessings with such actions as eating a piece of bread or smelling a flower. Bodily ritual and spoken prayer were wedded as one.

Besides the prayers of gratitude before enjoying an experience with one of the five senses, there were also prayers before certain ritual deeds such as the lighting of the Hanukkah or Shabbat candles; indeed, even the common daily task of washing one's hands called for thanksgiving. Blessing prayers were recited in gratitude for any number of reasons: for the safe return from a journey, for recovery from an illness, for being forgiven, for the coming of a feast or the beginning of a new season.

> Blessed are you, God of the universe,
>> who has preserved us and enabled us
>> to reach this season of: _____.

The concept of reciting a blessing prayer over a new house, a new pair of shoes or any new possession is a way of ritualizing the joy of the gift. We bless a new car, not because we need to claim it from the devil's domain, but because we delight in the feel, smell and joy of it.

The following prayers are intended only as the beginning of a pattern of prayer. You will be able to create your own in a short time. If you pray in this way, you will find your life filled to overflowing with gifts and wonders. Brief blessing prayers are a part of the heritage of every disciple of Jesus, for they were a part of his daily prayer life.

> I lift up my heart to you in gratitude, O God,
>> for this gift of a hot shower that refreshes me.

> I lift up my heart to you in gratitude
>> for this gift of a new day filled with possibilities.

> I lift up my heart to you in gratitude
>> for the gift of good health and a sound body.

> I lift up my heart to you in gratitude
>> for the gift of seeing a rainbow,
>> the sign of your eternal promise in the sky.

> I lift up my heart to you in gratitude
>> for the joy of putting on this new clothing.

> I lift up my heart to you in gratitude
>> for the deep and fertile smell
>> of rain-soaked earth.

> I lift up my heart to you in gratitude
>> for the ability to fly high above the clouds,
>> the fulfillment of an ancient dream.

> I lift up my heart to you in gratitude
>> for the gift of this glass of wine
>> and its taste of sun, grape and earth.

I lift up my heart to you in gratitude
>for the gift of music
>that delights my ear, my heart and my soul.

I lift up my heart to you in gratitude
>for the ability to read
>and for the wonder of words
>that speak to my heart.

I lift up my heart to you in gratitude
>for the expression of love I have just shared.

I lift up my heart to you in gratitude
>for the present pain I feel,
>which frames with greater joy
>the pleasures of my life.

An even shorter method of thanksgiving is the ritual of gratitude Jesus practiced as we find it in the Gospels. He simply raised his eyes to heaven, pronounced a blessing and gave thanks. Whenever you experience the giftedness of life, you could slightly raise your head and simply say, "Thank you!"

Of course we know that God is not just in the sky, but in the act of looking up we bodily acknowledge that the gift in which we are rejoicing comes from an eternal source beyond us. Without even naming that Divine Gift-giver we have professed the gratitude that should be expressed to our Creator.

These rituals of gratitude both enlighten and enliven us, for we are made conscious of the presence of the Divine Mystery in the very act of gratitude. When we give thanks for the gift of our eyes, our taste or our good health, it opens us to the immediate enjoyment of a precious gift that is easily forgotten until we are without it.

Planetary pilgrims who engage in these daily rituals find that they quickly become millionaires. All mystics are millionaires, for they are aware that they possess everything necessary at this moment to be happy. The whole beauty of creation is theirs to enjoy. As a result they find release from our modern epidemic of consumerism, the constant thirst for more. Rituals of thanksgiving become important tools for justice, for sharing our gifts with those who lack them. They encourage the planetary pilgrim to become involved in the greatest prayer of gratitude, that of giving others both material and spiritual gifts. The person who practices these rituals with discipline and delight becomes increasingly generous and grateful to God and to others. The mystic is perpetually busy with thank-you notes—written, spoken, sung and lived.

MINI BLESSINGS: RESPONSES TO LIFE

The use of the sign of the cross: the sign of the cross was part of the practice of early Christians and so is part of the heritage of all Christian traditions. The cross is also found as a sacred sign in several non-Christian religious traditions. To trace this holy symbol upon yourself or on some object invokes a universal mystery and so is part of the rich religious heritage available to all who desire to use it.

WHEN FASTENING YOUR SAFETY BELT:

Wrap me in your love,
    buckle me in your blessedness.

(sign of the cross +)

ON LEAVING YOUR HOME:

Protect this home and those who live here
    in the name of the Father,
    and of the Son and of the Holy Spirit. Amen.

(signing the cross on the door +)

UPON RETURNING HOME:

Thanks be to God, who watches over us.

(signing the cross on the door +)

IN TIMES OF DIFFICULTY OR MISHAP:

Grant me the grace to shoulder my cross.

(sign of the cross +)

or

Your kingdom come, your will be done.

WHEN SOMETHING HAS BEEN LOST OR FORGOTTEN:

May the lost be found as you grant me your peace.

WHEN WHAT HAS BEEN LOST IS FOUND:

From hiding places you bring forth the lost,
    blessed are you.

UPON GOING TO BED:

May I sleep with you
    and rise in glory.

(signing the cross on your pillow +)

IN A TIME OF ANGER:

O God, quiet my heart

and fill me with your compassion.

or

Empty my heart of anger and hate
and fill it with your peace and love.

(signing the cross on your heart +)

or

signing the cross on forehead: Cleanse me of angry thoughts
on lips: and of angry words
on heart: and fill my heart with peace.

(Take a slow deep breath, inhaling peace and grace.)

AT RECEIVING GOOD FORTUNE OR GOOD NEWS:

Bless us, O Lord, and these thy gifts
which we have received from thy bounty.

(This traditional meal blessing can be used in countless times of gifts and blessings.)

WHILE PREPARING TO SEND A LETTER:

Stamp this letter (card) with your love
and seal it with your peace.

(signing the cross on the letter +)

BEFORE READING A TEXT OR BOOK:

signing the cross on forehead: Open my mind
on lips: and my soul
on heart: and my heart to your grace.

ON PASSING A CHURCH:

Blest be this temple of God.

or

Holy is this temple of God.

(signing the cross on your heart +)

ON PASSING AN ACCIDENT:

Grant your help to those in need
and guard me on my way.

WHEN MAKING A TELEPHONE CALL TO A LOVED ONE:

May my words be rich in love,
and may this call bring peace and joy.

(signing the cross on the telephone receiver +)

UPON COMPLETING THE CALL:

Blessed are you who gives to us
such gifts that enrich our hearts.

THE RITE OF REMEMBRANCE

The Rite of Remembrance recalls not only the right to remember but also our duty to do so. At that ritual meal the night before he died, Jesus spoke plainly: "Do this in memory of me." As disciples and friends of Jesus, let us with faith, love and gratitude remember.

OPENING PRAYER

I pause, my God, along the busy roadside of my life,
    to remember you and your love for me.
Calm my body and my heart,
    heal me of the social disease of restlessness.
Come and sit here beside me as I pray now in silence.

a brief period of silent prayer

I lift up my heart to you, Source of all life,
    a heart quiet and open, yet eager for ecstasy,
    ready to be carried out of myself
    and into your divine heart, my Beloved One.

I lift up my heart to you,
    in gratitude for the gift of memories,
    that marvelous ability you have hidden deep within us.

I recall in thanksgiving
    not only such famous deeds of salvation
    as the liberation of Israel from slavery in Egypt
    and the resurrection of your son Jesus from the dead,
    but also the many deeds of love
    that you have shown to me, your servant.

pause for a personal litany of thanksgiving

THE REMEMBRANCE

With reverence and awe
    I bow down before you, Most High.
Holy, holy, holy are you,
    the Womb of all that we call holy,
    heaven and earth are full of your glory.

a bodily ritual such as a profound bow

I thank you for filling me as well with your glory;
    like Moses, I know that this place where I worship you
    is truly holy ground.
Pour forth upon me your Spirit, the Spirit of the Holy,
    to remind me that you ordained me in my mother's womb
    to be a priestly maker of sacrifice.
Anointed from above by your Spirit,

I also was called to be a minister of memory,
to remember how your son Jesus Christ
gave his body and blood, his very life,
that the earth and all that lives
might be healed of sin and separation.

I now remember how at that ritual Passover Meal
your son Jesus did something new.
To renew my memory of that cosmic consecration,
I now read the account of it
from the Gospel of Mark (14: 22-24):

> During the meal he took bread, blessed and
> broke it, and gave it to them. "Take this," he
> said, "this is my body." And then, he took the
> cup, gave thanks and passed it to them, say-
> ing, "This is the cup of my blood; all of you
> drink from it. This is the blood of the
> everlastingly new covenant, it shall be poured
> forth for you and for all."

for variety, one could also read
Matthew 26: 26-29, Luke 22: 15-20 or 1 Cor. 11: 23-25

With reverence I bow
and pray in silence before this sacred Memory
which holds within it such great mystery
and even greater presence.

a profound bow, followed by a period of silence

PRAYER OF THANKSGIVING

Blessed is this memory of the total outpouring
of the love, life and spirit of Jesus.
I remember that he did not come
to bring us rituals and ceremonies
but rather a way of life,
a way of total loving and surrender.
This is how my life is to be lived
if I am truly to be his disciple and friend.
May this memory which he asked that I recall
fuel my feeble heart to be strong in service,
to be bold in defense of the oppressed
and those who suffer from injustice.

I remember also the fullness of his memory;
that he not only died on the cross and was buried
but that you gloriously raised him up
from the grip of death and the tomb.

I remember that in his resurrection
    he was joined completely to you
    in light and splendor.

PRAYER OF HOLY COMMUNION

I now join myself in an act of holy communion
    with the body of my risen savior Jesus Christ.

silent communion

With faith I now join in an act of holy communion
    with all the departed who share his luminous life,
    the Shining Ones,
    especially those of my own family,
    and those who were my friends, teachers and neighbors.

silent communion

I now enter into holy communion
    with all who are part of Christ's holy body
    and share life on this planet with me now,
    especially those whom I love
    and who are a part of my life.

silent communion

I acknowledge with reverence and faith,
    that within his re-created body,
    risen and one with you,
    are all the peoples of this earth,
    women and men of all races,
    of all religions and political beliefs.
I now enter into an awareness
    that binds us all together in a holy communion.

silent communion

Your son Paul, the tent maker, tells us that Jesus
    is now one with all the universe in its many parts.
So I pause to be in holy communion
    with wide flowing rivers, with towering mountains,
    with green valleys and silent sands of the desert.
I enter into communion with fish of the deep,
    with birds soaring above the earth,
    with the variety of animals and all your creatures,
    with the sun and the moon,
    with the thousand-times-ten-thousand sister suns
    that compose the company of stars
    that you shaped into our galaxy
    and all the hundreds of millions of galaxies

that you have scattered in shining splendor
across the dark velvet vastness of space.

silent communion

Having kept the memory of Christ's death and resurrection,
I ask that this holy memory
which unites me with his mystical body
and brings me into holy communion
with all that you have created
will also become the pattern for my life.
May it be not only his Way but also mine.

Into your hands, O my God, I commend my spirit;
I offer my life, my work and my dreams.
Without you and the abiding presence
of your risen son Jesus Christ,
what I now prepare to do is impossible.

May the memory that contains such cosmic communion,
that holds your promise of perpetual presence,
perform that which is beyond my power.

CLOSING PRAYER

Now it is time to continue on my road of life,
and as I prepare to leave this holy place,
may I fill the pockets of my heart
with the memory of this prayerful remembrance.
So enriched, may I meet all that comes to me
in a sacred and priestly way.

Having remembered the mystery
of Christ's death and his resurrection,
I have been re-membered as part of his body.
May this new sense of my body,
one with his, risen and glorious,
call me to greater reverence this day.

Having recalled Jesus' final meal with his friends,
may the memory of it call me
to join others in full-hearted acts
of corporate remembrance of his death and resurrection.

Note: Icons, flowers, incense, lighted candles or other such aids will make this prayer
of remembering an act of worship by the whole person and not simply a men-
tal exercise. You may use other prayers found in this book, as well as readings
from Scripture as a means to expand and deepen this ritual.

The Triangulum Galaxy

The Andromeda Galaxy

SURVIVAL MANUAL FOR A COSMIC AMPHIBIAN

EQUIPMENT, EXERCISES AND INSTRUCTIONS

In the Hindu scriptures the warning is given, "The Way is narrow, as narrow as a razor's edge." Jesus likewise warned that the Way is narrow, and few are those who are able to walk its thin edge. In his parable of the seeds he also cautioned his disciples about the numerous dangers that await those who begin the sacred journey but for various reasons drop away. Regardless of all our good intentions, of our moments of insight and enthusiasm, the Way is difficult. As it has been said, many are called. But it's not so much that few are chosen; rather, few choose to remain steadfast in the face of the magnetic forces that can pull the sacred traveler off the razor's edge.

This part of the book is a survival manual for one who desires to travel the razor's edge. It would be useful to read the instructions in this manual carefully and more than once. You are aware of the rigorous training given to space pioneers, to astronauts and cosmonauts. They travel in space, an environment that often is not friendly to earthlings. Such navigation in space is impossible without specialized instruction and equipment for survival. So it is with everyone who desires to explore the vast regions of inner space.

You are a cosmic amphibian, designed to live harmoniously in the midst of both matter and spirit. The polarized realities of spirit and matter exercise great magnetic influences on the inner space traveler, and they form different yet unified fields. It is possible to be simultaneously caught in their separate gravitational fields. At the same time as you seek to walk the narrow way, you live in the midst of a secular society which holds to a belief in God while not expressing any need of God. Secularism proclaims the arch-importance of materialism and its rewards. While not denying the Divine Mystery, it says that one has no need of that power to live a full life. As a result, the activities of prayer and worship are given little value and, in fact, are often considered a waste of time.

If you seek to travel the razor's edge of inner space survival, you must begin with the survival knowledge that you will receive little support from your society. While physical exercise and proper diet are encouraged in countless ways to develop and help maintain the full potential of the human body, exercises that activate untapped inner potentials are not promoted.

While Jesus told his disciples that they were not of this world, he did not intend, so it seems, that they live outside the realities of this world. The striving of the secular society for material comfort, success and personal achievement is not evil. It is but a lower level of consciousness of the same reality sought by those who walk the Path. Rejection of the world as a way to God is truly a dangerous path, even though it has been encouraged for centuries by spiritual guides. For the seeker of the fullness of truth, the Way must embrace rather than reject all of creation, which includes the world, business, family and material goods as good. We need to let the words of the Creator at the end of each day of creation, "That's good," reverberate in our hearts. That which the Gospels call "the world" becomes a detour only when it is seen as the sole destination of life or proposes values and practices that are contrary to the messages the Divine Mystery has given to the children of this planet.

But in addition to the lack of support from society, as a spiritual pilgrim, you are also faced with the great paradox that your inner astronavigation cannot even count on encouragement from your particular religious affiliation! While they provide very important opportunities for communal support and worship (see Section Three for a discussion of the necessity of community on the Way) and a continuity with pilgrims of the past, on another level, religions are go-between services that provide their followers with a bridge between heaven and earth. Each of them has its bridge people whose work is to connect you with the Divine Source. If you seek to establish a direct contact with that Source by yourself, your journey may be given only a nod of affirmation, if that. While prayer is encouraged, you may be warned that a spiritual search is a dangerous activity.

Indeed, it is dangerous, and only a hero or heroine should set foot to the razor's edge. For your comfortable and familiar world may truly be shaken in a direct encounter with the Divine Mystery. As the Sufis—Moslem mystics—say, "Don't make friends with an elephant trainer if you don't have room in your living room for an elephant." Because of that threat many religious traditions are devoid of practices such as meditation and contemplation. Fortunate are those whose religious affiliation has an appreciation and a tradition of mysticism and the prayer of silence and solitude.

While a certain narrowness of religious vision is a reality, even a casual reading of the lives of the founders of the great religions of the world reveals personal inner quests for the Truth. They were travelers of the razor's edge who believed that the Divine Mystery was not limited only to the boundaries of their original religion.

The purpose of contemplative and mystical prayer is to provide the same kind of direct contact with the Divine Reality as the great religious leaders experienced. Such prayer and the entire spiritual journey requires great humility and continuous compass-checking. Humility keeps the spiritual traveler on course along a path where one can so easily be the victim of illusion, mistaking mirages for reality. From the Latin word *humus* for earth, true humility grounds the seeker in truth. Every pilgrim must travel along a path, which may be the spiritual tradition into which one was born or one that was chosen later in life. But it is impossible to make any progress by jumping from path to path, for roots are essential to growth. And humility produces in the cosmic amphibian a deep respect and reverence for the wisdom of a religious tradition and its customs. While a given religious custom may seem outdated and no longer potent, you can be sure that when it began it held great power for those who practiced it. If you can peel back the historical layers of time and see its core value, you may be able to again take up a traditional exercise in a totally new and nourishing way.

For the Christian cosmic amphibian, the compass for traveling beyond the boundaries of religion is the original words of Jesus. And if you are concerned that what you hear with the ears of the heart is not the same as what you hear from the pulpit, take out your compass and check your bearings. Christ also promised us an inner-guide, the Holy Spirit, who would teach us what was impossible to proclaim at that time. God did not stop speaking two thousand years ago but continues to whisper in each of our hearts and desires your journey home more than you do. Since each of us is unique, our personal paths will likewise be unique. A truly great religion is like an umbrella that is large enough to encompass the individual paths of all its members.

May the following instructions and suggestions for traveling the razor's edge assist you in the greatest expedition ever known. Such an adventure is not limited to those with strong bodies or clever minds. Nor must it be undertaken in one's youth; rather it is an enterprise that grows more exciting with advancing age. But like all great adventures and explorations, it requires dedication, courage and personal discipline.

SECTION ONE

EQUIPMENT FOR THE JOURNEY

THE LAUNCHING PAD: A PRAYER SHRINE

Travel in space requires a rocket or other spacecraft. And an extraterrestrial vehicle needs a launching pad to take off from this planet. Likewise, travelers of inner-space need a base to launch them on the journey inward. The importance of this prayer space can easily be overlooked since the journey is viewed as "spiritual." But earthlings are cosmic amphibians, a blend of matter and non-matter. And as the Spirit can transform matter, so the physical environment can have a great influence on the work of the Spirit.

In ancient times, every home had its shrine to the gods and goddesses. These were small altar areas where sacred images were displayed. To create such a shrine is thus to return to our religious roots. And just as the earth has its particularly sacred places— mountains, rivers and shrines of natural beauty—so the personal world of the planetary pilgrim should reflect the wisdom of creation.

Jesus said that God is spirit and should be worshiped in spirit and truth. But that truth does not exclude the need of a special place of prayer, an environment in which we are especially disposed to the Divine Presence, just as Jesus went off to the desert or the mountains to pray. The danger of all shrines and sacred places is the temptation to view what lies outside their boundaries as secular. The entire cosmos is God's temple and within it are billions of shrines. All land is holy land, but we easily forget that reality. Special, set-aside sacred spaces remind us that all space is sacred.

The typical home in the Western world has rooms for all the important activities of life. There are rooms for eating, sleeping, bathing, storage, relaxing and even a room for keeping your vehicle. While your entire home is a sacred place where you pray and journey to God in different ways, it can be invaluable to set aside a particular place for your inner exercises. This will be the pad which propels you on the Path and onto which you land on your return from exploring the Divine Mystery. For a fortunate few this personal shrine could be an entire room such as an unused bedroom or a small den. But for the majority it will mean a corner of a room.

HOW TO CREATE A PERSONAL SHRINE

You might, for example, choose a corner of your bedroom and set it aside as your prayer place. A stone slab could serve as a small altar, or perhaps you could create one out of wood. You may also find it valuable to have a small prayer rug to sit upon only in meditation or prayer.

If you are a highly visual person you may desire to use a variety of symbols, icons or images to grace your personal shrine. If you are not especially visually oriented, you might want to create a space which is void of all images. The very simplicity of an empty wall can help clear your mind and heart of clutter and help open you into prayer.

You may also find it beneficial to vary the design of your personal shrine or change the images in it with each of the four seasons. Because our technological culture often separates us from a direct contact with the changes that occur in nature with each season, altering the environment of your shrine can help make your prayer more natural and in harmony with God's creation. And since we easily become blind to what is "always" there, the introduction of visual changes for various feasts, holidays and special occasions has the power to cleanse the eye and so open the heart. To make use of flowers or other images on holy days and special occasions will also assist in making your personal shrine a "living" place of prayer. An unchangable prayer space can easily become a static one.

Understanding that personal tastes and needs will direct your choices in these suggestions, experiment with finding the kind of environment that can best open you to God in prayer.

SACRED IMAGES FOR YOUR SHRINE

A religious image, icon, cross or other sacred sign can speak ten thousand words about the purpose of your prayer space. Religious icons, particularly when they have been prayerfully painted or crafted, have the power to make the presence of God immediate and real.

We are not, however, limited to traditional religious images. If you view all the world as both good and sacred, as God's temple, it would be natural to select an earthen icon for your shrine. This could be a curved branch, a rock, a feather or a flower. And just as we have separated life into two opposing areas—seeing a church, synagogue or mosque as sacred space and an office, store or work place as secular—so we have also separated art into religious and secular. For the Japanese, on the other hand, a painted scroll of beautiful flowers or a scene from nature is often reverenced as a sacred image.

Icons are usually images of Christ or Mary, the mother of God, various events in the life of Jesus or images of former inner-space explorers, the saints. But since the invention of the camera, we have a host of hero images that can be used in your prayer shrine. Photographs of both living and deceased spiritual giants, perhaps even the "saints" of your own family, can inspire you to holiness and awaken within you the desire to give your life in service to others, in the pursuit of justice and peace.

Another awesome icon is the NASA photograph of the earth viewed from space. This sacred image was not available to previous generations and unfortunately is often considered today as just a picture of our planet. But contemplation of this image of the earth, devoid of nationalistic lines of division, has great power to move the planetary pilgrim to see that all life as created by God is one, is devoid of the countless lines of division and separation that, to a degree, have been created arbitrarily.

But we can become blind to the beauty and holiness of any sacred image. Variety helps prevent such dullness of vision. You may find it of value to frequently or seasonally change the images that you have in your shrine area. In summer, for example, you can use a flower in full bloom as a sacred sign; in autumn, a brightly colored leaf. Each season can offer a unique icon. You may also wish to cover certain images and view them only when you are at prayer. In past ages many icons had doors that could be opened and closed to reserve the icon for only reverential viewing. All images are doors that hold the power to lead you into another reality. Care must be taken so that sacred images do not become mere decoration rather than doorways.

While a great variety of magazines deal with interior design and home decoration, there is little in our culture that recognizes the beauty of ancient religious images. Have you ever seen a *Better Homes and Gardens* pay tribute to a home with a sacred shrine? As a result, religious images or a shrine area in a modern home can easily be cause for self-consciousness or even feelings of embarrassment.

For the early disciples of Jesus, such images meant imprisonment and even death. This has also been true for Jews and peoples of other religions during times of persecution and even for some of your planetary pilgrim companions today. The early followers of the Way of Jesus, as a result of persecution, became closet Christians who kept their shrines hidden. Or they used symbols, such as the fish, as secret signs known only to those of their own faith. You may wish to have your shrine in a closet, opening the door only when you pray or when visitors are not in your home. Your shrine may even be enclosed in a small chest or wooden box.

ALLIES FOR PRAYER POSTURE

The use of a prayer rug has already been suggested. The Zen tradition also uses a small pillow, or zafu, for prayer and meditation. A firm pillow allows you to be comfortable while seated on the floor. Most churches and synagogues use benches or chairs, but mosques, Buddhist and Hindu temples and other sacred places of Eastern religions are like old cathedrals in that they have only open space. To pray seated on the floor places the pilgrim in a position of humility, a position closer to the earth.

But, as we are called to "pray always," you will be at prayer in various places and in various bodily positions. And so it is important to also learn to pray well while standing or kneeling. Some traditions make use of a prayer bench or zazen (meditation) stool to help support the body while in the classical Carmelite kneeling position of sitting back on your heels. Age, health and a variety of other circumstances may make a straight-back chair or sitting with your back firmly against a wall to be the best prayer posture. When choosing a bodily position for your formal times of prayer, you should choose one that allows your whole body to pray, as well as your heart and mind. Find a position that is both comfortable and yet allows the body to be an alley to the heart by keeping you alert.

Your body will also be more at ease if you wear loose and comfortable clothing. In the morning you may find it helpful to pray before you dress for your day's activities. A bathrobe or other garment that is not constraining can facilitate a freedom of the body in this time of prayer. And you might choose the same prayer clothing at the end of the day.

A TRAVELING PRAYER SHRINE

If your work requires you to frequently be away from home, you can support your practice of prayer by having a traveling shrine. It could be as simple as an icon, a cross or a small folding shrine, which you might personally construct, along with a small vigil candle. These traveling sacred objects will allow you to center your attention as you pray or meditate in a motel or while visiting a friend's home.

A possible container for such a traveling shrine could be a wooden cigar box or a shallow wooden box with a hinged lid. Your portable shrine could be used to carry your favorite sacred images from your home shrine, or, if you travel often, another meaningful icon could be permanently fastened to the inside of the lid. The box might be large enough to hold a small vigil candle and your copy of this prayer book as well as any of the other prayer allies mentioned later in this section.

On some trips a very simple portable shrine carrier would be appropriate, such as a leather folder or pouch to protect your favorite sacred icon. Take a little time before leaving on your trip to reflect on what prayer allies might be helpful in keeping you connected to God while you are away from home. Give consideration to the season of the year, to the sacred or personal feasts that will take place during the time of your travel and especially to what prayer images or aids are particularly alive for you at the moment. It can also be very helpful to carry along some picture, image or note to remind you of the intentions that are close to your heart at home and of your prayerful unity with family and friends who have not traveled with you. And let the allies that you take along help remind you of your home prayer shrine.

The traveling shrine acts as a reminder that you are a person of prayer at home or away. It allows you to quickly focus your attention when in a strange environment that can easily distract you, making prayer on the road easier.

When praying in a space other than the prayer shrine in your home, you may find it of value to take more time than usual to center yourself before entering into prayer. One helpful ritual is to slowly draw around yourself a sacred circle before you begin. Cleanse the area of any energy that is not in harmony with the sacred. In some religious traditions, water is sprinkled around the area or sacred smoke is made to encircle the area as a sign of cleansing and to prepare oneself for prayer and meditation.

SACRED OBJECTS AND RELICS

Your shrine can also be the place where you keep precious objects that hold power for you, like a stone or some dirt from a sacred shrine where you experienced holy power. And as the Church has relics of her saints, so each of us has personal relics, special possessions passed on from parents and grandparents, friends or spiritual guides. Such relics as a family rosary, a parent's old prayer book or medal or a prized photograph of a distant or deceased loved one add to your shrine's holy power as a place of inner travel.

Native American Indians traditionally were given medicine bundles by their shaman which contained sacred objects, "good medicine," to protect them and assist them on their quests and journeys. In this spirit, you might place your sacred relics and holy objects in a small round basket with a lid or in a special box. This shrine basket or box placed within the shrine area becomes a kind of tabernacle.

PRAYER PEBBLES

Small smooth pebbles collected from the seashore or purchased at import stores can serve as prayer sacramentals. Before praying, take the pebbles in your hand one by one, pausing to remember friends or special intentions. Then place them in front of you in a half circle or other design. Let them be visual signs of the persons or intentions for which you wish to pray that day. When you have finished your time of prayer, leave them in their sacred pattern at your shrine. As you pass your shrine during the day or return to it at evening, they will remind you of your prayerful intentions and your communion with loved ones.

If you have used a particular stone for a period of time, it can become a relic that holds much power. It can then be passed on as a further way of sharing the prayerful energy with which you have invested it. For example, if you have prayed for someone who is sick, you can give that person your prayer stone after the recovery as a sign of your communion during this time of trial.

It was the custom of some Eastern spiritual guides to give their disciples a pilgrim stone to carry in their pocket. The disciples were told to rub the stone until it became smooth from constant wear, a sign of their intention to wear away the rough edges of their personality. To touch the stone in one's pocket on occasions throughout the day was a reminder of the real work of that day, one's inner transformation.

If you find that a particular attitude or pattern of behavior is holding you back from progress on your pilgrimage, you can make your pilgrim stone symbolic of that handicap-habit. You can feel it in your pocket or place it in full view at your work place to remind you to strive to practice the virtue that is opposite the negative habit you wish to overcome.

In the East, when the pilgrim seeker returned to his or her guide with a beautifully smoothed stone, the guide would smile and take the stone. Then the pilgrim was handed another rough stone and sent off to polish it. That ritual was a reminder that the work of inner transformation is never completed in this life. When you have mastered one destructive inclination in your life and your stone is smoother, there is always another rough pebble to replace it.

PRAYER NOTES

When you are asked to remember someone in prayer, you may find it helpful to write that intention on a piece of paper or index card. This prayer intention may be placed at your shrine as a visible sign of your desire to prayerfully hold that person's need in your heart. If a family member or friend has written to you and asked you for your prayerful support or simply has told you about a problem, you can also set that letter near your shrine. And since such prayer notes may pile up over a period of time, you might occasionally remove older ones and begin again.

A small spiral book can be used also for writing names of persons, intentions and global concerns that you wish to include in your prayer. Such a prayer book would not have to be read daily. It can be an occasional reminder of the many needs of others which you wish to make your needs as well. The very presence of such a prayer book would awaken your awareness that as a planetary pilgrim your prayer should be truly catholic and universal; it should include the needs of all the earth.

THE USE OF SACRED FIRE

Fire and light are among the most universal of all sacred signs. Our ancient ancestors often worshiped fire as divine. And in scores of great myths, fire was stolen from the heavens or given as a gift from the gods. Even the small and simple flame of a single candle can be a very important ally in your prayer. A vigil candle can make your prayer shrine come alive. A flickering flame can help make your prayer dance.

Caution should be exercised when using a candle because of the danger of fire. Your vigil light should always be placed in a glass container. And because a wick leaning against the side can break a glass container, it is wise to place it within another thermal receptacle. Prudence also dictates that you not leave lighted candles unattended.

But the potential hazard of any flame of fire also speaks of its potential power for awakening the inner fire of devotion, the desire for illumination.

Special prayers for the use and lighting of candles can be found on pages 214, 215 and 216.

THE USE OF INCENSE

The awareness that every planetary pilgrim is also a cosmic amphibian brings with it the knowledge that it is more than the mind that prays. As much as possible, the body should be invited into the process so that a whole prayer arises from the pilgrim. Incense is an excellent aid to more fully involving the senses.

The use of incense is truly ancient and is found in countless religious traditions. The power of smell is profound. It holds the magic to stir up memories, to create moods and to shape attitudes. The smell of rain on a spring morning speaks of freshness and new creation. The aroma of burning leaves in autumn has about it the scent of harvest and completion. Some scents can return us to our childhood faster than the speed of light. In a similar way, incense is the aroma of adoration and prayer that can quickly carry the whole person into a prayerful state.

In medieval Japan, sticks of incense were used by shoguns to measure the length of time granted for an audience. Likewise, incense sticks can also be a measuring device for a period of prayer or meditation.

The sight of the perfumed smoke of incense slowly rising is a visual sacrament of one's heart-prayers ascending to the Divine Mystery. Incense can carry away the eyes, nose and mind in a unified field of prayer.

Some traditional granulated incenses, such as frankincense which is burnt on charcoal in many church liturgies, should be used with discretion. They create billowing clouds of smoke and strong aromas. Most fragrances are also available in less-smoky stick form. Be mindful of neighbors and those you live with, as well as the sensitive sensors of smoke alarms.

Prayers for lighting incense at times of prayer can be found on pages 100 and 101.

PRAYER FLAGS

In the Tibetan Buddhist tradition, prayer flags, small pieces of cloth, are hung outside to blow in the wind. As the wind moves through the flags, it carries the prayers inscribed on them across the land.

They need not contain actual prayers but can be inscribed with symbols or even a single word such as Love or Peace. You can glue the cloth to a stick or hang it "laundry-like" over a string. Prayer flags can hang on tree limbs, porch railings or outside the window of your prayer shrine. And the color of the flag can be chosen according to a particular feast or the season in which it is celebrated.

Prayer flags are particularly appropriate as aids to your worship on special feasts such as Pentecost which celebrates the Wind of Heaven, the Holy Spirit. Anytime you pray out-of-doors would be a good time for prayer flags. Outdoor celebrations, house blessings, weddings or garden dedications would also be occasions for their use.

PRAYER FANS

The Spirit of God has frequently been imaged as a mighty wind, as in the great wind that blew over the darkness of chaos during the act of creation. There is a primal longing in the human heart for that Divine Wind, and so long ago the fan was conceived to re-create a holy movement of air.

Perhaps the first paper fan invented evolved from using a large leaf to make a breeze for cooling oneself. And personal hand fans have commonly been used in public meeting places and in churches until only recently when air-conditioning came into existence. Hand fans were also seen as sacred objects. From about 300 A.D.

until around the year 1300, fans were used at the Sacred Liturgy of the Eucharist. Their outward function was to fan away flies from the bread and wine on the altar table. But they also held a symbolic value since fan bearers from ancient times have accompanied royal persons to keep them cool and to keep insects away. The use of sacred fans then was a reminder of the royal nature of Christ, the Cosmic Lord.

Among certain tribes of native American Indians, hand fans made of eagle feathers were used to direct sacred smoke. They were also a sign to remind persons at prayer that their prayers were often held earthbound by their own selfish needs. The feathered prayer fan encouraged its users to pray for others so that their prayers might ascend to the Great Mystery in the sky.

Often when it is time to pray, the spiritual sojourner's heart is empty of enthusiasm, devoid of inspiration. When the heart's fire of devotion, so essential to any lover's prayer, has died down to glowing embers, a prayer fan is a prime piece of the pilgrim's equipment for rekindling it. As you fan yourself, pray that the Divine Wind blow through your heart and stir into flame your devotion and love.

You can obtain an oriental folding fan from any import store, or you can easily make your own. Just take a small piece of colored cardboard and cut out a circular or other fan-shaped design in about an eight inch diameter. If you wish you can apply a sacred design or image to the face of the fan. Then take a small piece of wood, like an ice cream bar stick or a tongue depressor, and attach it with a desk stapler.

Your prayer fan can be one of the sacred objects that you keep in your prayer shrine. It can be used often as part of your preparation for prayer, especially when you feel drawn to prayers of devotion.

PRAYER BEADS

Most Western pilgrims are familiar with rosary beads. The traditional rosary, which has been used for centuries, is a string of five sets of ten glass, wooden or metal beads, with a crucifix at the end. The *Hail Mary* is recited upon each of the ten beads in a set, and the *Our Father* is said between each set. The prayers are recited like a mantra or sacred word, allowing the mysterious reality of different events in the life of Jesus and his mother to sink into one's consciousness.

However, rosary beads may also be used for various other forms of devotion. Other prayers, for example, may be recited on the beads. The great prayer of the virgin mother of God was her song of thanksgiving: "My soul proclaims the greatness of God." This classic phrase or any prayer that awakens us to gratitude and to the greatness of God would be at home on a traditional rosary.

The planetary pilgrim can also use a rosary for a litany of thanksgiving. With each bead, recall a gift or blessing that you have received from the Source of all gifts. After mentioning the gift, you might repeat a word or phrase like *Gratias* or *Deo Gratias*, Latin for "Thanks be to God," to give a chant-like quality to your prayer of gratitude.

If you wish you can construct your own rosary of prayer beads by simply tying knots in a cord between each bead that you string. Making your own string of prayer beads can allow you to choose the kind of material, whether wood, stone or gems, and the shape of the beads. Besides personalizing your prayer, touching materials and shapes that feel right adds a special tactile quality to your prayer. As in Islam and in various Eastern religious traditions, prayer beads are used to allow your fingers to pray. Prayer beads, particularly personalized ones, help you to "get in touch" with the Divine Mystery, help you to feel your way into prayer.

BOOKS AT YOUR SHRINE

The great religious traditions of planet Earth speak little about the value of books as equipment for the spiritual quest since reading has only recently become a common ability. The art of reading and writing was long practiced only by temple priests, scribes and a fortunate few. Even kings and rulers often did not know how to read or write. But today, because of the marvel of the printing press and the increasing availability of education to both rich and poor, reading is an activity accessible to all who wish to learn.

And what a wonderful gift spiritual reading is for furthering your progress on the Path. Your prayer shrine is an ideal place to keep the sacred writings of the first and second Testaments of the Judaeo-Christian tradition. It is also handy to have present an individual copy of the classic prayer book of that twin tradition, the Psalms. These immortal prayers are rich beyond measure in their power to speak from the depths of the human heart in times of joy and pain.

Together with the sacred scriptures of your own tradition, you may find it of value to read sections of other holy books. Today as never before, the sacred writings of the great religious traditions of Hinduism, Buddhism, Islam, Taoism and many others are available at bookstores or can easily be ordered. Until recently many of the translations were difficult to read, but now excellent and very readable versions—and even editions in the original languages— can be acquired. Each planetary pilgrim will have to determine if these rich treasuries of inspiration are of personal assistance on the spiritual journey. But wherever one finds truth, the Spirit of God, who is the pen of the Divine Mystery, has been at work.

A good rule for any sacred reading is to read little but think a lot; read few words but create much prayerful space around them. A few sentences or a paragraph is often sufficient. Nor do you need to be in a hurry for intellectual insight into what you read. Rather let the heart understand, by standing under the text to let its light flood down upon you. Practice the art of surrounding your reading with silence. Take time to create silence beforehand to allow your heart to be cleansed of preconditioned ideas or discriminations so that you can truly hear and inwardly receive what is read. Then take time afterwards to allow the words to soak deeply into your consciousness.

Hearing with the heart usually happens in stages. First, we see and understand the words we read, but only as we have been conditioned to hear them—often a text's meaning has been determined by religious authorities over the centuries. In the second stage we move beyond previously held understandings of the text to new and personal implications it suggests. When we first begin to go deeper into the meaning of a text, questions begin to emerge. Because of the scientific inclination of our age, we may be tempted to ask questions like, "Is this true?" or "Did this really happen?" But a better question to ask is, "What is the hidden meaning of this—what is its meaning for me, at this time and place in my life?" At this second stage the planetary pilgrim should remember that the sacred scriptures are not so much guidelines for social and moral order as they are guideposts for the sacred journey back to the Divine Source. A good reader is one who knows how to read in-between the lines so as to decode the secret message of the Spirit.

The third stage of reading occurs when we have moved beyond the words and their literal meaning and have moved beyond even their deeper meanings. We reach the point where we hear only the voice of the Beloved speaking. When one is ready to listen not merely to the Bible but rather to the voice of the Beloved, one is then free to play with sacred words. One not only plays with the innocence of a child but also with the scholar's zeal for wisdom and with the reverence and affection of a friend of God. If the sacred scriptures are indeed, as we firmly believe, the word of God, then they surely must possess the divine ability to speak to people of all ages and of any age in history. It is not the message that is inflexible, it is a narrow interpretation that prevents them from being fresh fountains of life-giving water to those who walk the Path.

In summary, the reading of sacred scriptures, including those of other traditions, provides nourishment for the inner person, insight into the quest and confirmation that one is indeed on the right pathway. In addition, the writings of great saints, spiritual masters and contemporary authors who are attuned to the activity of the Spirit can supplement our spiritual reading and help make it a gift that truly can carry our hearts, intellects, imaginations and spirits to the heart of God.

THE CAPTAIN'S LOG: A JOURNAL OF THE JOURNEY

To record events was once primarily a priestly power since the ability to write was limited to an elite group. Although the ability to write is commonplace in our modern Western world, our use of this priestly skill is usually limited to personal letters and occasional notes. Often this is because our overcommitted lives do not allow us enough time or because we fear that we do not have enough skill. But keeping a log or journal can be one of the most trusted allies of the spiritual sojourner. As on any expedition or journey of discovery, carefully recording daily events and the nature of what has been encountered along the Way, as well as making maps of the uncharted territory, is important.

On his first expedition to the Americas, Columbus kept two logs. One was for the crew, in case they wanted to know about the ship's progress. The other was a secret log that held the exact mileage covered each day. It seems that the crew feared that if they traveled too far westward they would never be able to find their way back home again, and so Columbus doctored the records of distance they had covered in order to prevent a panic.

You may also wish to keep your pilgrim log private, sharing the more intimate parts of your journey only with close friends or a trusted guide. If so, take proper care of its safekeeping. This will be easier if you have a log book (hard or soft cover books with blank pages which can be purchased in art shops or stationary stores or even inexpensive spiral notebooks make excellent log books for your sacred journey), or perhaps you could gather all your log entries in a spiral binder. You may also wish to devise a code system for recording events which will both save time and assist in keeping your log book private property.

It has been said that the person who writes thinks twice. Having a planetary pilgrim log provides a way to observe your progress. It allows you an opportunity to express your feelings, motives and fears as well as your dreams. Keeping a log or journal can also be a means of self-direction, if you are able to keep a flexible mind. For example, when you encounter something that stalls your movement on your journey, whether it is a difficult interaction with another, a failure, mistake or loss, write down in your log all that happened and how you felt about it. When you are finished, read aloud to yourself what you have written. Try to listen as though you were another person, perhaps a wise spiritual guide. Then make note of this wise counselor's response.

As with the log book of any explorer, feel free to make note of such things as the weather and how it affects you, the state of your health and mood swings on good days and bad days, and especially those special events that can change the course of your journey. You can also use your log book to record the quotations from scripture or from your favorite authors that you found to be especially significant at a particular point in your journey. As you write down important words or passages that you have read, you are also inscribing them more deeply in your consciousness, making their energy more fully your own. By recording them in your log book you can quickly locate them if you need to refer to them again at a later date.

The keeping of a journal is also an ongoing confirmation that you are indeed on an expedition, a journey of cosmic consequences. In our busy world, this will not be an easy discipline. It is better to write a few lines or inscribe a few coded symbols each day or several times a week than to write long pages and end up giving up the practice because you don't have enough time. Perhaps the best way is to establish at least a minimal daily discipline and make longer entries when you have more leisure or at times of great discovery and insight. Occasions of crisis, trouble, suffering or the sense of being lost, along with the high moments of great gratitude, victory, celebration and blessings, are other important times to journal.

One of the key tasks of any explorer is mapmaking. Your log book can also serve you in that work. Dr. Ira Progoff, who pioneered journal keeping as a tool for self-growth and spiritual progress, suggests that you make a simple map of your life, from childhood up to this moment. This personal map should contain fifteen or more significant events of your life. You can make symbols to express their meaning for you or simply write them down and draw lines to connect them.

Dr. Progoff suggests that you also include on your map the paths you could have taken in life but for one reason or another chose to go in a different direction. This would include decisions about things like whether or not to study some subject, to learn how to play a musical instrument, to develop a gift or talent or even to travel to far-off places. The reason for recording untraveled paths on your map is that you may wish to explore them at another point in your life.

As with the other equipment for your inner journey, this log book can be kept in your prayer shrine. Your entries can then be part of your daily prayer period. I have called it a captain's log since you and you alone are the captain of your inner space expedition. It is your responsibility to know where you have been and where you are going. And your log book can serve you in some surprisingly insightful ways if you can develop a faithful discipline.

DISCIPLINE AND
WILL POWER

Discipline is essential for anyone who wishes to achieve a goal, whether as an athlete or an astronaut, an artist or an actor, a soldier or a saint. Discipline is the mother word for disciple; it is a key ingredient for providing impetus for the disciple starting on the Way. While the word sometimes has a negative ring, discipline is really no more than directed behavior toward accomplishing an aspiration. And it is often only hard work until we get the hang of something. As small children we had to learn the discipline of proper table manners so that we would not offend others and so that we might learn how to make a meal a graceful experience. When we eat as adults we are unaware of any discipline being involved since our eating behavior has become second nature.

The Way calls for conversion of heart and transformation of mind. Practically speaking, that means that we need to form new behavior as well as new ways of thinking. Discipline is a principle part of that transformation process for any planetary pilgrim. Again, in the beginning it requires attention, time and exercise of the will. But with the passage of time, like table manners, it also becomes natural and even unself-conscious behavior. Since discipline is intimately connected to the will, it would be wise to take a closer look at this important power source of human behavior.

WILL POWER, THE ENERGY SOURCE

The great spiritual masters of history have consistently called for two simple yet challenging exercises. The first is to strive to make your daily life more simple and therefore more free of complications and unnecessary desires. The second is to strive to develop your inner resources and powers. The twin processes of discipline and the development of your will power address both these admonitions.

This process first requires that you acknowledge that you have a free will, that you do indeed have the capacity to choose. Then the art of discipline is directed toward having your life's energies revolve around the choices of what is important in your life. As an explorer of inner space, for example, you might discipline yourself to regularly do things that support your spiritual journey, like setting aside time for prayer, and not doing things that may get in the way, like mindlessly reading the newspaper or watching TV during your spiritual practice's "prime time." Discipline thus allows for greater simplicity by freeing the planetary pilgrim's energies for movement along the Way. It prepares you to be more one-pointed and more fully attentive. It leads you to cultivate the quality the Gospels call single-heartedness.

The will is the inner faculty strengthened by the exercise of discipline. To "switch on" this power source of the will is to feel a thrust of energy that carries an enormous capacity to perform deeds you may have thought impossible. The use of will energy has often been seen as an inner brake system that represses certain aspects of the personality. Rather, like an arrow shot from a bow, the creative will is an energy source that directs and propels our inner powers toward the goal that we have freely chosen and does so while using the least amount of our total energies. The blossoming of your power of will leads to self-mastery. And while getting a master's degree in the arts or sciences is a great achievement, becoming a master of the inner way is the greatest attainment to which we as human beings are called. Since many are called but few choose to remain on the Way, it is necessary to develop your will power in order to create the determination that will keep you faithful to the Path even when it leads through barren deserts and wastelands.

When one is traveling in a strange, uncharted land, the capacity to be spontaneous, to respond creatively to whatever comes up, is critical. For the planetary pilgrim who is in quest of the Divine Mystery, such openness to the unexpected, such willingness to be surprised, is crucial. The development of your will power does not repress such free self-expression but paradoxically gives birth to it. A healthy inner-directed person is more able to drop social controls and personal defenses, rituals and other restraints and to be spontaneous when the situation calls for it. Such a balanced person can control behavior, delay the enjoyment of natural pleasures and comfort or restrain eager impulses when the needs of others or the goals of the quest require it. For the aim of self-mastery is ultimately to restrain one's own impulses in the service of the Spirit's free movement in one's life.

The following exercises are intended to assist you in the development of that great inner energy source, your will power.

ACCIDENTAL EXERCISES

An important initial principle to remember in the development of your will power energy is that every muscle, organ and faculty of our mind-body-spirit can be developed by exercise. And each of us has numerous daily opportunities to exercise our will power toward self-mastery. You can strengthen your will by freely choosing to respond generously to life situations that require sacrifice, such as being asked to wait for something or having to stand in line at a checkout counter. Use such accidental or unplanned occasions as an exercise of your will power by freely choosing to wait with patience and graciousness. You can choose not to react with anger when cut off in a traffic jam, or to respond with flexibility in adjusting your schedule when your child gets sick or some unexpected work comes up at the office. While small and seemingly insignificant, each of these accidental exercises can strengthen your will toward greatness of heart.

1. PERFORM EACH EXERCISE WITH ATTENTION AND LOVE

Be vigilant not to approach these exercises with only half a heart. Invest each of them not only with a fullness of attention but also with all the love you can.

2. FIND THE HIDDEN PLEASURES OF DISCIPLINED BEHAVIOR

As you perform your various exercises, experience the pleasure of the flow of power from within you. Take legitimate delight in your newly discovered inner powers.

3. MINOR MARVELS LEAD TO MAJOR MIRACLES

Realize as you practice these seemingly insignificant acts of the will that life's large battles are won in increments. Self-mastery comes in the daily minor victories over self and its constant pull toward self-gratification.

INTENTIONAL EXERCISES

As well as accidental exercises it is helpful in forming a strong and healthy will to intentionally choose certain activities that are more beneficial than their alternatives. Such intentional exercises could include reading a book or writing a letter instead of watching television, eating a healthy meal rather than junk food, taking time for prayer rather than reading the morning newspaper, working one evening in a soup kitchen instead of seeing a movie or consciously choosing to conserve or recycle earth's resources. Such acts of the will, as with accidental exercises, should be done with full attention, with great love and care.

Some writers on the will, such as Boyd Barrett, suggest that you carry out a number of simple tasks with as much precision and persistence as possible. These could be such daily chores as dusting, doing the dishes or sweeping the floor or something as totally nonproductive as mindfully getting up and down from a chair thirty times. A planetary pilgrim might add a mantra-like quality of dedication and devotion to such repetitious tasks.

1. MAKE AN ACT OF DISCIPLINE PART OF YOUR DAILY DIET

Each day choose to perform at least one unnecessary or distasteful action for the sole reason that it is difficult for you, that it is something you would normally choose to avoid. Everyone's life has many such "I'd rather not" sort of obligations from which to choose.

2. REMEMBER TO DO SUCH EXERCISES WITH GREAT GENEROSITY

For such undesirable duties not to become a burden, however, they must be done with a generous heart. Each exercise of discipline, whether it is accidental or intentional, should be given your full attention and carried out with great love and devotion directed toward the person, object or action involved.

3. LEARN TO NICELY SAY "NO"

Another key element in the formation of a disciplined life is the exercise of saying "no" to engagements or requests that are not possible for you to take on. To practice this necessary exercise is often difficult and involves a certain amount of risk, for saying "no" may bring the disfavor of those who have asked something of you. Contemporary life is complicated by countless commitments and endless work. While technology has greatly extended opportunities for travel and communication, it has not extended the number of hours in a day beyond twenty-four. And so, we all need to determine priorities according to the basic life choices that we have made, according to what we feel is the central work in our lives. But when we do need to say "no," it must be done with deep affection directed toward those who have made the request or extended the invitation.

4. PRAYER AS AN ONGOING EXERCISE OF STRENGTHENING DISCIPLINE

Consider such activities as morning and evening prayer and prayer before meals as opportunities to strengthen your will. And as you choose them over other activities, do so consciously and with great devotion.

CONCLUSION

The planetary pilgrim's daily life is a fertile field of opportunities for the ongoing exercise of the will. The will, in turn, is a primary power source for propelling the prayer pilgrim on the Path. While will power is usually seen as energy to get things done, it is also a marvelous tool for reshaping our hearts and minds, even for letting go of our compulsion to get things done. For example, because accomplishing a task is such a rewarding experience, we often respond to being interrupted in our work with curtness. By continuous practice you can use your will power to resist being angry at interruptions and to reform inner attitudes so that you might begin to see with new eyes. You can discipline yourself to call these interruptions by a new name: visitations. It has long been believed in several religious traditions that the gods came disguised as unexpected strangers; you can exercise your will to be open to seeing each interruption in your day as a visitation of the Divine Mystery.

Ultimately, perhaps, discipline and the development of the will and our other inner powers only set the table for prayer. We are only truly nourished by the graceful presence of God. But certainly, the exercise of our gifts and resources is essential to disposing ourselves fully to the Divine Presence, and it is integral to our most fundamental calling as spiritual sojourners.

IMAGINATION AND INTENTION

Among the greatest allies of the will in the development of your inner powers are the abilities of the mind to imagine and to set an intention. These rich inner resources are given to you as aids for finding happiness in life and as power sources for your sacred journey. And one of the principles of the Path is that every planetary pilgrim has the inner resources for making pictures in the mind and for setting those images into motion.

The power of imagination is not the same as daydreaming, which is idle use of this dynamic power source. Buddha, five centuries before Christ, began his written teachings with the words, "With your thoughts you make your world. Think evil thoughts and darkness and evil will follow you as surely as the cart follows the ox." Thoughts and their cousins, mental pictures, are electrical blueprints which possess great power. Every idea is only the first act of a whole unfolding drama which potentially may be performed. Ideas and images have a hidden power to manifest themselves outwardly.

Therefore, if you desire to perform some act of sacrifice or prayer, you can greatly increase the energy behind that desire by first imagining yourself performing that action. Picture it as vividly as possible and feel the sense of pleasure that comes with doing that activity. Since our minds are often crowded with thoughts, it is important that you clear space for this seed-idea or image to fill as much of the total field of your consciousness as possible.

EXERCISES FOR PRE-IMAGING BEHAVIOR

1. BLUEPRINT YOUR DESIRED BEHAVIOR BEFOREHAND

Before you retire at night, create within your mind an image of yourself seated in your prayer shrine the next morning wrapped in prayerfulness. Allow your imagination to taste the sense of peace and fulfillment that comes from such communion with God. Such a mental blueprint can make it considerably easier to remain faithful to your discipline of meditation.

Then, before departing from your prayer shrine, briefly image yourself sitting there again in the evening. Envision your heart overflowing with gratitude for the many gifts of the day. Picture yourself in prayerful thanksgiving for the grace you received to perform with love the deeds of that day. In that image-idea will be much motivation for returning to your prayer shrine at the end of the day.

2. BEHAVIOR BUILDS ON THIS BLUEPRINT

Before leaving your prayer shrine after your morning prayer, take a few moments to pre-image a specific task or activity of your day that may be difficult. Create an inner motion picture of yourself performing that action with great love and care. Picture a pathway for grace that enables this blessed blueprint of will power to become a reality.

3. THE BLUEPRINT AND YOUR BODY IN PRAYER

The position of your body can call forth as well as support your images and thoughts. For example, the ritual action of a profound bow and the idea of adoring God can mutually reinforce and feed one another in creating a heartfelt adoration. And the posture of sitting as still as possible when you meditate strengthens the image of yourself as perfectly at rest and encourages peacefulness. Likewise, your thoughts and mental images can powerfully influence your bodily posture. Think elevating thoughts and envision noble deeds and your body will correspondingly open and extend.

4. WORDS WORK WONDERS

If you desire your prayers to be devotional, to be filled with love and affection, then remember that ideas and words tend to awaken corresponding emotions and feelings. Words on fire with divine love often evoke images of devotion. And if you envision your heart aflame with a love for God, words of devotion are likely to spontaneously arise in your prayer.

The choice of powerful words can assist not only your prayer but also the lifestyle that flows from your prayer. It can greatly reinforce the discipline of proper pilgrim behavior. The same inner law that applies to prayer also applies to your practice of non-violence, peace and justice. Words of kindness, compassion and affection also deeply influence your interrelations with your companions aboard planet Earth.

5. REPETITION RENDERS REWARDS

If you wish to drive a nail into a board, you hammer the nail in with repeated blows. An action or attitude likewise becomes an integral part of our lives through repetition. This inner law is well understood by advertisers as well as by dictators. To repeatedly perform something makes it easier to do and makes one better at doing it. Similarly, the more one visualizes a desired attitude or behavior, the more likely it is to blossom into reality.

Every good habit brings the freedom of the 4th of July! When prayer is hammered into your consciousness by frequent imaging and repeated practice, it becomes more and more second nature. Rather than having to remember to pray, prayer tends to spring spontaneously into your heart and upon your lips. As a result, your conscious mind is more free to concentrate on an activity. At the same time, your prayer becomes more integral with your activity.

6. A COMMUNITY OF CREATORS OF CHANGE: A SUMMARY

The discipline of prayer and meditation, as well as the other behavior essential for remaining balanced on the razor's edge of the Path, is the responsibility of a whole cast of characters who are part of your inner community.

First, your inner artist creates full-color images of a desired behavior. With complete and careful attention, that artist within paints a clearly defined image-idea in bold colors on the full canvas of your mind.

Next, your inner poet carefully selects the right words to invest the image-idea with power and desire. The images and words then creatively interact with each other to produce new behavior.

Following that, your inner carpenter hammers each new behavior into a habit by continuous repetition. A good carpenter does not half-heartedly hit a nail. Each time, therefore, that this carpenter of the heart hammers home an action or intent the structure of one's inner temple is reinforced.

Your child within now has the space to take delight in the playfulness of the game of holy habits. That child who never dies makes games out of the various accidental or intentional exercises of the will. And the inner child becomes absorbed in the play of perfection, bringing the full attentiveness of childhood play into exploring the new prayerful possibilities that these exercises create.

And your inner lover is constantly romancing each image, idea and act with as much devotion as your heart can bear. Such lovemaking blossoms into spiritual fruit. For the love of God begins with love of what is truest in oneself. If you truly love yourself, then you desire only the best for yourself. This proper love of self should also prevent you from failing to achieve what you desire in life. The power of love is proclaimed in all the scriptures, and when it is applied to the process of reforming your life, it can truly work miracles.

DEPARTURES FROM YOUR DISCIPLINE: FAIL-SAFE FAILURES

Mindful of the parable of Jesus about the fate of the seeds that fell on rocky ground or among thorns and so did not grow to full maturity, we can understand how many are reluctant to even begin the adventure of the spiritual quest. Many also begin with great zest but at some point experience failure in their spiritual disciplines. They then often become discouraged and slip back into their old patterns, giving up their dream of the quest.

It is inevitable that in traveling the Way you will occasionally wander off the path. And so it is prudent to remember this principle of the inner journey: there is no way to travel the razor's edge without sometimes slipping off. Indeed the way is truly a High Way that calls the pilgrim who travels it to progress upward in evolutionary spirals. It is, in the words of the Psalms, "the path of perfection." But what pilgrim is perfect?

Failure, however, must be embraced not only realistically but also with great love. Each time you stray off the path, drawn by the powerful magnets of materialism, by the lure of the sirens of desire or power over others, you must embrace the failure honestly. But then, having recognized your mistake, the surest progress is made on the pilgrim path by simply returning once again with a smiling, if not humble, heart to your discipline of prayer.

What difference does it make whether you slip from your spiritual disciplines ten thousand times as long as you wholeheartedly return to your practice of prayer each time? So constantly keep before you, especially as you begin to use this book, this success principle of a planetary pilgrim:

SUCCESS FOR THE SPIRITUAL SOJOURNER IS NOT IN NEVER HAVING SLIPPED BUT IN SPEEDILY SPRINGING BACK ONTO THE RAZOR'S EDGE

This important guideline for the journey is based on the same principle found in a coil of wire. It quickly returns to its original form because it has been forged into that shape. The more you shape your life in harmony with the Way, the easier it becomes to spring back from slips in discipline or behavior. The only real failure in prayer is to finally abandon your practice because you have failed to remain totally faithful in your daily disciplines of meditation and deeds of love and compassion.

THE PILGRIMAGE AS PERPETUAL REVOLUTION

The spiritual revolution of Jesus was unique in that it called for a continuous revolution rather than a one-time event. His call to reform our lives was a challenge to invest ourselves in repeated resolutions to do the impossible, to love God with all our heart, mind, soul and body.

Such total surrender in love to the Divine Source requires great dedication, as well as the elastic ability to continually spring back. To have a spring in your spirit, like the springs and shock absorbers in your car, not only makes the potholes and bumps of life less jolting, but it also saves wear and tear on the space vehicle of your soul.

The presence of your prayer shrine, and perhaps the plainly visible presence of this planetary pilgrim's prayer book, will encourage you to spring back until such readiness to return to God becomes natural.

THE WAY IS
A COMPANION WAY

All travel, both in outer space and inner space is dangerous, and the wise space traveler is well prepared and makes provisions that it is not a solo journey. Today's explorer of intergalactic space must by necessity be part of a team that includes not only companion astronauts but countless technicians on earth who make possible the journey. Likewise, the pilgrim who is exploring inner space must also have companions.

It is wise to frequently recall this principle of pilgrimage travel: the journey back to the source is not a solo flight. It is easy to image yourself as a spiritual Lindbergh on a heroic solo flight, struggling single-handedly on a mystical adventure. But realistically, that's not the way to travel the Way. It's not likely to provide the energy to take you all the way home, to form you according to the Way of holiness. In fact, to attempt any work alone in this life, especially seeking a holy-wholeness, is to discover that you are de-formed. The secret of holiness is that the Path is a Companion Way.

The first thing Jesus did after coming from his desert solitude was to gather around him a small group of companions, making his life communal. Jesus, Buddha, Mohammed and Moses were community-makers. They saw the necessity of companions on the Exodus experience, the path from slavery to godliness. The Moslem sage and poet, Rumi, summed up the Islamic vision: "Gather with the followers of Reality that you may both win the gift and give yourself up generously." Fortunate, then, is the pilgrim-traveler who has found a close companion, one who also seeks Reality, with whom one can share life's journey as the Way.

But for the North American pilgrim-traveler of inner space to acknowledge that the Way is a Companion Way will not be easy. American heroes are soloists, the Lindberghs and the Lone Rangers we admire. Even our saints are soloists who stand in icy isolation on their pedestals. Yet to be a true seeker in God's design seems to require abandoning the arch-American trait of rugged individualism by seeking a communal arch-pilgrimage.

The acronym A.R.C.H. provides a key to the Companion Way.

AFFIRMATION: This first of all means being supported in your efforts to surrender your little self, which always wants its own way. The dictator-ego is constantly inflating its self-importance and feeding its self-indulgent hunger. Companions are reflective; they are mirrors which allow you to see yourself in ways that are impossible as a soloist. Companions also affirm you by praise, that soul-food which spurs you to ever greater effort.

REFORMATION: This is the reshaping of your life according to the virtues proclaimed in the Gospels. Reformation is quickened by others who show you the effects of your selfishness or rudeness. Companions reveal the cracks and faults that the ego likes to justify as "my unique personality." Walking the Way with others who seek to be loving, prayerful and compassionate, fuels your efforts to grow in love.

CONFRONTATION: Again, companions can be mirrors that lovingly confront you with your blind spots. There is also the confrontation of conflicting inner desires. I desire to pray daily, to feed my inner-self with wholesome food. I also desire to get the job done, to be successful and to accomplish all the numerous tasks necessary in daily living. In the wrestling match between desire-to-pray and desire-to-get-the-job-done, guess who usually wins? The Companion Way calls you beyond personal agendas to a concern for another's needs and to the invitation to prayer contained therein. Companions can also be comrades-in-arms in the struggle for balance by confronting you with the question, "Isn't it time to pray?" or even "Isn't it time to play?"

HUMILITY: Sharing the daily Path with companions develops humility. It provides numerous opportunities to perform true "secret service." All service is significant, some service is spectacularly significant. To take out the trash, to prepare supper or to do the dishes with love are acts of significant service. To abandon your family and job to give your life to feed the poor in Ethiopia can be both significant and spectacular. It can also be dangerous since it gives rise to the possible disease of fame. Companionship allows for hidden yet significant acts of kindness and service in which no news team of TV cameras and reporters would be the least bit interested.

The "H" of arch-pilgrimage or companion spirituality also stands for humanity. Not only is fame dangerous to those who seek to be holy, so can seeking to be spiritual. Those who venture forth on a spirit quest need to remember that we share a heritage of an unwholesome spirituality which considers the flesh to be evil. The quest for holiness has a distorted tradition of thinking that by abandoning the world, family, sex, the daily affairs of business and those God-implanted hungers of our bodies we can become holy.

Good friends or companions remind you that you are not an angel in disguise, because they see so well your human imperfections, like the mini-sins of your thirty second attacks of impatience, tiredness or fear. What you can hide if you are alone is impossible to conceal when you travel with others. Companions reveal that we are either sinning saints or saintly sinners.

The saying, "Your best guru is your lover or marriage partner," then makes sense, if you are fortunate enough to have one who shares your thirst for the divine mystery. And nowhere, to my knowledge, in the collected words of Jesus does he speak about the necessity of today's much sought after guide, the spiritual director! It seems that he saw companionship and communal life to be the normal guides to prayerfulness and holiness.

PRINCIPLES FOR COMPANIONSHIP ON THE QUEST

If you are seeking to grow in holiness and lack a mutual companion who shares your search, how would you go about forming a community?

1. YOU NEVER "MAKE" COMMUNITY, YOU DISCOVER IT

Step one begins with the knowledge that you never create community, rather you discover that you are already part of a community! Like amnesia victims, our primary task is to remember who we are. It is remembering that we already share a community of life with all creation.

2. LIVING ALONE DOES NOT PREVENT COMPANIONSHIP

Even if you live alone, you exist within a global, if not cosmic, community. You are one with all humanity, the good and virtuous as well as those who are evil and destructive. Planet Earth is one home, where we all sleep, walk, work, pray, love and pilgrimage together to God. The gift of sharing life and prayer with others is a visual sign of that larger and cosmic community in which we all share membership.

3. BEING A CREATIVE AGENT IN THE REDISCOVERY OF COMMUNITY

You can be a creative agent of community by inviting those with whom you work or live to become more than a "natural" community. Together you can transform any aspect of your common life into a spiritual reality by sharing meals, work, prayer, recreation or whatever you do, in the spirit of Christ. If such common living is impossible, then find a small group of others who pray, study or seek God together. Or if none exists, form your own. What our hearts hunger for is usually not unique; others are seeking the same thing and only need someone to start the shared process.

4. A PERSONAL COMPANION FOR THE QUEST

You can also open your heart to discover an intimate companion with whom to share the Path. Such a soul friendship allows for an exchange of spiritual energies that can heighten and enrich both of you. It can be a class in the school of loving that helps carry both of you home. Some of the factors that hinder such arch-holiness are fear, lack of imagination and your cultural formation in rugged individualism, which says that such assistance is a sign of weakness rather than an act of heroism on the quest. Never underestimate the powerful cultural influence of the ideal of independence in your life.

5. SOLIDARITY WITH OTHERS WHO PRAY

Together with these efforts to create a corporate pilgrimage to God, the greatest expedition anyone can venture upon, find ways to be in solidarity with other seekers, especially those who pray. When you form a solidarity with those who pray, you will find it easier to be a person of prayer yourself.

Private prayer does not exist. All prayer is communal even if it is personal prayer. When you pray alone, you can be reminded of the fact that you are not apart from others by a simple act of communion. Before you begin to pray, join yourself consciously with others who are praying. It is especially helpful if you can image particular persons with whom you are connected or have a friendship. This can be a spiritual community or any group with whom you share the same dreams of holy-wholeness and the work of peace and justice.

Moslems face Mecca when they pray. You can stand for a moment before you pray and face in the direction of your companions in prayer, perhaps making a slight bow of reverence. If you know the hour of prayer of your companion community, your own prayer can be reinforced by joining them at that time. You can also be in holy communion with them even if you are not in formal prayer then. For a brief moment, no matter what activity you are engaged in, pause and link up with them as an act of solidarity. See the following page for the prayer of sacred circles to assist you with this act of communion in prayer. You may also find the following exercise to be valuable as a preface to your personal prayer. It is an exercise for communion with your companions on the journey who at this time are some physical distance away.

THE HEART-THREAD LIFE LINE

By using the inner resource of your imagination, see in your heart a sacred spool of thread. You can begin by creating an image of this thin, invisible thread in your favorite color. Then reach out with this sacred thread and tie it, with great love, to another thread that issues from the heart of a companion who is not present physically.

Make the knot secure, then move on to tie your thread to the heart of another companion who may be hundreds of miles away. That knot securely tied, move to another, and another, until you have completed crisscrossing the country, joining those who share your pilgrimage into inner space. Don't worry; like magic, your heart's thread, light as an angel's breath yet stronger than steel, can cover vast distances and leap over high mountains. It can span vast oceans to reach other threads yearning to be connected.

CONCLUSION

Share with your companions the books, tapes and other resources that you find helpful. Connected and confirmed by letters, telephone calls and visits, keep open those critical communication-communion lines that link you together. To find friends to share this great adventure is truly a divine gift, and, as such, great care must be taken not to lose it. As you seek the life-support system of companions in your journey into inner space, remember that God desires to give you that great gift more than you desire to receive it. When tempted to go it alone, keep in mind Eden's wisdom, when God spoke to Adam, "It is not good for one to be alone." With those words in your heart, resist the temptation to close your heart to community because of the pain of the positive asceticism of constant selflessness required for any companionship, the pain that must be embraced by any pilgrim who wishes to achieve the end of the journey.

SACRED CIRCLES:
A RITUAL OF COMMUNION BEFORE PERSONAL PRAYER

First, take time to enter into communion with your body. Be aware of the flow of your breath and the life-giving circulation of blood. Quietly sense the unity of body and mind as billions of messages are exchanged among the various life-centers of your body. Be present to all the activity which makes possible the unconscious but essential functioning of your whole person.

Second, move outward to touch all those whom you love. Form an image of these persons in your mind's eye and embrace them with peace or wrap them with your heart-thread. Before leaving this second circle of communion, unite yourself with your personal companions on the spiritual path.

Third, ask God to unite you with those who struggle to pray. Seek to create a single chorus of praise. And make an intention that any who are in need may share richly in the gifts of the peace, grace and light of God contained in the prayer you are about to begin.

Fourth, with a desire for union, move next to those of your local community, to members of your congregation, parish, diocese or larger association. From that circle, move outward to embrace all those of your country, your homeland.

Fifth, extend your awareness to the wider circle of all earth's citizens. Seek to be one with all the people of this planet regardless of race, religion or political position. This encompassing communion, because of its vastness, may not hold the same emotional force as the circle of your close friends or family. But seek to open your heart to as complete a sense of oneness as is possible.

Sixth, seek to be one also with the earth itself, with oceans and lakes, mountains and valleys, forests and deserts. Enter into communion with trees, flowers and plants, with birds, beasts and fish. Awaken within your heart a burning desire to feel your body and the body of the earth as one.

Seventh, finally expand your awareness outward from the earth, and be in a holy communion with the sun, moon and planets, with all the stars of our galaxy and all the billions of galaxies of our universe. One with all that God has created and is creating, desire with a whole heart to be one with the cosmic Christ and with all the community of heaven; desire to be one with God.

Now consciously in touch with the divine energy that flows throughout this cosmic mystical body, enter deeply and with devotion into your personal prayer.

SECTION FIVE

MEDITATION
AND MINDFULNESS

As the astronauts and cosmonauts who journey into the mysteries of outer space require spacecraft or interplanetary vehicles, so the spiritual pilgrim has need of a vehicle or method to journey inward. Meditation or silent prayer—which is an integral part of the daily prayers in this book—is such a vehicle. Some form of this important prayer is taught in each of the great spiritual traditions of the world.

Since the mid-1960's an entire library of books has been written about various methods for meditation. While the methods and practices are many, they all are directed toward the same end, namely, to still the flow of thoughts and desires that keep the mind and heart constantly occupied, and thus to make one more fully available to God.

Many shy away from the idea of meditation, believing that it is only for special people. In reality, everyone meditates; only the subject of meditation differs. Those who desire to be olympic athletes literally think, eat and sleep their sports. And persons who believe that money is the source of happiness also meditate daily, as thoughts about making and investing money constantly absorb their minds. For spiritual seekers, the Divine Mystery is the subject of meditation. There is a saying in the Upanishads, the scriptures of India: "If men and women thought as much about God as they think of the world, who would not attain liberation?"

While it may be said that God is at the heart of all our desires and is present in all our activities, God is also beyond anything we can put our fingers on. As Jesus told us, God is spirit and should be worshiped in spirit and truth. And while the Spirit is at the heart of all matter, the Spirit is also beyond all matter and form. The Spirit cannot be contained by the concepts and thoughts of human minds since those concepts by nature of our humanity involve matter. Although they are not solid matter, our thoughts are still not spiritual. The thoughts that fill your mind as you read this page are actually electrical units of energy which can be measured by machines.

In silent prayer or the prayer of meditation, the pilgrim seeks to still the endless river of thoughts and so to find the center from which all thoughts arise, the center within which peace and the Divine Mystery reside. The following exercises suggest one way of meditation. If you presently do not meditate and desire to do so, they can provide a vehicle for the essential journey inward.

A METHOD OF MEDITATION

1. SIT STILL AND QUIET THE BODY

The first requirement for any journey inward is to quiet the body which so easily absorbs the countless energies of life that surround it. Without straining, intend to sit with your head, neck and back erect. If possible sit on the floor since chairs tend to create the need for constant shifting or a dullness of the body. It is thus easy to become distracted or sleepy, as opposed to being alert and awake, fully present and available to God. As was suggested in the section on equipment for inner space travel, a cushion or prayer bench can help you sit comfortably yet alertly. If you need a chair, try sitting on its forward edge so that the upper body can be in a straight line. If helpful, as you begin, you can lightly rest your back against a wall or the back of a straight chair.

For a few minutes, simply notice what's happening in your body without trying to change it. Be aware of where you are stiff or tense, where you are dull. Then, without slouching, let your body be supported by the earth or the chair; let it become quiet.

Practice this exercise.

2. WITH GENTLENESS BEGIN TO BREATHE DEEPLY

As you breathe, be conscious of the act of breathing that you normally take for granted. Bring your attention to your nose as air passes through your nostrils as you inhale and as you exhale. At first simply notice your breath without any attempt to control it. Then gently let the breath become fuller and deeper. Do not strain, but let your breathing be slow, even and deep.

Then use your power of imagination to visualize the air that you are breathing out as dark or gray, as if it contained the nervous energy, negativity and even the blocks to stillness that may exist within you. Image the air that you are inhaling as a pure, clear stream, luminous and full of peace. Without stress, draw out of yourself all impurities and dis-ease as you exhale. And as you breathe in, fill yourself with peace and with the abiding presence of the Divine Mystery who breathed life into the nostrils of Adam and Eve and who like a mighty wind blew over the dark chaos before the cosmos was created.

In short, breathe in everything that is of God and breathe out everything that is not of God. With each breath, image the air growing lighter and more luminous until you feel that you are filled with light and peace.

3. HAVING PREPARED YOURSELF, REST IN THAT PEACE

Practice sitting in stillness absorbed in peace.

If you have tried this exercise, you have no doubt found that for a while the mind was able to be at peace. But at some point a thought or string of thoughts appeared as if from nowhere and occupied the attention of the mind. It seems that the secondary organ of our personality, the mind, finds the present moment to be a boring place and so races into the future with planning and ideas. Or it retreats into the past to rerun old tapes of past experiences.

Trying to sit still without thinking only awakens us to the awareness that we do not think. Rather, we are thought! Ideas and thoughts visit us regardless of whether they are invited or not. But if our thoughts are electric blueprints, with enormous power to become reality, it is important that we learn how to regulate their flow and their presence within us if we aspire to a life of high consciousness. And from the perspective of prayer, it is important to be able to create the inner spaciousness necessary to simply be with God.

The problem, then, is how to stop this throng of thoughts from filling your mind. The methods differ from tradition to tradition. Moslem mystics, the whirling dervishes, dance them away. Some seekers chant them away, while others still the mind by bringing it to rest upon a sacred image, a candle flame or a mandala. Still others propose the use of a single word or phrase that is repeated over and over with great devotion. The word can be a name of God, a phrase from a Psalm or other book of Scripture or a word of great power like love or peace. For each of these methods it is good to remember that the ultimate intent is to be absorbed in God, whether in the ecstasy of God, the presence of God or the name of God.

In some traditions this word or mantra is given to you by a spiritual guide. But ultimately the choice of a sacred word is yours to make. It is often helpful in making the choice to simply set a prayerful intent for the right word to come to you. The important thing, though, is to find a word that quickens and heightens you and has the power to take you to God. It is also important that, once you find a word that leads you into prayer, you do not switch from sacred word to sacred word, seeking one that will work better than the other. Choose one after prayerful reflection and, unless there is a very clear reason to change, remain faithful to it in and out of season.

4. GO INWARD AND BEGIN TO SILENTLY REPEAT YOUR SACRED WORD OR PHRASE

As you do this, let your mind rest solely upon your sacred word. Invest it with as much devotion and attention as possible. Inevitably in this practice, a thought or idea will rise up into your consciousness. Do not resist it or attempt to force it out of your mind. Remember a basic law of not only meditation but also life: what you resist, persists. And instead of attempting to push it away, quietly and with great devotion simply turn your attention back to your sacred word.

Practice this exercise.

PRINCIPLES OF THE PRACTICE OF MEDITATION

1. THE PRAYER OF MEDITATION IS OFTEN REALLY THE PRAYER OF DISTRACTION

As you strive to sit in stillness you will find that countless thoughts, bits of memory, brilliant ideas for future projects and even holy thoughts will continuously arise from the inner darkness. Let go of your previous notions of what this type of prayer should be like. And keep in mind the following important rule for those seeking the razor's edge path that leads to the heart:

2. NEVER JUDGE YOUR MEDITATION OR PRAYER

The reason most people fail in their discipline of meditation is that they judge themselves failures when they find it impossible to still the constant flow of thoughts through the mind. Judging their meditation as a waste of time, they stop and turn to an easier and more satisfying form of prayer. Regardless of how many times you find that your mind has locked onto a thought and that you have been carried away with it, as soon as you become aware that this has happened, with great gentleness and attention return to your sacred word or phrase.

3. ALL INNER WORK OF MEDITATION SHOULD BE NO WORK

This third principle of silent prayer is an important one. What is sought in the nuclear core of all prayer is not to be achieved by sheer force of will, by laboring or forcing the mind to concentrate. The method of achievement should mirror the desired achievement. The purpose of meditation is not to be able to concentrate on God but rather to be absorbed into God. As a sponge absorbs water, so our mind should be absorbed with the sound of the sacred word and, beyond that, absorbed in God's presence. No hard work is required for this to happen, only the gentle discipline of bringing your attention back again to your vehicle word or phrase.

4. AS YOU MEDITATE, SEEK NO REWARDS, POWERS OR GIFTS

It is important that each time you come to this prayer you divest yourself of seeking any profit, even the reward of being at peace. A pilgrim meditates not to change patterns of behavior, to be happier, more healthy, powerful, wise, holy, closer to God, or for any other reason, but only as an act of love. If we come to prayer seeking any profit, we come not so much with dirty hands as handicapped. Coming to prayer with an agenda, however noble, ultimately gets in the way of the mysterious divine Way. A simple intent to be available to the divine activity is about all there is room for in silent prayer. If you wish a reason to pray, then give the time solely as a gift to the Divine Source of all your gifts. What more perfect and unselfish gift can you give to God but the gift of your time?

5. GIVE AS MUCH TIME TO THE CARE AND NOURISHMENT OF YOUR INNER PERSON AS YOU DO TO THE OUTER

The inner person who is half of the cosmic amphibian of body and soul, has many of the same needs as the outer person. Daily we bathe, wash, brush our teeth and groom the body. Some also exercise and tone the muscles, circulatory system, organs and glands of the body by various activities. The body is fed with proper food and nourishment. If you could give as much time and energy to your inner life, you would be a holy and healthy person. For meditation to properly nourish you, it should be practiced for fifteen to twenty minutes in the morning and in the evening. In many ways this is the ideal, and if the evening period is impossible, then at least try to meditate for twenty minutes in the morning. If twenty minutes is impossible, then ten minutes would be a good beginning. No amount of time spent in this prayer of meditation is ever wasted effort!

6. THE PURPOSE OF MEDITATION IS NOT TO FIND GOD, WHILE THAT MAY HAPPEN, BUT RATHER TO LEARN HOW TO LIVE IN GOD

A contemplative is one who is absorbed in God. A mystic is one who tastes, feels and experiences the Divine Mystery. The prayer of meditation is the classic and ancient method to become what you have been designed to be: a contemplative mystic. By daily practice of meditation the pilgrim learns how to maintain mindfulness of the presence of God. A way of being is achieved through silent stilling that slowly changes the way you view life. A mystic is not so much someone who sees visions but one who has a new vision of life, seeing it as saturated with the sacred.

What often prevents the living out of this dual birthright is the hyperactivity of our secondary organ, the mind. It is constantly busy making judgements and feeding the ego with distorted images of reality that affirm its importance. This ego-self is not the real self, that truest identity which is often buried deeply beneath your personal, cultural and religious ideas about what is real. The mind is extremely clever at creating justifications for any behavior that protects this little self of the ego. It is able to foster fears that insure its continued separate existence, to raise walls that protect you from the work of every planetary pilgrim, the reformation of life and denial of self in opening to Self.

7. THE BENEFITS OF MEDITATION USUALLY COME SLOWLY SINCE THEY FLOW FROM A CHANGE OF PERSON THAT IS PERMANENT—THEY CREATE A CHANGE IN LIFE THAT WILL NEVER BE LOST

Since the changing of consciousness is usually a slow process—even if it is a permanent one—the planetary pilgrim must be prepared not to expect instant results. While change does occur, it is often imperceptible. At times we can experience a quantum leap in consciousness, but those who are in a hurry for results usually get in the way of real change and invariably become quickly discouraged.

With fidelity to the long and slow reformation that is achieved by meditation, you will slowly become aware that negative thoughts may easily be replaced with other thoughts. By your daily practice of meditation, your words and behavior will change permanently because the divine activity has transformed your heart.

8. PEACE AND THE PRESENCE OF GOD ARE THE RESULT OF THE PRAYER OF THE HEART, MEDITATION

The peace that flows from the prayer of meditation is not the absence of conflicts in life but rather the ability to remain centered in the ebb and flow of life's tensions. Those who have found that inner sacred center possess the peace which is based on the presence of God.

ALLIES FOR THE PRAYER OF MEDITATION

While meditation or silent prayer is the simplest of all prayers with regard to method, it can be the most difficult of prayers because of the discipline required to remain faithful to its practice. There are, however, allies that aid in the practice.

1. CREATE A PEACEFUL ENVIRONMENT FOR MEDITATION

Choose a quiet place to meditate, especially as you begin the practice. Wear comfortable clothing, remove your shoes and create about you an environment that encourages repose and stillness. When you are more skilled in this essential work of a pilgrim of inner space, you will be able to find your peaceful center in the midst of noise and activity.

2. ASSIST THE PRACTICE OF BEING SINGLE-MINDED BY DOING ONLY ONE THING AT A TIME

A great ally in this inner work is to practice the discipline of doing only one thing at a time. Having more work than we can accomplish in the time we have available, it is easy to fall victim to attempting to do several things at the same time. This temptation is particularly strong when doing some chore that does not require your full attention. But even in complicated tasks we easily allow the mind to be elsewhere, dealing with other matters than the one in which we are involved.

Do one thing at a time. If you are talking with someone, give that person and what is being said your full and undivided attention. If you are walking, then walk. If you are eating, simply eat your food. Sharing a meal is really a very complicated task since it involves both the act of eating and engaging in conversation. But you can bring your attention back to the food by frequently remarking about the taste of the meal and the beauty of the food and the table.

3. WHENEVER POSSIBLE, REINFORCE YOUR MEDITATION BY MAKING HABITUAL HUMAN ACTIVITIES INTO SABBATICALS

The Sabbath was intended to be a day of no work and re-creation. And a sabbatical is a period of time when one is freed from normal labors and responsibilities in order to be re-created. As an exercise to support your meditation and also to allow yourself to be re-created, go for a walk and think only about walking. With each step, simply feel the earth or sidewalk beneath your feet. Focus your entire attention on the act of walking.

This kind of single-minded exercise can be practiced when you take a shower, eat an apple or put on your clothing. You will find that each of these seemingly routine activities is really extremely rich in the quality of life. And your enjoyment and ability to practice these exercises can be greatly increased if you do them at half your normal speed. As you slow down these habitual acts, it will be easier to give them your full attention.

4. USE WORDS TO REINFORCE YOUR ATTENTION AS YOU
   PRACTICE A SABBATICAL EXERCISE

Another way to assist in giving full attention to whatever activity you are involved in is to use your power of imagination and look upon what you see before you as a motion picture. In this process you become the narrator of the film. While walking or driving alone in your car, narrate the action as your eyes move from scene to scene. To practice this simple exercise for even a few minutes can heighten your sense of awareness and mindfulness.

The absence of words in those activities that normally are filled with them can also increase your mindfulness. Eating, walking or working with someone in silence, for example, can allow the environment to flood your mind and create a heightened sense of being one with the world around you.

5. THE PRACTICE OF MINDFULNESS CAN INCREASE YOUR EXPERIENCE
   OF LIFE SO THAT YOU CAN LIVE MORE FULLY

The purpose of life is to enjoy it and to find within it the Source of life. When we believe that happiness depends upon the right conditions or on the right amount of possessions, it forever remains beyond the horizon. Our mind is busy with the defense and enlargement of the little self, the ego, and with the endless problems of making a living and all that sharing life with others entails. As a result the beauties of creation, the joy of simply being alive, the taste of our food, the wonder of walking and innumerable other joys are eclipsed because we do not give them any attention.

CONCLUSION

When you have learned to discipline your mind and to live in the present moment—which is the fruit of mindfulness—you are more able to experience life. If this heaven and earth are full of the glory of God, then should it not be possible to experience—at least to some degree—that glory? Are we not called, in the words of Psalm 33, "to taste and see the goodness of God"? It is only out of such an appreciation of the wonder of life that a full and true gratitude arises spontaneously from deep within our hearts, a gratitude for the support of the earth when we walk, for the food that has given up its life that we might be nourished, for ten thousand other things and for the gift of life itself.

The Divine Mystery has countless names, and in our tradition the title of God can bring to mind many possibilities. But even if the pilgrim were to give God only four-letter names, like Love or Life, the possibilities of experience and appreciation are unending.

PILGRIM'S PROGRESS AND CLASSIFIED INFORMATION

Any manual about the exploration of inner space would be incomplete without a warning about the release of information concerning your journey. This warning is intended to raise consciousness concerning pitfalls and not to be taken as a hard and fast law. The following suggestions should be carefully considered by the user of this manual according to his or her particular point of reference.

Jesus pronounced a cryptic counsel, "Do not cast your pearls before swine." That warning echoes advice from the Orient that one should exercise great caution in sharing the experiences or knowledge of one's spiritual journey with another. When something is shared, it should only be done with a sojourner who is on a parallel path of that mysterious journey. Or you can reveal something of your journey with a person you know to be advanced in spiritual knowledge and whom you have learned to trust.

What makes your prayer, meditation and other pilgrim practices top-secret is not that you have anything to hide. Rather, the reason for keeping such information classified is because of the damage that may be done to your progress if you are not well-founded in your spiritual exercises. There is even the danger that the negative opinions of others may cause you to abandon valuable practices.

Jesus also instructed that when you pray you should do so as if the activity you are involved in is top-secret. His words about praying in secret carry implications beyond not making a public demonstration of your prayerfulness. If your prayer is intimate communion with the Beloved, then you should exercise the same discreet and reverential silence as you would in any intimate love affair.

The gifts of prayer are precisely that—gifts. And while one is responsible to return tenfold for every gift received, that return does not imply a discussion or revelation of what you do in prayer or what is done to you in prayer. Jesus is the arch-pilgrim, the pattern for those seeking to become one with God. And nowhere in all the pages of the Gospels does he reveal the inside of his prayer life. We do not know what happened on the mountain tops or deserted places where he withdrew to be in intimate communion with his God. Rather we see in the words and actions of his life—in his compassionate behavior, his harsh attitude toward narrow, legalistic observance of laws, his openness to outcasts and sinners, his delight in feasting and life—the results of his prayer.

A planetary pilgrim best shares his or her prayer and spiritual exercises with others by sharing the fruits of that inner journey.

OTHER ESSENTIAL EQUIPMENT

THE SPIRIT GUIDE

Traditionally those who set foot to the Path do so under the loving guidance of a teacher. Among the many names given to this person are: guru, spiritual director, spirit guide, shaman and teacher. The purpose of such a guide is to point the way, to encourage and support you in your efforts and to provide necessary information and understanding for your progress. He or she also warns you of potential danger spots, the swamps where one may easily become bogged down, the cleverly concealed pits into which one can easily stumble. In the fields of sports and the arts, the function of a personal coach has its origin in the ancient role of a teacher of the Way in calling forth from the student more than he or she believes is possible.

In short, such spirit guides are helpful not only because of the wisdom of the Way that they possess but also because they can break through the arbitrary limits we tend to set upon our inner powers and because they can short-circuit the clever excuses we invent for our lack of discipline.

In light of the shortage in our contemporary society of those learned in the arts of the Spirit, fortunate are those who have a personal spiritual companion and guide. But any who dedicate their hearts to becoming life-long pilgrims of the path should take heart. **The** teacher, the Divine Mystery, is ultimately the spirit guide for each of us. And the Divine Mystery uses a variety of persons, events and even animals and plants as channels for communication.

Rule One: BELIEVE THAT YOUR TRUE TEACHER IS EVER EAGER TO ASSIST YOU, CAUTION YOU, ADVISE AND STRENGTHEN YOU IF YOU BUT HAVE EYES AND EARS THAT ARE OPEN TO THE MESSAGES

God can send you the messages that you need through the words of an author in a book, the words of a song, the sight of some wonder in nature or any number of other agents. Keep your ears and eyes open.

God uses a host of assistant teachers in your lifetime to give you all the information you need at a particular moment to move onward in your journey. Rare is the pilgrim who is given a complete message outlining the path in detail. Instructions come in bits and pieces, in sizes and shapes that we are able, at any given moment, to digest and assimilate.

Your spirit guides may at times be saints, prophets or holy persons who long since have been dead but whose recorded words speak directly to your heart and awaken your thirst for God. Some scriptural scholars maintain that the prophet of Israel, Isaiah, was such a spiritual teacher of Jesus of Nazareth, since the words of Jesus so often seemed based on those of the holy prophet. A parent, spouse, friend or lover may also hold a temporary teaching position. If you are mindful at each critical turn in your journey, you will receive instructions. So, again, keep your eyes and ears open.

Rule Two: HUMILITY IS THE DOORWAY FOR DISCIPLESHIP AND ALSO THE SECRET OF STUDENTHOOD

Since the Divine Mystery desires to direct you away from those activities, exercises, methods, behavior and work that may block your homeward journey, the wise pilgrim is open to any messenger. It is not by accident that in fairy tales, birds, fish and other animals are messengers who assist those on great adventures. If one is not humble enough to be guided by a mere bird, a dog or a cat, or the insight of a garbage collector, the journey may lead to a real dead end. With humility, keep your eyes and ears open.

Rule Three: IF YOU WISH TO BE A SAINT, COMMUNICATE WITH THE COMMUNION OF SAINTS

Parents, teachers and those who have loved you in life, love you beyond the grave. They, more than any earthly teachers, desire that you reach your birthright destination and are eager to assist you. Although they lack the official title of saint, these holy dead are nonetheless saints. They go wherever love draws them. And so, in the absence of other guides, do not fail to call upon their assistance. Since your normal sense organs are not designed for such communication, you must be sensitive to the slightest touch of the heart, to intuitions, feelings or apprehensions that are beyond the merely rational. Your inner eyes and ears—as well as your heart—must be open.

Rule Four: SINCE THE DIVINE MYSTERY IS YOUR PRIMARY TEACHER IN THE CRITICAL MOMENTS WHEN YOU NEED DIRECTION, LET GO OF YOUR INCLINATION TO CONTROL AND OVER-CALCULATE AND LET YOURSELF BE NAVIGATED BY THE HIGHER SIGNALS OF YOUR AUTOMATIC PILOT

This last rule for guidance is perhaps the most difficult since we resist letting go of control and seek rational answers to ways out of the fog. To follow the communications of your inner counselor is to blindfold reason and be drawn magnetically along the Path. It requires enormous trust and love as well as the ability to be as weightless as a leaf upon the wind. Pray for such willingness to let the Divine Wind, invisible and intangible, lift you up and carry you forward.

THE ALLIES OF INNER ENERGIES

THE MAGIC MAGNETIC ART OF THE TRAVELER OF INNER SPACE

While we have spoken of the value of creating images to assist in developing discipline, the great human gift of imagination is also important equipment for other aspects of the journey into inner space. To properly utilize this gift, the planetary pilgrim needs to remember the uncommon-sense fact that the earth, our solar family and the whole universe are not composed of blocks of matter but rather of energy.

While such common objects in your world as trees, buildings, machines and land appear to your senses to be solid and separated from each other by space, modern physics tells us they are really more like particles within particles, all sharing in a great web of energy. These objects have different frequencies of energy which interact, which one might say are in constant communion. These frequencies continually affect and influence each other.

Energies that vibrate at a similar rate of speed usually tend to be magnetically drawn to each other. It is important to be aware of this principle of attraction when you must begin some task but do not know how to go about it. First create, even in the roughest form, a thought blueprint of what is desired. Be conscious that your thoughts are also forms of energy which attract and are attracted by idea-thought energy of a like kind.

The Eastern concept of karma and the Judeo-Christian notion that "as you sow, so shall you reap" are both readily understood in the light of this principle of magnetic energy. Think evil or do evil and, without failing, you will draw evil to yourself.

Rule One: CONSTANTLY MONITOR THE QUALITY OF THE ENERGY FIELD OF YOUR THOUGHTS, FEELINGS, DESIRES AND FANTASIES—KEEP YOUR PERSONAL FIELD OF ENERGY AS PURE, LOVING AND PEACEFUL AS POSSIBLE

The Way is narrow and difficult. The path of life is filled with potential dangers at every turn. Meditation and reflection are aids to monitor the thoughts (energy units) that appear in your mind. You are not responsible for a dark thought's unwanted appearance in your consciousness. But if you feed it, house it and nourish it with encouragement, you will invite other dark energy. Our primary and ongoing spiritual work is the alignment of our hearts and minds with goodness and truth.

Heed the advice of Jesus: "Do not let the sun set on your anger!" And consider the words of Buddha: " 'That one was angry with me, attacked and defeated me, robbed me.' Those who harbor such thoughts will never be free from hatred." Both Jesus and Buddha proposed that you fill your heart with love (positive energy) for those who harm you. Jesus said quite plainly, "Love your enemies." And Buddha adds, "Hatred never puts an end to hatred; love alone can end hatred. This is the unalterable law."

Rule Two: WHILE THE FINAL DESTINATION IS BEYOND YOUR PRESENT VISION, SEEK EACH DAY ONLY THE GOOD FOR YOURSELF AND OTHERS

Seek the kingdom, the age of God's peace and justice, and all you need will come to you. Make your life that of a perpetual pilgrim, letting go of any possession, person or occupation that hinders the sacred journey, that restricts the flow of divine energy into your life, and you will receive a hundredfold today and life everlasting tomorrow. All the wisdom of Jesus' words is based on this law of magnetic radiation of energy. Seek only the good, and you will draw to yourself all that you need for happiness and life. And further, a genuine concern for the well-being of others is the best way to draw grace to yourself. The pursuit of happiness is best achieved not by running after it but rather by the passionate quest of the Good.

You hold the power to create your life. The source of your happiness is within you.

CONFRONTATION WITH THE FORCES OF EVIL

PRINCIPLES FOR CONDUCT WHEN CAUGHT IN A FIELD OF NEGATIVE AND DESTRUCTIVE ENERGY

Rule One: REMEMBER THAT WHEN YOU ARE CONFRONTED ON THE PATHWAY BY THE PRESENCE OF EVIL OR BY STRONG FIELDS OF NEGATIVE ENERGY FLOWING FROM ANOTHER, WITHIN YOU IS AN EVEN GREATER POWER OF LIGHT AND LOVE

No planetary pilgrim journeys alone; we live in a complex and crowded world. You will thus inevitably encounter those who are angry and caught in hatred, unable to control their dark thoughts. You will encounter many who do not yet understand the cosmic laws of the positive and negative forces of the universe. Do not be afraid of the presence of dark energy, but do be extremely cautious.

By your frequent prayer, your daily meditation, you will be reminded that the love of God is at work within you. Christ is one with you, speaking and working in communion with you. At your fingertips are resources of enormously creative divine power. Resist the impulse to return dark energy for dark energy, hate for hate, injury for injury.

"To those who are good, I am good; to those who are not good, I am also good. Goodness is power," said Lao Tzu in the 49th chapter of the *Tao Te Ching*. While this is indeed divine wisdom, it appears to be foolishness to those who are not on the Path. For weary millenniums the world has returned aggression for aggression and anger for anger. You need only recall that acid is not neutralized by adding more acid. Only when infused with its opposite, an alkaline solution, is acid tempered.

Rule Two: USE THE LUMINOUS ENERGY GENERATED BY YOUR MEDITATION AND PRAYER AS AN ALKALINE AGENT TO NEUTRALIZE THE DARK AND NEGATIVE ENERGY CONFRONTING YOU

When in a confrontation with the energy fields of anger or hate, recall that the divine light blazes like a cosmic nuclear furnace within your heart. The real spiritual battle is not to give in to returning violence for violence. While it is a great challenge at times, we all have the power to activate the divine energy that lives within us— and our daily prayer helps bring us into contact with the source of that energy and increases our readiness to respond out of love in the midst of a confrontation.

Send forth long luminous fibers from your heart-star and slowly wrap the other person or persons in these glowing fibers of love and light. As you envelop them in strands of divine energy, wish them all the good they are capable of receiving. Look upon them with eyes flooded with love and compassion. See them as yourself, part of your body. In short, love them.

Whenever you feel threatened by fearful situations or persons who seek to do harm to you or others, remember the commission given by Jesus to his disciples: "You are the light of the world." You can repeat these words to yourself like a mantra, with great faith and confidence. And picture rays of compassion flowing forth from every pore of your body, blessing and healing, imparting positive energy to all they touch. And even if you are hurt, seek to never return injury for injury, blow for blow. Such planetary pilgrim advice truly is intended only for heroes and heroines.

Rule Three: IN ANY CONFLICT YOU BECOME THE WEAPONS THAT YOU USE—THOSE WHO MAKE WAR AGAINST DRAGONS BECOME DRAGONS THEMSELVES

If conflict is essential, carefully select your weapons. If you are foolish enough to use the same weapons as those who attack you, you will lose even if you win. If you know in advance that conflict is ahead of you, create an inner blueprint of how you wish to engage in the conflict. Design with prayerfulness only weapons of light, craft only shields of love and wear no armor but the presence of God so that you do not turn into the evil forces that you fight.

CONTINUING EDUCATION

THE PILGRIM AS TEACHDENT

The term "teachdent" is a hybrid name for one who is both teacher and student. In our Western world we have arranged education with a closure point called graduation. The unspoken implication is that we have left behind the need to be a student. In this age when new knowledge is expanding at the speed of light, such an attitude of being beyond studenthood is not only extremely limiting but also harmful.

As a teachdent, a planetary pilgrim must not only be willing to remain a student for life but also must be willing to share what has been learned on the Path, even when that learning has not been formal. Of course, it is easy to abuse the role of being a teacher. But without presuming to be an "authority," each of us is called, at one time or another, to be a channel to guide another on the Path. We need an openness to the Spirit drawing to us those who can benefit from what we have learned. And we need the trust that the Spirit can speak through us in ways that can advance another's journey.

But being a teachdent also implies that each spiritual sojourner must be his or her own best teacher and student. Among the mystics of Islam there is an expression, "If the student is eager and the teacher is strict, one can learn anything." That saying holds the secret of education after one has finished formal education. And following from that truth are several principles for a pilgrim's continuing education:

Rule One: IF YOU WISH TO BE FED CONTINUOUSLY BY THE WISDOM OF YESTERDAY AND THE INSIGHTS OF TODAY, NEVER ABANDON THE CHILDHOOD DELIGHT IN ASKING QUESTIONS

As the body and its many organs have need of food and nourishment, so does the inner person with its intellectual and spiritual organs. To be constantly curious about the why, what and how of things—questioning the origins of even the unquestionable—helps safeguard one's studenthood. Feed your mind with the fresh food of new ideas. Welcome not only attractive ideas but even disquieting thoughts that are contrary to your personal or cultural preferences.

The question mark is a power tool that haunts you until you have found a way of looking at a situation that will allow you peace without having to compromise. Awaken it frequently enough, and it will be a constant companion to aid your way.

Rule Two: IN A VISUAL AGE, MAKE USE OF MOVIES, VIDEOS AND TELEVISION, BUT DO NOT ABANDON THE GREAT GIFT OF READING

In the daily prayers in this book there is a place set aside for reading. While you may not be able to take that time during each period of prayer, it does have the purpose of reminding you to read. For unlike the flow of film, reading a book allows you to stop and reflect upon an idea that you have just encountered. Books also allow you to return and re-read something that was important.

As a new era emerges, new insights and ideas flourish. As recent research and study of scholars unlocks implications that are underlying in traditional religious texts, the possibility of these texts speaking to you is greatly enhanced. If you do not continue your education in those subjects that directly touch upon your spiritual quest, you will be handicapped in the most important work of your life.

Rule Three: ATTEND WORKSHOPS AND SEMINARS THAT DEAL WITH THE PARTICULAR PILGRIMAGE UPON WHICH YOU ARE TRAVELING—MAKE USE OF ANY CONFERENCE THAT YOU BELIEVE WILL BE OF ASSISTANCE

As with a book, a workshop or a seminar can be a place to pick up the next message for your journey. And one of the added values of conferences on prayer and various other disciplines of the Path is that they bring you into contact with others who are traveling the Way. Even if you do not learn anything new intellectually, you will usually find your enthusiasm and dedication renewed, your convictions strengthened by being with others who seek what you are seeking.

Rule Four: THE WISE PILGRIM IS CAUTIOUS OF FADS AND NOVELTIES THAT CONSTANTLY APPEAR LIKE TRAVELING CIRCUSES ALONG THE WAY

Take care that in your desire to find "your" way you do not move from one "in" movement to another. In a culture where anything old is suspect and the new is welcomed merely for the sake of its novelty, beware of religious bandwagons.

While most new trends have some truth about them, there is a real temptation to escape from a dull disciplined life onto the merry-go-round of new movements and so slip backwards, if not completely off the razor's edge.

Beware of spiritual sideshow barkers who promise something too good to be true, because usually that will prove to be the case. Be wary of those who use marketplace methods to promote spiritual practices and gifts. Be cautious of those selling secrets hidden since the beginning of time and other gifts that are asleep in your own heart that require a "special" awakening.

THE MOST IMPORTANT PIECE OF EQUIPMENT TO PREVENT FALLING OFF THE RAZOR'S EDGE

THE MAINTENANCE AND USE OF A BALANCE BAR FOR THE TRAVELER OF INNER SPACE

While this Survival Manual could contain countless more sections of instructions for traveling the Way, it will conclude with this one. It deals with what is perhaps the most important piece of equipment for your journey, the balance bar. As Jesus said, "The Way is narrow"; it is as narrow as a high-wire. And no serious aerialist would walk the high-wire without a balance bar.

Balance then is one of the supreme virtues of the pilgrim. Balance, the fruit of meditation and prayer, is but another name for peace. The pilgrim cannot remain atop the narrow way by being rigid, for not being able to adapt dooms a devotee to falling. Rather, you must be able to sway back and forth, constantly in touch with your center of gravity, respectful of gusts of wind, even slight breezes that may topple you from the Way. And, again, when playing with the issues of balance, the give and the take, the use of a balance bar is essential.

Rule One: ALWAYS CARRY THE BALANCE BAR OF HUMOR WHEN YOU CLIMB TO THE NARROW WAY OF THE SPIRITUAL HIGH-WIRE

Because the spiritual quest of the planetary pilgrim is so serious, it cannot be taken seriously. Unlike the astronaut who must at times be deadly serious or find him-or herself dead, the spirit-naut must be able to laugh at mistakes and errors. Woe to any who set forth on the quest without the balance bar of humor.

Your balance bar will assist you when the strong gusts of incongruity make you sway from side to side. Jesus was called a drunkard and glutton, which he never denied. At the same time, the crowds called John the Baptist a life-denying ascetic. To feast and rejoice while the gloom of doom hangs upon the world, while evil preys in every corner, is one of the paradoxes of the path of holiness. To deny surface pleasures in order to make way for joy to shine through is another prayerful paradox. It is also a humorous irony that the holier you become, the more of a sinner you become. For what you once may not even have considered a fault, like being upset and angry with another, can bring your progress on the Path to a complete stop as you draw closer to the light.

Rule Two: NEVER LEAVE HOME WITHOUT YOUR SPONTOON

Whether at home or abroad, at prayer or play, always take along your spontoon, which is another name for the pilgrim's balance bar of humor. The term comes from the Italian word "spluntone," which means to blunt, to remove the point. Originally the spontoon was a short weapon or pike carried by 18th century French infantry officers used to blunt an unexpected attack. As a weapon of the inner space adventurer, the spontoon is the sign of the virtue of spontaneity, the ability to deal with the unpredictable with humor and good-naturedness. If you can travel the Path with it constantly at your side, you will be able to withstand the "slings and arrows of outrageous fortune," to remove life's sharp points of contradiction that so easily can pierce you.

To carry a spontoon will shield you from arrogance, the sin of taking yourself and your prayer too seriously. It will remind you that God, not you, is really in charge of making daily assignments and determining lessons for the Way. Religion is not your business, even if you are a professional, ordained person. It is God's business and God knows best what will bring you progress on the Path. And the balance bar of humor will help you to travel evenly and lightly along the Way.

If you carry a spontoon, you will not be able to grip too tightly your life situations or even the discipline of prayer and the spiritual exercises and goals that you have set for yourself. Hold to your spontoon and let go of trying to manipulate life, others or God.

Rule Three: DO NOT HESITATE TO BE HUMOROUS IN YOUR CONVER-
              SATIONS WITH GOD OR TO BE FUNNY IN YOUR PRAYER
              AND WORSHIP

It is understandable that this rule appears to be heresy, for humor and the holy seem as far apart as heaven and hell. Since much of religious tradition does not associate humor with a house of God, it will not be easy to apply rule three in your spiritual quest. Previous ages have made places of worship somber and serious. Anything lighthearted or funny was seen as sacrilege.

An important gift of the blended Judaeo-Christian tradition is the Jewish folk practice of addressing God as one of the family. If parents can be chided for their occasional contradictions or failures to provide, then why not the Divine Parent? The familiarity of such ongoing conversations with the Reality which is closer to you than your skin yet beyond the boundaries of space can make formal prayers meaningful. Do not hesitate to be Jewish regardless of your formal faith. Feel free to poke fun at God and to be playful in your prayer.

Rule Four: HUMOR BRINGS ABOUT HEALTH OF BODY AND SPIRIT—
IT IS AN UNEQUALED ESCAPE VALVE WHICH RELEASES
THE FLOW OF DIVINE ENERGY

Laughter and humor have been proven to relieve pain and help cure illness. They create chemical compounds that strengthen the immune system and increase general health and well-being. Humor softens the shock of surprises which abound along the narrow edge of the Way. While we find some surprises to be delightful, others cause us discomfort because they leave us out of control. Humor helps keep the flow of divine energy going, and it releases the energy necessary to creatively respond to the surprise packages of our life situations.

And the ability to laugh at yourself when you make an error is a sign of the kind of humility that gives birth to holiness, to a wholeness that flows from viewing yourself as part saint and part clown. The burden of always having to be respectable, of always having to be on top of things or always having the right answer, is not only a burden too heavy to bear, the weight of it will pull you off center and cause you to slip from the razor's edge.

A Self-Humor Exercise: This exercise requires you to be semi-spontaneous, for it is best performed when you find yourself caught in an unexpected moment. But for now, think back to a time when you found yourself surprised by an unplanned event or a time when a mistake caused by your lack of memory or concentration made you lose your balance. Experience again, as clearly as you can, how ashamed or angry or guilty you felt, and then just laugh out loud at your predicament. Take as much pleasure as possible in the humor of your forgetfulness or in the surprise raid of the Divine Mystery into your life.

This exercise should be repeated until a humorous appreciation of your mistakes or a sense of gratitude for unexpected gifts becomes a natural response. The more frequently you make the intention to respond with laughter to situations that catch you off guard, the easier you will find it to respond with humor rather than irritation, resentment, grief or shame.

Rule Five: PLAYFULNESS AND PRAYER ARE SIGNS OF THE TRUE
PILGRIM OF THE ABSOLUTE WHO KEEPS ALIVE THE
CHILD WITHIN

The sacred and the spontaneous are twin sisters of the Way. The spontaneous is the unpremeditated energy which has its roots in humor. It is very different from the premeditated energy of jokes or funny stories. Humor breaks out from the spontaneous combustion of head-on collisions between the absurd and the absolutes of life. Like God's creative energy, the spontaneous is self-generated and therefore provides a mystic taste of the Divine Presence.

Rule Six: IF YOU FEEL YOU HAVE LOST THE CHILDHOOD GIFT OF HUMOR AND SPONTANEITY, PRAY AND WISH FOR IT, AND IT WILL AGAIN BE YOURS

The power of the wish is truly great. To wish is itself a prayer that engages some of our deepest inner powers. This law of how things take shape was known long ago and so became an important part of fairy tales, in the form of the magic wish. But every wish is magical and magnetic; it draws to the one who wishes the reality which is desired.

Wish for whatever change you desire in yourself with all your heart. State your wish in positive terms and repeat your intention with loving attention. Then be prepared for a wonder. If you desire to be more humorous, to see the humor in your humanity, the comedy of your behavior, then wish for that gift of humor. Wish for the gift of being spontaneous, wish for the gift of laughter, and make each of those wishes faith-filled prayers.

The Nebulous Cluster in Serpens

DESTINATION: PLANET EMMAUS

To simply sit in the evening and look out at space into which we are traveling at a speed of 43,000 miles an hour, is truly awesome. The night sky is filled with stars that sometimes seem so close that you could almost reach up and touch them. In that interstellar sea, the closest star is Proxima Centauri. Yet if you could travel aboard a Voyager spacecraft—which is the fastest space machine we have yet launched, traveling at one ten-thousandth of the speed of light—it would take you 40,000 earth years to reach our nearest neighbor, Proxima Centauri.

Since the space between us and the galactic suns far beyond Proxima Centauri is so great, we measure the distance not in miles but by the speed of light. A light year is the distance light travels in one year, 5,787 trillion miles. The vastness of the nighttime vista is heightened when we realize that traveling at the speed of light to the center of our own galaxy, the Milky Way, would require a journey of 30,000 light years. And if we wished to visit the galaxy M31, the closest neighboring spiral galaxy to ours, that journey would require 2,000,000 light years!

To reflect even momentarily on such facts has the power to bring every pilgrim to his or her knees in an act of adoration. The prayer of adoration and wonder may be **the** prayer of the 21st century. What fire, thunder and the mystery of birth once invoked in the primitive person, the magnitude of space awakens in us. And in looking out the window of an ordinary night sky, those three great questions again flood the mind, "Where did I come from?" "Where am I going?" "Why am I here?"

Like the disciples on the road to Emmaus, we also have heavy hearts. Like those two spiritual travelers, we look back at our planet Earth from the perspective of the NASA photograph and see war, hate, violence and exploitation, the apparent victory of evil over good. The two Emmaus pilgrims wondered seriously about the fate of the future. As they looked back at Jerusalem, the world they knew, their hearts were filled with doubts that the promised age of peace and justice had really arrived. Jesus, their spiritual master, had proclaimed with enthusiasm that the Age of God had dawned, yet evil seemed triumphant in his execution as a common criminal.

As they traveled to the village of Emmaus, they were discussing these sad realities when a stranger joined them and began to share in their discussion. The stranger pointed out to them how the trials and misfortunes that caused their hearts to doubt were necessary elements in the dawning of the new era. While they were discussing these things, the evening approached, and so they urged the stranger to stop and eat with them. In the breaking of the bread they suddenly realized that the stranger was the Risen Christ. Their sorrow was transformed into joy, and they returned in great haste to Jerusalem to tell the others about their encounter on the road to Emmaus.

You and I are pilgrims traveling aboard our planet, in the company of the sun and the other planets, outward into space. We know that in our lifetime we shall never reach Proxima Centauri, our closest star, let alone our neighboring galaxy, M31. Yet in ten thousand different ways we are able to visit Planet Emmaus. This planetary place is not listed on any galactic map, yet it does exist. To be a traveler to Emmaus is to continuously seek a rendezvous with the Risen Christ so as to experience what those two disciples did on their journey.

But if we expect Christ to appear as he does in our imagination or in the images of art, we shall never find Planet Emmaus. Ours is a journey solely of faith, without any personal experience of the promised presence of Christ, a lonely pilgrimage into the darkness of inner space. But if we have an openness of heart, a willingness to encounter the Divine Mystery in as many different ways as there are stars in the sky, then a rendezvous with Planet Emmaus awaits us.

The pilgrimage for each of us is but a journey of return to where we began. We know that "we are dust and that to dust we shall return." But we are star dust! The iron in our blood, the nitrogen in our DNA, the calcium in our teeth—all that we are made of was created in the blazing hearts of the stars. Yet we are more than flesh and bone; we are also something else which is beyond destruction into dust, something eternal which we call spirit.

Our final rendezvous with the Divine Mystery is anticipated each time we find ourselves overjoyed at being swept into the gravity field of Planet Emmaus and experience our Divine Beloved, who promised such experiences to those who believe. For the first three centuries of Christianity, the followers of Christ showed no interest in making pilgrimages to the historical places of his birth, life or death. Apparently they had no need to pilgrimage to a particular place because they experienced the Emmaus encounter with their Beloved in the midst of their daily journeys.

If our faith is to be a living faith, we also need firsthand encounters with the Risen Christ. We need to discover our own Emmaus experiences at such occasions as breaking bread, sweeping floors and changing tires, in all deeds of service and compassion and all acts of communion and expressions of love. And along with these encounters with Christ, we need to be open to meetings with other planetary pilgrims. Each time we meet sojourners, we should greet them with joyful recognition. Such wayside meetings may also be opportunities to encourage and confirm these companion pilgrims on their unique pilgrimages into inner space. Whenever you do this, you will find your own journey reconfirmed by an experience of solidarity. On occasion, mutual sharing of methods or knowledge of the inner journey may be valuable too. All such pilgrim encounters on the way to Planet Emmaus are sacred meetings.

We are aware that not only at night is the sky above filled with the vista of our pilgrimage in space. But at every moment of the day the sky is crowded with clusters of stars, even though the light of our single daystar prevents us from seeing them. And to look up from earth at any time is to be faced with those three great questions, "Where did I come from?" "Where am I going?" "Why am I here?" May the prayers and personal rituals of this book help you to keep those questions alive in your consciousness. While answers to them will always remain just beyond our reach in this life, perhaps it is the energy of those questions that keeps us moving on our journey into inner space. And while we await the final answer to the question, "Where am I going?" for now perhaps we can answer, "Planet Emmaus."

INDEX OF THEMES FOR PRAYERS AND PSALMS

Praise, 126, 184, 188, 197
Prayer, 95, 96, 97, 100, 101, 102, 103,
    111, 124, 128, 129, 131, 136, 137,
    138, 139, 172, 176, 180, 181, 183,
    184, 189, 190, 195, 206, 208
Presence, 96, 100, 102, 103, 111, 129,
    144, 171, 172, 182, 187, 188, 190,
    196, 199, 215, 224, 226
Priest(ly), 96, 102, 139, 190, 223, 226
Prisoner, 108, 115, 136, 141, 156, 160,
    162, 164, 185

Quest, 124, 200
Quiet, 128

Redeeming, 102
Reform, 136
Re-member, 121, 226
Renewal, 136
Restless, 97, 119, 223
Resurrection, 107, 110, 126, 142, 144,
    223, 225, 226
Rhythm, 153, 154, 155
Rise, 100, 101, 110, 141, 144, 146, 151,
    179, 185, 206, 223, 224, 226

Sabbath, 114, 117
Sacrament, 101, 110, 132, 215
Sacrifice, 96, 139, 140, 190, 223
Saint, 109, 132, 181, 183, 200
Salvation, 129, 205, 223
Savior, 144
Scripture, 98
Seed, 109, 141
Servant, 102, 145, 176, 223
Service, 96, 101, 189, 195, 224
Silence (Silent), 97, 101, 126, 129, 141,
    145, 150, 164, 181, 223, 224, 225
Shrine, 96, 101, 111, 124
Slavery, 99
Sleep, 116, 120, 126, 137, 155, 164,
    199, 221
Snow, 110, 113, 123, 125, 126, 137
Song, 97, 103, 107, 109, 112, 120, 128,
    141, 182, 185, 188, 198
Soul, 96, 98, 99, 103, 108, 138, 161,
    171, 173, 182, 204, 222
Spirit (Holy), 95, 96, 97, 100, 101, 102,
    111, 126, 129, 136, 137, 138, 139,
    145, 146, 147, 168, 169, 171, 180,
    186, 202, 217, 223, 224
Splendor, 96, 107

Spring, 107, 108, 109, 110, 111, 120,
    126, 129, 136, 150, 173
Stars, 96, 134, 135, 170, 178, 215
Stillness, 97, 124, 129
Stranger, 96, 134, 139, 144, 191
Summer, 113, 114, 115, 116, 117, 118
Sun, 109, 110, 114, 115, 139, 141, 146,
    153, 178, 182, 186, 225
Support, 151, 216
Surprise, 133, 149

Temple, 122
Thanksgiving, 197 (Also see Gratitude)
Thoughts, 194
Trust, 141
Truth, 96, 150, 164, 195, 198, 200

Unity, 125, 139, 188, 216

Vestment, 96
Victory, 130, 144, 151
Virgin, 108, 136

Waiting, 131, 155
Water, 98, 142, 182
Way, 130, 138, 183, 195, 224
Willing, 201
Wind, 108, 120, 123, 137, 145, 146,
    148, 178, 179, 182, 185
Winter, 107, 108, 113, 120, 123, 124,
    125, 126, 173
Wisdom, 98, 125, 135, 140, 162, 187,
    194, 205, 217
Womb, 116, 139, 223
Wonder, 124, 133, 148, 170, 201, 217,
    220
Word, 98, 100, 114, 125, 128, 132, 134,
    147, 169, 173, 201, 206, 217, 220
Work, 103, 113, 116, 117, 118, 158,
    169, 188, 189, 190, 191, 203
Worship, 96, 100, 102, 122, 138, 139,
    205, 214, 223

Yearning, 122, 141
Young, 112, 133, 149, 150
Youth (fulness), 102, 133, 145, 149, 150,
    162, 182

Zeal, 99, 101, 144, 145, 184
Zest, 99, 117, 170, 171

The second part of this volume is a comprehensive manual for those on the path of prayer. It has valuable practical exercises and instructions for creating a personal prayer shrine and on the practice of the prayer of meditation. It suggests such allies to personal prayer as the use of incense, sacred fire, icons and sacred images, prayer beads, flags and fans and a journal for the journey.

Characteristic of quality hardcover books, this edition of **Prayers for a Planetary Pilgrim** is carefully constructed to withstand the wear of daily use and will lie open flat without falling apart. It is sewn along the spine, and the flexible leatherette cover has the "feel" of a guidebook that will become a trusted companion on the prayer pilgrimage home to God.

Edward Hays is a Catholic priest who for over twenty-three years was the director of a contemplative center. He is a storyteller, artist and internationally known speaker on such topics as prayer, contemporary spirituality, liturgy, community, ministry and the home as a "Domestic Church." An author of twenty books on prayer and incarnational spirituality, his travels throughout the East provide fertile ground for the blending of Eastern and Western thought. His many stories, essays and prayers have a wide range of appeal among peoples of various religious traditions.

FOREST OF PEACE
P u b l i s h i n g

Suppliers for the Spiritual Pilgrim
PO Box 269
Leavenworth, KS 66048-0269
1-800-659-3227

ISBN 0-939516-10-1